The Other Song

Discovering Your Parallel Self

Rajan Sankaran MD (Hom)

HMP
Mumbai, India.

Please note:

This book is for educational purposes only. It is not meant to be used for self –diagnosis, therapy or treatment.

First edition: 2008

ISBN: 978-81-903378-2-3

Printed by : **Thomson Press (India) Ltd.**
Plot No. 5/5A, TTC Ind. Area, Thane Belapur Road,
Airoli, Navi Mumbai - 400 708.

Published by :

Homoeopathic Medical Publishers

20, Station Road, Santacruz (W), Mumbai – 400 054, INDIA
www. rajansankaran.com

affectionately dedicated to my father.

A Note to the Reader

Recent discoveries in homoeopathic practice have led to a completely new way of understanding the human being, concepts that can be applied universally. This book intends to introduce the lay reader and all those interested in knowing about the human psyche to these concepts.

It is not the purpose of this book to teach homoeopathy or therapy. Such teaching needs to be imparted systematically and in recognized institutions. It would be highly risky to practice any therapy without a proper, systematic and rigorous training. At the same time this book should not be used to superficially classify oneself or others.

To perceive what lies at the depth of each one's being is a process. Such a process needs to be done by someone well qualified, skilled and trained. It demands of both, the therapist and the one undergoing the process, a completely open mind, free from all prejudice and knowledge including what is given in this book.

...

Thank You

While I am grateful to many friends and colleagues for help in the preparation of this book, special thanks are due to **Dr. Kanan Khatau Chikhal**, who has worked with me on the book right from the first draft, and to **Dr. Mary Gillies, Susan Cortes, Prof. Usha Subramanian** and **Dr. Roger Morrison** whose editorial inputs have been most valuable. Some parts of this book are borrowed from my earlier books, 'The Sensation in Homoeopathy' and 'Sensation Refined' which were very competently edited by **Dr. Rashmi Jaising** and **Dr. Antonia Desouza** respectively. My thanks are also due to my many friends and colleagues who read the initial drafts and offered their valuable feedback. These include **Dr. Linda Johnston, Cheryl Feng, Rachna Toshniwal, C.Y. Gopinath, Hema Rajshekhar** and **Rajiv Mehrotra**. Thanks to **Dr. Divya Chabbra** for her constructive criticism which is much valued. Thanks to my two in-house ego-antidotes, my children **Soham** and **Sahaj**. And special thanks to **Dr. Meghna Shah** whose intention, efficiency, effort and encouragement has made so much of what I do possible and a joy.

Many thanks to all my patients. Their trust in me was a very big motivation for all my work. Heartfelt thanks to those who have so kindly consented to have their detailed case studies reported here.

Many thanks to **Anjali Menrai** and **Cheryl Feng** for the artwork and cover and to the excellent cooperation from Thomson Press particularly **Ms. Neha Patwardhan** and **Mr. Surendra Babu**.

Prelude

What is it that makes each one of us who we are? What is it that makes us feel, perceive, experience and act in a manner unique to each one? Wherein lies this uniqueness and its source? What is it that generates stress in each of us?

Questions like these are not merely interesting and intriguing but are also vital to an individual's understanding of his persona. And "Know thyself" is but the way to "Heal thyself".

I went to Country X for a seminar. The process of going was interesting. I applied for a visa and was told I would have to go to Delhi for a private interview. I wrote to my hosts in Country X to ask if they could talk to their ministry to arrange that I be allowed to talk on the phone for the visa interview. They left a message with the ambassador, and then told me to speak to him on the phone. When I phoned him, however, the embassy said that he was away on holiday for one-and-a-half months. The vice-consul didn't do phone interviews. So I wrote an e-mail. There was no response for ten days. What to do now? They said they would arrange for me to speak to the vice-consul. "We don't promise. However, send your papers." So I sent them the papers, but there was no response for two weeks. Three months after initiation of the procedure there was still no result.

Now I was supposed to leave in a week for a big world trip of seminars. All my papers were held up. I made 30-35 phone calls. They told me the visa was ready. I sent somebody to pick up the papers at 9 a.m. They made him wait until 4 p.m. and then told him to come the next day. The next day the same thing happened. They said my papers were not ready. The papers were for a different Sankaran, who wanted to go on the same day. Then they asked for a bank paper, which would take a week to process. In the meantime, the ambassador was back, so I phoned him. I said, "Give me my passport back, with or without the visa." He said, "You are an honored guest, you must go!" So again I sent a man at 10 a.m., and he got the visa at 7.30 p.m. Throughout the day they would say they were putting the visa in his hand, while he would say he was still waiting outside.

Why am I telling you this story? This is a typical stressful situation, and it provides a good opportunity to inquire into the nature of stress. If we can perceive what stress is in this given situation, maybe we can get an idea of what stress is in general. Surely, I was very stressed in this situation - but what was happening within me which I labeled as **"stress"**? What did I feel and experience throughout this process? I could observe that simultaneously there were different things going on within me. It was like there were different levels of experience within me.

I had a need for visa so that I could go to that country. I needed my passport back so that I could go to the other countries on the lecture tour. I needed the passport back within a particular time so that I could take the scheduled flight. I had to calculate what to do in case I did not get the visa. What changes I had to make on the itinerary. A practical mind was working out these facts. This was one level of my experience at that time.

On another-namely, an emotional level-I was angry and anxious. The anxiety led to physical symptoms like palpitations. I was very upset.

At another level, I was imagining what was happening. Why was it not working out? What could be the reason? Several theories came to my mind. But one prominent thought was whether this was deliberate on the part of the embassy. Was it a conspiracy?

I can now see that this kind of suspicion and perception is not limited to this particular situation and it is something that is familiar to me in other situations of my life, past and present.

But if you were to ask me to go deeper into myself and ask *what I was actually experiencing in the moment?* - not what feelings I had, or what imagination I had about the situation, but *what was I experiencing?, what was I feeling in the very core of my being?,* for the most part I (like most of you) am not aware, not conscious of it. However I let myself go into that experience and observed it and came in touch with a deeper level of experience. It was a sensation I could feel intensely within my whole being.

I could only describe it as a kind of gagging. The word alone is insufficient to describe my experience. It was a choking, a constriction that went up my chest into my throat. To fully express it, I needed to make sounds and gestures. If I went deeper into this sensation, I would see it as a part of an experience of being caught, trapped and overpowered.

This sensation (and the overall experience) actually had nothing to do with the ambassador, ministry, visas or conspiracies. It transcends the barriers of time and space. It is an experience I have had many times in my life and that I will have in any future stressful situations. This experience has no name, no fact and no emotion to it. It intrinsically has to do with my unique, inexplicable experience of reality.

This experience is a part of a deeply embedded pattern within me. The deeper I perceive this pattern of experience in my life, the more I realize my state and the root of my stress. This is not only true for me, but it is true for you. Awareness of this pattern is the path to liberation from it.

We all desire to minimize our stress and suffering; we desire peace. We try to find the solution to the problem we see as the cause of stress. We may try to avoid situations that are stressful. We attempt to change our job, our partner or our location. We try and change ourselves. We read self-help books. We meditate. We go to religious services. We talk with people about our problems. We seek professional help. I am sure you are familiar with whatever you do to deal with your stress.

When we have an argument with someone, when we feel hurt in a relationship, when we are having difficulties in our work or when we face a business loss, we tend to see the problem as being outside of us, something which we need to solve. We analyze the issue and find logical explanations or reasons why such a situation has occurred and what we should do about it. We could say,

"The problem between my wife and me is that she simply does not understand me; I think we need to go to a counselor." We tend to justify our emotions; for example we may say, "It is natural for me to be anxious when business is so bad" or, "who would not get angry if your friend does like that?" We classify situations, give people labels; sometimes we even give a name to our own state. We could say, "That man is a dictator" or, "I have an inferiority complex."

None of these attempts to solve the issue has lasting effect. The reason is simple: We have not got to the root of the issue. The problem is not outside, but it is in our experience of it. When we communicate with others, we reason or we argue but we do not see that we are not getting through. We are saying something, but it is not what we say that is important. What is important is where it is coming from. And that is from a deep level within us which we are not conscious of. And till that level is touched by us, within us, our communication and dealings with the outside world will remain problematic, superficial and ineffective in the deeper context of our inner peace.

Let us use an everyday example to illustrate this idea. You come home from work and see that your parking space has been taken by someone else, a neighbor perhaps? Your emotions are excited. This is not the first time he has done this. You have told him before politely, but he has done this too often. What happens? At one level you know what needs to be done and this level is matter of fact. There is no stress here, only a calculation. But at another level there is anger, "How dare he? What does he think of himself?" This level is stressful, your nerves are excited, and your mind is working overtime. When you look into this experience, you will see that this stress does not come from the situation, but from your perception of it i.e. your innermost experience of that anger, your feelings of being victimized, trapped, caught, helpless against a stronger opponent in your struggle to survive. Or your experience of apprehension that the parking space will be lost to you. Or your experience of fear to face the rudeness of the neighbor when you confront him with what he is doing, your desire to avoid the rudeness since you are very sensitive.

Whatever be your experience, you realize that this experience is not limited to this situation but transcends this and applies to you as a whole and for most of your life. That this experience is who you are. That is the stress for you; it is the constant source of stress.

At some point we do realize that stress is not from the outside of us, but from the way we perceive and react to reality. And this is unique to each one of us. In fact, it is the way each one perceives and reacts to reality which makes him unique, gives him his individuality. Thus our stress is inseparable from our individuality.

Most of us realize that, ultimately, to minimize stress, it doesn't help to change our outside circumstances, but that we need to perceive where the stress is coming from. Psychologists, therapists and others do a lot of work on this. We are familiar with the ideas that stress comes from incidents like your father beating you when you were twelve, from constantly arguing with your wife, from feeling like you don't have enough money and so on. But what I discovered is that while these may be the situations in which you feel stressed, your experience of stress arises from something much deeper and that experience is unique to you. What is more profound is that this unique experience is also expressed in areas of your life that are not considered stressful; it actually underlies your entire experience of life.

In my work as a physician and a homoeopath, I definitely need to know as much as I can about the inner processes of each individual who comes to me for treatment. This has certainly been a strong motivation for my work, but at least equally has been the desire to discover what lies at the core of my own self.

In my practice I repeatedly see people go deeper into the experience of their stress, their disease, their joys, their grief, and each time, a characteristic pattern, unique to each person, is revealed. Such a pattern exists in me, in you, in everyone. If you increase your awareness of this pattern, you will experience less stress and more peace.

You can experience the truth of these ideas through a simple process of enquiry. Not a process where you analyze or classify, but a process in which you go deeper within and observe your experience in the moment. The depth and totality of this experience is the truth.

We go deeper by asking the *what* of something and not the *why* of something. When we ask ourselves, *why* something is this way or that, we come up with reasons that may seem like the truth, but these reasons can always be debated on whether they are true or not. On the other hand, when we ask, "what is?" deeper and deeper, we uncover the true inner experience where there is no room for interpreting, theorizing or analyzing. It is a process of pure observation of what is deeper.

We need to realize that part of the essence of the concepts in this work lies in the notion that our behavior and our feelings stem from something much deeper in our beings. They are rooted in a very basic, inexplicable experience unique to each one of us. This experience is not emotional or intellectual; it is a sensation felt in the body and mind simultaneously, one that is constant, one that colors our whole experience of life. This sensation is our constant companion, the other song that keeps singing within us. A song that resonates with something in nature, be it an animal, plant or a mineral.

The awareness referred to here is not an intellectual understanding or an observation of a behavior or thought pattern in ourselves; nor is it a flash of realization, or an interpretation by someone else.

It is a process. It is a process of going within the self without the mind, of going into the depth of one's experience over and over again. It is a process that can begin now and extend over several months or years. It is a gradual awakening to one's inner world. It is a silent, nonverbal, nonintellectual process, where one can hear what the other song is that is playing within and become aware of how it has shaped everything in his life.

The ideas in the book have had a considerable impact on the homoeopathic practice. They are not theories, they are observations from daily practice and life confirmed by colleagues all over the world. *All case examples written in the book are ones that have been successfully treated with Homoeopathy and helped by the interview process.* However the concepts are universal and, once understood, they can be applied in any field of human involvement.

Origins

By way of a background to the book and to trace for you the path I have travelled, let me briefly explain Homoeopathy and the development of my ideas.

In 1790, a German physician Dr. Samuel Hahnemann made a very significant discovery. At that time cinchona bark (from which quinine is derived) was very well known and used for its curative effects on malaria. Eager to discover what gave the bark its curative power, Hahnemann tested this substance on himself whilst he was in a healthy state. He saw that it produced within him symptoms similar to those of malaria i.e. chill, fever and sweat. This led him to the clue

that drugs can produce certain symptoms and signs in the healthy individual and can cure someone with the same symptoms. This was the beginning of Homoeopathy which is based on the principle: "Like cures like".

After this, Hahnemann started testing several drugs on himself and some volunteers to ascertain what effects they could produce on healthy people so that he could use these drugs when he found similar symptoms in sick people. He started recording accurately the elicited signs and symptoms of each drug tested on healthy volunteers, in a book called the Homoeopathic Materia Medica.

What Hahnemann also discovered is, that disease is not localized but affects the whole being. Therefore when a person is sick, it is not merely a part but the whole of him that is sick. Likewise, a drug affects the whole being including the mind. The homoeopath thus treats a person keeping these factors in mind.

During the consultation a Homoeopath records all the symptoms as well as the patient's state of mind. This is then matched with the symptoms of the various remedies in the Materia Medica and then one single remedy which is the closest match is given to the patient.

Hahnemann recognized the need to also use certain substances which in their natural state would be poisonous, for he foresaw their utility as great remedies but there was no way he could use them in their pristine form so he decided to dilute them. To his surprise, he saw that the more he diluted the substances (with vigorous shaking) the more their medicinal effects increased. This process of serial dilution of a drug substance is termed "Potentization".

The serial dilution was ca rried to such an extent that hardly any substance was left in these dilutions. Yet they were found to act powerfully. This led Hahnemann to conclude that diseases are states that are not material but dynamic. Healing also happens dynamically. He postulated that there is a **dynamic life force within each of us, the vital force at which level disease and healing happen. Disease is the disturbance of this force unique to each individual and manifested as a state of mind and through different physical symptoms.**

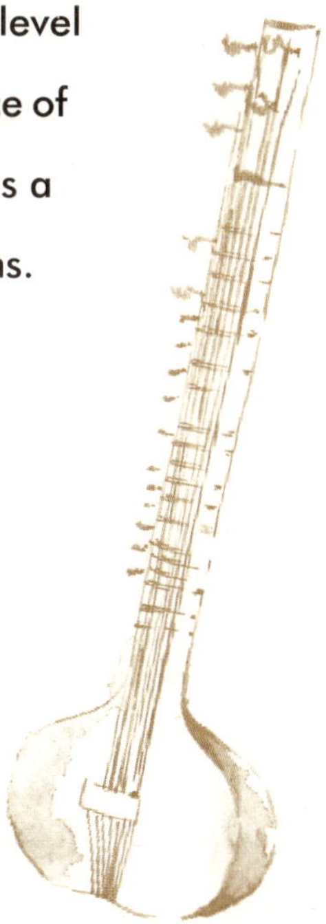

Sickness can be compared to a sitar [1]
whose correct tuning has been disturbed.

Naturally, there will be discord. However it is the faulty tuning itself and not the individual notes that need to be

[1] A stringed musical instrument

addressed. Similarly, homoeopathic treatment is at the same time **holistic and individualistic**. The inner disturbance needs to be corrected and restored to health and balance. A person's state of being, his perception of and response to the world are an essential part of his individuality. These are as integral to his disease as the pain in his limbs or the ulcer in his stomach.

In Homoeopathy everything that a patient says, however queer, rare, peculiar and strange becomes a symptom. For example, in a cold room if you feel hot it is a symptom. If we understand this deeper, a symptom is an inappropriate response to the existing situation. It is as if the person is perceiving and reacting to a different reality than what is actually there. In a cold room he reacts as if it is a hot room.

Disease was thus seen as an affection of the whole person, as a posture adopted as a survival mechanism to suit a particular situation that is perceived rather than real. This posture makes us react to reality in an unsuitable and disproportionate manner due to our false perception of it. Naturally this in turn produces a constant stress in us. For example, when a man is being chased by a lion, the posture of running fast, being afraid, etc. is appropriate since his survival depends upon it. However, if he is in such a state, with no lion to justify it, or he adopts such a posture even when chased by a little dog, or if he is in such a panic that he cannot think (a reaction that is in excess of what is needed in the situation) then this is disease. It is as if he were functioning on a false perception of reality, a **"delusion"**, which makes him react in an inappropriate manner. This is the root of his stress. This delusion is further reflected in a person's fears, dreams, hobbies, and colors all aspects of his life akin to colored lenses he wears at all times.

The patient, a boy of 10 years, was referred to me by my colleague for treatment of a very severe and chronic skin problem. He had boils on the extremities which were very painful and itching. For the past month he could not even sit or stand. He was carried into my consulting room, crying, his boils full of pus.

Describing the itching, the mother said it was so bad that the boy wanted to tear away his skin. With his hands clenched, he would shriek from the severity of the itching, almost like an insane person. He would say: "Kill me, I can't take it, I don't want to live." Whenever the itching became too much he would say: "Give me a knife, I want to stab my arms."

As a child, the boy had been very dependent on a particular Goddess. He used to compose and sing songs in her praise. With the itching, the boy had become angry with the Goddess and would say: "I have done so much for her and this is what she has done to me!" Once having said this, he tore up the picture he had of the Goddess.

He was very sensitive both in mind and skin. He could not tolerate even a drop of water; he did not like bathing and was thirstless. The itching with its accompanying violence was not continuous, but spasmodic. There was cruel behavior. He would say: "I will become mad."

In this case we can see the following symptoms on the mental and general level:

- Violence
- Abusive
- Striking
- Cruelty
- Impulse to tear
- Desire to cut, mutilate
- Impulse to stab himself

The main feelings connected with this state are:

- Forsaken (by Goddess)
- Tormented feeling (by Goddess)
- Feels he has suffered wrong

From these feelings come the violent reactions. He has skin eruption and reacts as if he were in a situation where he is tormented and forsaken by the person he is serving and on whom he is dependent (the Goddess).

From this we can see that the boy's fixed perception (delusion) was that he was being tortured and tormented by the Goddess to whom he was so devoted. This reaction was one of violence with the impulse to destroy. (The Homoeopathic remedy Hydrophobinum – which is made from the saliva of a rabid dog – has this exact perception and reaction. And this remedy healed the boy.)

Incidentally I examined the history of the mother during her pregnancy and got the following story.

The mother had a severe toothache throughout the pregnancy. This was her second pregnancy. Her first child was stillborn. Since the beginning of the second pregnancy the mother had felt that something terrible would happen. She would pray all the time. The baby was ten days overdue. This made her panicky and extremely tense. She would stand before the picture of the same Goddess and with her hands clenched, she would cry: "Why are you doing this to me?"

The feeling is the same : "troubled by someone she is dependent on, a sense of injustice, forsaken feeling".

I started noticing this phenomenon in several cases. One of my first observations was: If the mother had a very intense state during the pregnancy, the child almost always has the same state.

Disease sets up several conditions for feeling okay. Due to these conditions (compulsions) and obsessions (fixed feelings) our ability to react to the situation becomes restricted. This restriction is the measure of our disease. When such a restriction is present we are no longer open to what is in front of us. Good health allows man to be in the moment and to react appropriately and proportionately to the situation he faces. If the situation calls for achievement he will achieve. If it demands that he remains passive so be it. Neither achievement nor passivity is a condition of his good health. He is free to react in accordance with the situation. Health signifies freedom, spontaneity and being in the present. The spirit within is free to fulfill the requirements of the situation.

Once I understood that disease is a false perception of reality, I recognized that the type of situation perceived can be classified according to the depth and desperation of the perceived situation. I could categorize ten such possible types.

A situation can be perceived as one of the following:

1. It is perceived as sudden and acute, and there is a desire to flee from the situation because one's very life depends on it.

2. It is perceived as suddenly critical, but if one made an immediate intense effort he could regain his security.

3. It is perceived as a situation that can be worrying for him but never hopeless. The feeling here is that life is a steady ongoing struggle.

4. It is perceived as a situation that he would try to overcome sometimes and at other times he would just accept it.

5. It is perceived as a difficult situation where he feels trapped in and occassionally threatened by.

6. It is perceived as a difficult situation ensnaring but not life threatening, and so he has to just accept it and hide his problem since it is a perceived weakness.

7. It is perceived as a situation where time is short and there is a sense of being hemmed in and therefore a desire to break free before it is too late.

8. It is perceived as a situation that feels chaotic and out of control and one has to stretch beyond one's capacity to control it or to restore order.

9. It is perceived as a sense of obvious disgust with oneself and the situation, where the person chooses to preemptively distance himself from society, thereby feeling isolated.

10. It is perceived as a situation that seems impossible and hopeless giving rise to an impending sense of destruction.

Let us take the example that while driving on a highway your car breaks down. There are ten typical ways of viewing any demanding situation, and each individual's reaction will fall into one of them:

1. The situation calls for panic; I desire to escape as soon as possible. I will abandon my car if necessary in order to get a safer, less precarious area.

2. The situation is a crisis; I need to make an intense effort to solve it quickly. I will examine the car forcefully and determinedly, all the while rapidly pushing the buttons of my cellular telephone to get a towing company out immediately.

3. The situation presents a problem that is solvable; I will make an optimistic effort to solve it. I will carefully look for the cause of the breakdown, summon what I know about the workings of cars, and attempt to get the car going.

4. The possibility of solving the situation is doubtful; I will likely attempt to solve, give up, but then try again (alternating state). I will move around the car carefully, looking for the problem, while thinking, "Gosh, I really don't know much about cars"; return to the driver's seat feeling defeated; then rouse myself to exit the car, to take another look in case I missed something.

5. This is a situation for which nothing can be done; I will find another way (of getting home). I will make little or no attempt to examine the car, because, after all, only mechanics know how to fix cars; I will straightaway reach for my cellular telephone to call a towing company.

6. This type of situation is harassing or persecuting; I feel unfortunate and am sure that such situations always seem to happen to me. As I circle the car, I am more occupied with such feelings as if I weren't so poor, I could afford a better car; if my husband loved me more, he would see to it that things like this didn't happen to me, etc., than I am with taking practical steps to get help for me and my car.

7. The situation just has to be solved, whatever it may take. I will apply superhuman effort to solve it, as if my life depended on it. I will pop the hood, get tools from the trunk, and work determinedly, even doing things that I am not strong enough or knowledgeable enough to undertake, regardless of the surrounding hazards of cars speeding by at close range or the pelting rain.

8. There is a very limited window of opportunity to solve this type of situation; to get the car working again will be a racing against time. I am acutely aware that darkness will be coming on, I am in an area that will become increasingly isolated as the rush-hour traffic ebbs, and the towing companies will not be open much longer.

9. This type of situation is always very dangerous and hard to solve. I will think of all the reasons that it will be difficult or impossible to get a towing company to come all the way out here and fear that I will be forced to remain here, where I am stranded and at the mercy of criminals, wild animals or bad weather.

10. This type of situation is always totally hopeless and always makes me angry and frustrated. I am certain that when a car breaks down this badly it is beyond repair. The good feelings I had about this car are ruined, because it is now just another unreliable car. I will feel like taking a hammer to the car, certain that I'll just have to junk it.

Reaction Pattern (indicates nature and degree of the perceived situation)
The panic type
The crisis type
The possible type
The persecuted type
The doubtful type
The fixed type
The chaotic type
The claustrophobic type
The isolated type
The impossible type

Another Classification

Just as each of us is stuck in our view of the depth and desperation of the situation in front of us, we are also stuck in how we see the situation essentially or the type of situation we perceive. The type of situation we repeatedly perceive and thus create for ourselves can be a competition, a need for structure or the loss of something within us, or a sensivity reaction to something.

For example, let us take a situation wherein a young woman is disappointed in love because her boyfriend has left her for another person. This situation can be viewed by three women in three entirely different ways:

- The woman left for another could view the situation as one of competition, where she compares herself to the other woman and thinks, "In what way is she better then me?" The situation could provoke a desire for revenge, feelings of jealousy, or the urge to one-up the other person. She could feel victimized.

- Another woman in the same situation experiences the incident as a loss. She had viewed her boyfriend as a support that she could trust and depend on, someone on whom she could lean; and suddenly she finds herself at a loss, empty, and alone and wonders how she is going to support herself.

- Another woman could see the situation as a shock, something that just came out of the blue, completely unexpected. She is very sensitive, hurt and reacts to this shock with a kind of numbness.

In the above examples you can see three different ways of experiencing the same situation, namely by viewing it as a competition, fearing that it brings a threat to or loss of structure, or with a sensitive reaction. These disparate responses bring to mind the three kingdoms in nature, namely animal, mineral, and plant. The animal way of viewing a situation will be as a competition, a struggle for survival. The mineral way will be to feel a need for or fear losing part of one's structure. And the plant way will be to be sensitive and reactive to the external stimulus. Thus we can have people who are animal type, mineral type and plant type. What is interesting is that each one of us is stuck in a particular type and we will view every situation in our life according to our type.

Remedies in homoeopathy are mainly derived from three sources i.e. **plants, animals** and **minerals.** They are used singly and a patient would need a remedy drawn from a particular plant, mineral or animal. Remedies would be dictated by the symptoms. If the symptoms of a patient indicated a particular remedy, the homoeopath would give it no matter which kingdom it belonged to. However with some research I saw that people who needed remedies from each of these kingdoms differed fundamentally in the way they perceived and reacted to reality. Here are the main issues of the 3 kingdoms which we try to understand in cases.

Plant Kingdom	Animal Kingdom	Mineral Kingdom
Sensitivity and reactivity.	Comparison and competition and a struggle for survival.	The formation or loss of structure.

(Each of these kingdoms is described in greater detail in later chapters)

To define it more sharply I examined the subdivisions within each kingdom and this opened up a whole new way of looking at homoeopathy. For example, within the animal kingdom one could identify what is a snake type, or a spider type or a bird type. Now I started looking at remedies not merely as a collection of symptoms but as embodying the spirit of something in nature, and therefore a part of a system. I understood that the symptoms of a particular remedy that are in the Homoeopathic Materia Medica are not just accidents or random effects but they represent the source itself.

To cite an example – a cuttle fish (Sepia) in its natural environment has its defense mechanism in hiding behind its own ink and escaping by swimming backwards when faced by a predator. On the same lines it is seen in the testing of Sepia (the remedy from the cuttle fish) on healthy people that the person in his dream is escaping by running backwards. What is interesting of course is that the subject probably knew nothing of what he was taking and yet it seems as if the animal expressed itself through his dream!

I understood that the Homoeopathic Materia Medica is the human expression of the source itself. The remedies from various sources heal humans with similar states within them. These states, which we call disease, must also be, like the remedies, from one of the three kingdoms.

This led me to the next level of perception – and that is **'Sensation'** where I saw that a human being's deepest issue was a very specific state that was not even human! It was something **'Non-Human'**. What was abnormal was to be human and yet have a part within that was a plant, animal or a mineral and being confined within that perception. It then became my mission to identify ways of discovering the particular state that dominated each person.

Consequently I refined my case taking to reach this level of sensation. For example, a particular patient is asked a question in relation to some situation he faces, "So how does that feel?" and he says, "It feels like a captive in a cell." At that point I ask that one question – "What is the experience of being a captive?"– which takes the leap that is required to go deeper, one more step towards the sensation. To many of my readers this question may perhaps sound weird or ridiculous. You must think that it really does not require rocket science to figure out how a captive feels in a cell –

but one would be amazed at how each experience is different from another. For example, for one it could be an experience of, "I am stuck and I can't move." This is a sensation expressing sensitivity and so he would require a plant remedy. For another the experience may be like being under some other powerful being, like you're victimized by some one. This is a victim-aggressor issue that would require an animal remedy. And for yet others it could be a sense of incapacity, "I lack a sense of capability within to get out on my own." What he is saying here is that he lacks the structure that is needed. This person would require a mineral remedy.

I began to see how a delusion when examined deeper gives an inner sensation which is not human specific.

Consequently my case taking also proceeded in this fashion where patients normally began with the **"Name"** or diagnosis of their problem. Then they would furnish me with more details as **"Facts"** of their symptoms such as what seems to aggravate or ameliorate their complaint, what kind of pain they experience locally etc. Then they would describe how their illness made them **"Feel"** .They spoke of emotions like anger, irritation etc. At this point I would channelize questions by asking, "How does that feel?" Each one would describe their own **"Delusion"**. And an experience in this delusion is their **"Sensation"**. And when describing their sensation they would use their hands indicating that they had arrived at the **"Level of Energy"**. As I focus on this movement of their hands, a different language emerges from within, the voice of something in nature, the whole **'Other Song'** unfolds itself beautifully.

After the whole phenomenon is understood the important thing then is to find the source (remedy). The shift that began for me lay in the depth of the case taking process when people expressed their inner **'Other Song'**. Sometimes we heard songs that we hadn't heard before and we started prescribing more and more new remedies. Healing happened at a deep level, more than I had seen earlier.

What is significant is that the patients too apart from just receiving a remedy, realised as they expressed themselves during the interview process, that it brought them in touch with a core aspect of themselves. Improved self-perception and self-awareness made them realize their body, mind, their physical symptoms, emotions, dreams were all connected at this deep core level. This awareness was not intellectual but experiential. And they would remark, "Oh yes! This is the same experience that I had in the other situation."

A patient, a man of about 40 years came to my colleague, Dr. Chatterjee, for treatment of diabetes and weakness. He described his weakness as a lack of stamina. This was especially felt when he played his favorite sport of badminton. On being asked to describe the game, he said that it is a game that involved very high speed and stamina so that you are ahead of your opponent and after you tire him out you need to make one final shot where he least expects it and then the opponent "is finished by this smash." He demonstrated this by raising his right hand up above his head and then bringing it down with force and speed. On being asked about himself, he said he likes speed in general and likes to drive his motorcycle very fast, winding his way very quickly in the traffic so that he is ahead of all the rest. His favorite entertainment was to watch the animal channel on television, and he was most fascinated by the wild cats, especially by the cheetah. He described the cheetah as an animal of great speed and stamina and one that brought down its prey by the final smash of its paw after a long chase. He demonstrated the action of the cheetah by using exactly the same gesture of bringing down his palm very quickly and forcefully, the same gesture that he had used to describe the game of badminton. At that point he realised the same pattern in these two instances. It is intriguing to see how closely the patient's energy pattern reflected the source in nature and how that energy pattern colors his way of being, playing and choice of recreation, and how his disease (diabetes, weakness) is an expression of the opposite of this sensation.

This awareness even before taking the remedy helped them to experience a sense of freedom. It is almost as if sitting across you could hear the click in their consciousness. This "aah" phenomenon of their observing and seeing all aspects of their life as one, seeing the common thread through everything was a great potent healing agent. Some said that this was one of the deepest experiences they had ever had.

I concluded from this that our problems and conflicts, emotions and complexes, dreams and delusions, were all only expressions of a deeper inner state or turmoil existing at the level of sensory experience which has non-human-specific qualities in it drawn from other sources. Every self-expression contains the words and the gestures that indicate the sensory experience behind it. If we identify and focus on that, then the other world, the 'Other Song' opens up and you see something you know, whose presence you had only sensed, now standing completely revealed.

The Source Of Stress

All of us seek peace in the form of harmony, contentment, happiness, joy, health, serenity, balance. Peace denotes the absence of conflict, of the turmoil and stress that conflict brings. It is a state where we cease to be at war with ourselves or with the world.

Most of us know this state because we do experience it now and then in our lives. Most of the time, however, we do not. Although we know that fulfillment lies in sustaining this state of harmony, conflict all too often and too readily recurs and peace is lost. The resultant stress, which is an inherent part of our life, affects our health, our relationships and our work space. In short it affects the way we feel and act.

In our attempt to reduce stress levels, we indulge in various strategies that come naturally to us. The most common one is to try and change the external situation out of the belief that the cause of our stress lies there. For example, if our stress is about money, we try to earn more and generate new avenues of income.

When stress arises in relationships, we try to manipulate the other person or end the relationship itself. We hope to find in someone else a stress-free relationship. When stress takes its toll on our health, we adopt different techniques and therapeutic modalities to deal with it.

Another path we tend to adopt is to avoid the cause of stress altogether. If that does not help, we divert our mind from the cause of stress. Sometimes we try to escape from the scene and in the worst-case scenario escape life itself.

All these measures relieve us by releasing the stress. However, these measures work temporarily and only partially, if at all. The main reason why they are ineffective is because they aim at external reality which we attempt to avoid, escape or rearrange. This rearranging of external circumstances is like attempting to straighten your shadow while you yourself remain bent!

Stress does not arise from external circumstances, but from the individual perception of these circumstances. The truth is that the external reality is not the 'cause' of most of the stresses and conflicts that occur in our lives.

If we were to analyze life's extremes or observe the hardest of external realities, we would find an absence of internal conflicts at these moments. We know what the facts are and we also know exactly how to respond at such times. (It is a well known fact that the incidence of suicide and mental illness drops during wartime.)

If your house is on fire, there is no conflict in your mind. You know what best to do and you do it. There is a certain unity and harmony within. A single inner voice suggests the action to be taken. There is often little inner debate or turmoil at such times. You are not worried about the situation; all you focus on is the 'action' and you just act!

Thus, it would be safe to say that in a really tough situation where there is a vivid external problem, the mind innately seems to know 'what' to do (to the extent that it even knows 'how' to do it).

So then, how does the conflict within an individual arise?

It arises when the external reality differs significantly from the individual's perception of that reality. When such a disparity between inner and outer reality occurs, there is a threat to unity and harmony. Instead the person experiences duality and conflict. He experiences two inner voices: one voice saying what it actually is; the other perceiving, from his view point, quite differently and so talking with a different voice. For example, an individual may be prosperous financially, and may objectively seem to have no grounds for anxiety on that score. However if his own perception is that he is needy and financially insecure (a mismatch between outer reality and his own perceptions), he will experience two contradictory voices within him. It is this inner debate, this conflict within, which creates stress.

Another example could be that of a girl who constantly feels unloved by the whole world. Objectively, she has her parents who love her; the institution that she belongs to also takes good care of her; and yet she dwells on the feeling that nobody loves her. Subjectively she feels unloved. The voice of outer reality ('what is') is contradicted by that of her 'inner reality' (what she perceives to be the case). These two contradictory voices create turmoil and stress at every level in her.

So we gradually move to the concept that our underlying stress is, not about 'what is' (the external situation) but more about 'what appears to be' (our individual way of seeing and experiencing that situation).

When our individual perception differs markedly from the actual situation, we are in effect suffering from a delusion. This false way of seeing (delusion) is like wearing life-long colored glasses that we never seem to take off. We view all situations in the same 'colored way'. It becomes the routine way of perceiving our self and our world.

In any given situation, our mind and body tend to first perceive that situation and then evaluate what it signifies for our survival. We thus know how to adapt and respond to the situation. This is in a way an automatic process.

For example, when an insect stings you or a mosquito bites you, your senses perceive it and you automatically swing your hand to swat the insect. There is no conflict, no duality. There is action in the moment. The perception and the reaction are appropriate and in proportion as there is no distortion of reality. The incident or the situation leaves no trace or after-effects. This is health in terms of adaptability, freedom to be in the moment, where the mind and body know what to do and how much to do.

If your house is on fire, you might experience anxiety and fear, but these emotions would be in proportion and would evoke specific and appropriate responses. They would disappear when the situation is gone. However, when a person acts from a delusion he does not recognize the actual reality. Instead the latter is colored and shaded by his perceptions of it. In doing so he reacts inappropriately or disproportionately. The situation evokes something in his mind, excites memories of the past, reminding him of several things that have happened to him before. Moreover, the present situation confirms and reaffirms his delusion, and so the totality is more deeply etched in his memory for the future. Because of his 'deluded way of seeing,' a part of him is unable to live in the moment, in the present reality. However, another part of him is unable to deny that reality, the 'what actually is'. This duality causes deep, internal conflict resulting in stress. His inappropriate perception and reaction, and not the situation itself, is the basis of the stress.

If we are able to live in the moment, we perceive the situation as it is. There is thus no conflict and the situation can be tackled and dealt with almost automatically, like swatting the mosquito. The situation remains an experience and does not become a problem. A situation becomes a problem only when it is shackled to the past, and when it confirms a false perception of reality, thus fixing it even more firmly in our mind. Each situation then becomes a problem, connected to a lifelong problem, and a delusion that rules an individual life. Whatever the situation, it will always be viewed in a certain light and reacted to from this false perception of reality.

Each one of us has our own delusion which influences our life, on the way we work, and our interpersonal relationships. Emotional states, fears, hatred and even joy are based very much on this delusion. It also gets represented in our dreams, nightmares and fantasies.

What is interesting to observe is that these delusions are shared by the entire human race and are therefore nonspecific to the individual. They are universal in nature, finding expression in mythology, fairytales, literature, art, movies and all other forms of the human imagination.

We view all our experiences in life in the light of our personal delusion. We resonate with certain periods or events in history and mythology which match our way of seeing. We identify with certain characters in novels or films whose way of acting and reacting in some way corresponds with our own story. Thus the delusion takes us beyond our personal experience and connects us to other individuals throughout human history.

For example, a young man describes his state as being unhappy at his work place. This is his feeling. When we inquire further and ask him to describe this unhappiness in depth he describes his experience at work as being similar to that of being captured and tortured. When asked to describe the words 'captured and tortured' the images that come to his mind are those of African slaves taken to America, concentration camps during the Second World War, and the way the conquerors treated their captives.

These pictures of people who had been captured and tortured are from different eras and thus have been a part of human experience (and therefore consciousness) through time immemorial. Once we realize this, we understand that this experience is not limited to the individual, but is truly universal. Although the individual describes a deep level in him that is personal and private, the turmoil he describes is common to all and can be traced in all human consciousness. So even while reaching a plane that is intensely personal and individual, we find that plane to be common to all humanity.

Delusion therefore is not limited by time and place. It repeatedly manifests itself in different eras through different people in human history. It has existed in various forms since the beginning of human civilization. Expressions may vary, but the same pattern is manifest.

For instance, individuals who have the urge to be the most powerful can be seen in every era, and in every country. Examples range from Alexander the Great and Julius Caesar to Hitler. This demonstration of power in the use of capture, torture and the rule of fear is seen in all countries and cultures over time. This is why mythology is of contemporary significance. Shakespeare portrayed human delusions vividly, as personified by the characters in his plays. His plays communicate these truths and remain valid to us in a remarkable way that seems timeless. Our delusions cross the barriers of time, place, language, nationality and culture.

Attempts are made by many to find the origin of these delusions. Some attribute them to childhood incidents and traumas; others trace them back to past lives. It is understandable that we seek to find the source of these recurring and repetitive patterns of perceptions and behavior. In doing so, however, we follow a linear path of cause and effect: And this occurred because that happened. But then, what caused that to happen? And so on. Sometimes our ongoing question of Why? yields answer in the form of brilliant guesses. More often it yields only theories, as we can never be sure. We can only surmise.

There is a question that is far more fruitful than Why? and that is the question What? The only knowable, accessible truth is 'what is' in the present moment. Why the present reality is the way it is is not ultimately knowable to us. The 'what' is more than enough for us to seek, to perceive clearly.

Truth then is not the "why" but the "what" of something.

What is "Is"

The **"Isness"** of the moment is the entire truth. Isness signifies the totality of a phenomenon examined in the deepest possible way, in the moment, outside and inside, superficial and deep, as deep as you can go. The complete phenomenon in the moment is the only and entire truth. Every "why" is but a theory.

There are two branches of inquiry into the nature of things:

1. One way is the way of reasoning and understanding. It involves thinking, surmising, using logic, postulating etc. It seeks to find the cause of things, and to label and classify these things.

2. The other branch of inquiry is the way of pure observation. It seeks to just witness what IS without thought, analysis or attempt to find the cause or the category. The observation is pursued as deeply and as finely as possible. The totality of the observation is accepted as the knowable truth.

The latter way is the one we are following here. Stress is seen not as a cause and effect phenomenon but as an experience. We do not ask what caused it but what the experience of it is. If we encounter fear for example, we do not ask what the fear is for, or whence it arose. We ask what the experience of the fear is. That experience, when deeply observed, will be seen to be a consistent experience (a sensation) in the person's life, not only in his fear, but also in his headache and other spheres. This, and not theoretical causes, is the truth for the concerned person.

There are forms of psychotherapy that aim at making an individual aware of his delusion or show him his fixed patterns of perception and behavior. But the danger of this is that such a concept could be understood intellectually, not experientially.

The poet William Cowper (1731-1800) expresses it beautifully :

"Knowledge and wisdom, far from being one,
Have oft times no connexion. Knowledge dwells
In heads replete with thoughts of other men;
Wisdom in minds attentive to their own."

The Task.Bk. vi,88-91

The comfort born of intellectual understanding is transient and ineffective in the long run. The reason is very fundamental: a delusion is not intellectual. It does not arise out of a thought process, nor does it stem from emotions. It arises from a much deeper plane. Emotions are in fact the expressions of the delusion and not its source.

In fact when we examine deeper, delusion (the way we perceive a situation) is not confined to the mind, nor does it arise from it. The delusion itself is a part of a much deeper experience, a sensation that encompasses mind and body at a far deeper level, making it 'felt in our very bones,' so to speak. Such an experience is far deeper than a 'mind' experience. It is even deeper than being a specifically human experience, since it is not confined to the mind. It is an experience the human shares with animals, plants, and minerals and the things that make up this earth. For example, when a human being experiences a sensation of being attacked as if by a lion, it is an experience that is common to humans and animals. Other sensations are even more basic (e.g. gravity, pressure, contraction, expansion) and are shared in common with all things on earth including the minerals. Sensation is not just intellectual, emotional or physical. It in fact underlies of all the three.

The Experience and Not the Situation

Are we ready to observe that the sensation takes myriad forms of emotions, situations, symptoms, pains etc?

Are we ready to see?

The sensation assumes so many disguises. It is so absurd, so illogical, so much out of place and yet it is a person's deepest and most constant experience. It is as if he were wearing yellow colored glasses. He describes a car as yellow, a building as yellow, and a person as yellow. If we forget the object of his description but see only the color in it, we will see the same color in all that he describes. This color is the sensation. Often we get lost in what is being described, whether it is a situation, a dream, a hobby, etc. and we forget how it is being described, which is constant and common to all the descriptions. Which is essentially him and not the situation.

A man of about 45 years came with a certain physical ailment, which he said prevented him from having a one-point focus on anything. He said that he was much stressed. When asked to describe the stress, he said he was in a very responsible position. He was the head of his organization and he was the head of his family. However, he seemed to be speaking at this point from his mind, from his intellect, and not from his inner experience. So I asked him that in that moment what the most stressful situation for him was. He said that it was his fight with a local mafia leader over some property issue. On being asked to describe his experience in this situation of the fight, he said he felt like a man fighting against a big, strong, turbulent sea. When I persisted and asked him what is the experience to be in such a situation, he said it was a fight for survival. It was him versus the ocean. On being asked to describe a fight for survival, he said that that was how he experienced any stressful situation: it was him versus someone, or something, a fight to the finish. Then he described several situations in his life where he refused to back out of a fight even if it meant that he would risk his life. In one incident where he was attacked by a robber he showed us how in that situation all he had was a one pointed focus on the robber and then he showed us how he took his hand and brought it down on the robber with a massive force. Later on he described his fascination with lions and described the action of the lion with the same expressions and gestures. Then I could hear the animal song within him and especially the song of a lion. What initially seemed to be the stress of heavy responsibility (this was the situation) turned out to be the inner experience of a decisive fight for survival.

That constant, the sensation, is what we need to tune our ears to hear, that is the destination to which we need to guide the seeker. There lies that switch that suddenly opens the door to another world hidden behind. It is such a new world, just unimaginable!

The trick is to ask for the experience in any given situation, physical, mental, dream-like, linked to the past or an imagined future. For example, a woman says she had a fight with her father. Our question is what she experienced in the fight. She might mention an emotion like anger or hurt or a delusion like being tortured or betrayed. We need to go further and ask what the experience of anger is. Not what the anger is about, not when, not why, not who but "How does anger feel? How is anger experienced? Where is the anger felt? How is the speed? How is the direction?" and most importantly, "What is the sensation?"

The experience of anger will be: **unique, individual, the expression of her other song.**

In this case she likened the anger to choking. When asked to elaborate, she described the sensation as being tied, bound, suffocated by a vice like grip which was choking the breath out of her and she was fighting to survive.

She was describing (unknowingly) the energy of a constrictor snake like the python!

On the face of it, her fight with her father has logically no remote connection to her sensations of being choked, suffocated etc. And yet it is her truth. This is sensation.

People are fluent about what makes them angry and are often more than willing to tell you the entire story or pin the blame on others or on circumstances or even on themselves. But when you ask them to tell you the experience of anger, or how the anger feels, they fall silent and look puzzled since it is a level they are not aware of. Certain hints are conveyed as they express themselves, in the form of metaphors, idioms, certain peculiar words, images or gestures. These give a clue to the underlying experience or sensation behind the emotion or situation.

This pattern or sensation, from which our delusion arises, seems almost to be the voice of the spirit of something within us. It rules a part of our human life and colors our experience. It sounds like a discordant note. One can use the analogy of two voices singing two differing melodies inside us at the same time. One melody is human and is in its proper place. The other melody is simply out of place inside the human being. Thus, these two voices sing together and what a conflict! If we are to attempt to remove or eradicate this stress we need to go to this deepest level of awareness.

The Two Songs

What it is to be a Human?

"Man is the only animal that blushes. Or needs to."

Mark Twain, Following the Equator (1897)

The human is a social being. His existence is dependent on his being a part of a social group. This is common to many animals. What is distinctively human is that, though belonging to a group, each human is an individual, makes individual choices, harbours individual ideas, can think independently and has his own ego. This ego is a part of man's survival instinct; in fact it has been responsible for his development and progress. If we all thought in the same way we could not progress. It is this ego that also contributes to our ability to convert disaster into opportunity and suffering into a catalyst for change. As long as the right balance between the group identity and the individual identity is maintained, as long as the ego is an instrument of creativity and progress, even of spiritual growth, then the human is healthy. This is the human song. In health this is the only song that should be playing; the human is wholly human.

It is interesting to see how all of us as humans have similar qualities and features, similar fears and aspirations, similar thoughts and feelings, and yet there are so many individual variations. A very important component of this human variation is that each one of us possesses an aspect which renders us unique. It is this aspect, however minor, that is not human-specific which characterizes each one of us.

One can also express this by saying that different qualities exist in different proportions in different individuals. For example, one person may have more aggressiveness; another may prefer the colour black, another may have a very strong sweet tooth, etc. These individual variations are not isolated, random phenomena. When we collate all these 'out-of-proportion' features in the perception and reactions of a given individual, we see a clear pattern. That pattern is a reflection of another phenomenon, of an entity which seems to manifest a completely different energy from that of his human life in society as outlined above. Thus there exists a duality. On one hand, each individual has his life as a human being, singing his own human song. On the other hand, upon looking deeply, we find that simultaneously in each person there is also a whole different story from a completely other, nonhuman world inside him that seems to sing another song altogether, a song with its own specific but very different melody.

The Hidden Song Within

This second melody plays concurrently with our natural human song. It influences our life and interferes from time to time, colouring our external story. (It is as if there is another spirit residing within us.)

This other spirit inside us is in itself melodious and complete. Yet is out of place, simply because it is not innately human but is a reflection of a pattern that we have borrowed from nature: from the plant, animal, or mineral kingdoms which I would term the source. This different song in a human being only creates disharmony, a conflict, because there is another song that is already playing in us which is our 'human song'. This other song or our other world of sensory experience is a stranger from another kingdom that lives within us. A stranger who has been with us for so long that we think he is a part of us, like a guest who now talks like he owns the place.

Even though our borrowed song occupies only a small fraction of our energy system compared to the human part, it is this fraction which differentiates one human from another.

This borrowed song plays simultaneously with the normal human song. Often the normal human song is at the forefront in our daily life while the other song gets relegated to the background. However it keeps showing up through the words and metaphors we use most often and that characterize us. It also reveals itself in the sensations we experience and express in various situations, along with the gestures we use to indicate these inner feelings and sensations.

Sometimes it so happens that people try to make this song the main song of their life, by choosing a career or a situation or a partner where this song can be comfortably played. A person, whose song is an aggressive one, might choose a profession which needs that type of aggression (such as police officer).

He can thus live both his songs in his daily life thereby ensuring some degree of harmony in his life. But for the most part we are not able to live more than a small percentage of the other song in our daily life. Under such circumstances the human being expresses the other song in his pastime, hobbies and interests and especially through dreams.

There are things innate and spontaneous to man such as the pursuit of something higher. Man strives for higher achievements through work, a higher love, fulfilling his 'role' in his immediate surrounding, spiritual growth: all things that nurture his ego. Man is also a social animal; he lives in interaction with other human beings, as part of a family, a society, a culture, a nation. There are also some anxieties that are very 'human': an anxiety about security, about the future, about his position in society, etc. All these differentiate man from other animals, and these can be said to compose the human song. This is the only song that should be playing within him; this should be his essence. This song is common to all human beings.

Yet each individual is remarkably different from another. What differentiates us is that any one of the 'human qualities' becomes highly exaggerated, so much so that it attains nonhuman proportions. For example, survival is an issue with human beings as well as with other animals. But other animals are concerned only with survival and nothing else. Their entire existence revolves around survival. If a human being also becomes overly occupied with survival, a shift has taken place right in his very centre. His central energy and sensation are deviated, tending more towards a pattern characteristic to a specific animal. He continues his human existence limited by this deviated energy. His natural desire to pursue human goals is in conflict with an energy that compels him to be occupied with survival. In this way he is severely restricted by the issue of survival which has also become innate to him.

An 'animal song' begins to play deep within him alongside the human song, both distinct, one human and one nonhuman, and they are not in harmony with each other. The result is turmoil. The nonhuman song is harmonious in an animal, but in the human being where there is already an original human song playing, the addition of another melody creates disharmony.

Thus every human being is a part of human society, but buried deep inside him is a specific and distinct nonhuman energy that makes him stand apart from other human beings. As an analogy one can visualize a roomful of men, all from the same race, of similar height and build, all dressed in grey suits. But each one of them has something different about him: one wears a strange hat, another highly polished shoes, a third one a loud tie, a fourth one a red coloured clown's nose etc. The nonhuman part is as absurd and stands out as much as a clown's nose or a strange hat as it is equally inappropriate.

However, when this nonhuman song is not allowed any form of expression the internal turmoil heightens. The nonhuman song becomes more intense and demanding but it is humanly impossible to allow it expression. This part which is suppressed crystallizes as physical and mental pathology which, being a manifestation of the nonhuman song sings the same tune. The human and the nonhuman parts co-exist but in turmoil.

It may also happen that often we are so busy singing this other song, that our human song remains unsung. This might perhaps be the spirit behind the lament of Rabindranath Tagore in his poem **"The Song That I Came To Sing"**:

"The song that I came to sing
remains unsung to this day,
Even today I am still practising the notes,
And only have the wish to sing.

I can't get the right note yet,
it is still not coming together,
Only in the inner recesses of my life
remains the restlessness of the song."

Gitanjali 13, trans. [literally] Rajan Sankaran

Tagore reiterates this feeling further:

"I came out alone on my way to my tryst.
But who is this that follows me in the silent dark?
I move aside to avoid his presence
but I escape him not.

He makes the dust rise from the earth with his swagger;

he adds his loud voice to every word that I utter.

He is my own little self, my lord, he knows no shame;

but I am ashamed to come to thy door in his company."

Gitanjali, 30 trans. Tagore

We can say that this 'other song', this non-human melody expressed in the human can be best heard through the language of disease. And the language of the disease in a person can be heard in the way he voices his complaints, the exact sensation of his aches and pains or other complaints. It can also be seen in his perception of his situation, the words used to describe it, and the effect of the situation on him coupled with his reaction to that situation.

Let me illustrate this concept with an example.

A woman of about 50 consulted me for migraine headache and chronic backache.

I asked her to describe the headache exactly. She was very expressive and described the headache as tightness. As if there was something tight around the head that got tighter and tighter. I asked her to go deeper into the experience. She closed her eyes and went into a kind of hypnotic state and described how after getting very tight she feels as if all her limbs are dissolving and there is a kind of blanket around her. I encouraged her to go further into the experience. She said that when it gets very tight, then there is rocking. And then it opens and then there is a light feeling of floating and flying. The whole process was exactly described. I asked her what the blanket was. She said it was a part of her. I asked what the effect of the migraine on her was. She said she has stopped developing and was actually metamorphosing in the reverse direction. This was a strange word for her to use. I asked her to describe the word "metamorphosing". She said it was like the butterfly. And then she described the lifecycle of the butterfly in exactly the same terms as she described the headache, namely the tightness, the limbs dissolving, the breaking free, the flying (the larva, pupa, the adult butterfly). She herself could see this and remarked indignantly, "I am not a butterfly!"

Another instance that comes to mind is that of a young girl of 25 whose main complaint was irregular bowel movements. She suffered alternately from constipation and diarrhoea. On being questioned how this affected her, she replied that the constipation made her look fat. For her, looking fat signified not wearing good clothes and feeling less attractive. Asked further about the 'less attractive' feeling, she explained that if she stood next to a fat person she would not like it because it reflected on her. People would say 'fat and fat.' Similarly, in the office she did not mix with the people she called 'sideys'. For her, a 'sidey' was someone who was dull and unattractive. Being seen with them 'reflected' on her. If she was spotted with them it meant that she was like them. Since the word 'reflects on me' came up very often I tried to understand it from her perspective.

She said that 'reflects' was a word commonly used to indicate anything that reflects back like glass since it reflects what is inside and outside of it.

She further explained that in life she had a set picture of how her life should be and had a set image of the way she looked. Everything had to be in that set order; only then could one stay focused. She was asked to describe the word 'focused.'

"'Focused' is the opposite of 'blur'", she said. She expanded on this: "Blur' is the time when you take off your glasses and you cannot see. 'Focus' is when you put them back on and everything seems to be in order again. '" When asked about stressful situations in her life, she narrated the story of a relationship that did not work out. It affected her profoundly because she was so involved that she had almost forgotten who she was. Everything came down to 'what he was, I was', and she had become him.

The situations in her day to day life that she found particularly stressful were attending meetings and making presentations. She experienced severe anxiety, as she was extremely conscious of her image and appearance; she felt people were looking at her and that reflected on her.

This attitude of hers is typical 'glass-like' behavior. With 'glass' (behavior) in general, one has to be careful both inside and outside (in her case it is her presentation anxiety) so that it does not break. Moreover, it reflects what is inside (her issue with friends) so it really does not have anything of its own, but just reflects what is in front of it (as had happened in her relationship whatever he was she had become).

When each peculiar, individual aspect of the person is explored to the level of energy and sensation, we will find that they all speak the same language and sing the same song. When the main complaint is examined in depth, when the person's dreams, hobbies, emotions, childhood, fears, ambitions, etc. are probed deeper, each of them will lead us (amazingly) to the same sensation, though superficially they seem to be so different. For example, a person may have a headache which is described as starting from one point going in a circle and returning to the same point. This peculiarity of the headache must represent the 'Other song'. When we ask about the stressful situations in her life, she refers to problems she has with her husband. Asked to describe her experience during the problems, she says it all seems to go in circles and comes to the same point again, nothing moves forward. Essentially her experience (sensation) in the headache is the same as her experience in stress and in all individual aspects of her life. What individualizes her is the 'Other song'. To see and to confirm what the other song is, one needs to look at the totality of the person and go into each area of the person, to see where he is different. Probing this difference will bring us to the sensation in the case.

It is important to know that this concurrent other song exists. It is amazing to see how one can recognize the 'Other song' word for word, note for note, melody for melody. It is intriguing how we try to harmonize and live our external life in congruence with this internal melody. Nonetheless, when this is not possible, we live a different life outside and inside. This creates dichotomy and disharmony which is the root of stress.

In trying to confront and understand it, the best question to ask is not 'why something is' but rather 'what something is'. We can see the 'Other song' playing and we can recognize it. We can also with awareness tone it down once we know what it is. Awareness dilutes the melody, dilutes the 'hidden force' within us. As emphasized earlier, this awareness is a gradual process, a nonverbal, non-intellectual process. It is a process of constant awareness of the experience in the now. That is the only perceivable, knowable truth. All else is just theorizing. The truth has to be examined in depth and in totality at the deepest possible level.

What is happening now, in the present moment, is the only knowable truth. It has never quite happened before. When you see each experience as unique, only then will you ever know what truth is. The total experience of the present moment perceived at its deepest level is the only knowable truth. Why? How? Where from? These are only speculations that serve no purpose.

The Levels

Once I was at the breakfast table with my 4-year-old son and my wife. All three of us were relishing watermelon, and I said, "Wonderful! It is very tasty, juicy, and nice to eat." My wife nodded and said, "It is good for health; it has lots of essential vitamins and minerals." My son, on the other hand, pointing to some parts of the fruit, said, "Look daddy. This is my castle; this is a frog, and this one a tortoise."

It struck me that each one of us was experiencing the watermelon at a different level. I was experiencing it emotionally, with feelings of like and dislike. My wife was experiencing it intellectually, in terms of the facts of it, its advantages and disadvantages and calculations. And my son was experiencing it through his imaginations. One can see that there are many levels of experience. With some research I could identify seven levels of experience. We often deal with different situations in our life through different levels. For example, when we go to the bank and make a transaction we are at an intellectual level. When we are watching a sentimental film we are usually at an emotional level of experience. When we watch a science fiction or a historical movie we are often at an imagination level of experience. However we find that for the most part we are usually stuck in one given level of experience during a certain period of our life.

The Levels	
Level 1	Name
Level 2	Fact
Level 3	Feeling
Level 4	Delusion
Level 5	Sensation
Level 6	Energy
Level 7	The Seventh

Before going further into these levels of experience, an understanding of the general concept may be helpful.

Concept of the Levels

Recall the time we first learned to draw as children. We began by drawing lines, and then slowly came triangles, squares, circles. Gradually we were taught to copy things around us: objects, houses, trees, people, etc. As we progressed we were taught to qualify the subject of our drawings. The faces we drew developed expressions showing a happy or sad person. Next we were asked to create drawings from our imagination, scenes from nature, a marketplace, a picnic, etc. Later on as we graduated, we learned to abstract, and we were able to express our moods and experiences through different shapes, forms, and colors. Our experience, whether mental, physical or spiritual, could be conveyed through this medium of abstract art.

- One can see that in our first step of initial drawings of lines and shapes we could not convey anything. These drawings had nothing more than a name attached to them: this is a line; that is a circle and so on.

    - This is the 1st level, the level of name.

- The next step, where we were taught to copy, has to do with fact, there are things that exist around us and we replicate them.

    - This is the 2nd level, the level of fact.

- In the third step, we draw a happy person, a sad person and we put in the adjectives or feelings or emotions.

    - This is the 3rd level, the level of feelings.

- In the fourth step, we create situations from our imagination, situations that may or may not exist, or situations we may or may not have experienced.

    - This is the 4th level, the level of delusions.

- When we reach this stage, where we can abstract, we are able to convey our sensations (mental and physical) as well as describe some kind of energy in the form of patterns and shapes.

    - This is the 5th and 6th level, the level of sensations and energy.

In this way, when learning art, we gradually progress from what can be simply named to something that has no name but only energy.

This concept of the levels can be applied to our day-to-day activities, interactions, thought processes, and perceptions also.

For example, when looking at an object such as a mountain:

- One person would want to know the 'NAME [Level 1]', e.g. Mount Everest.

- Another would want to know 'FACTS [Level 2]', e.g. the mountain's height.

- In another person the mountain would evoke 'EMOTIONS [Level 3]' such as happiness, joy. Such a person would not be too keen to acquire the facts about the mountain.

- In some, the mountain could stimulate a vivid imagination of flying or visions of heaven. This is the level of 'DELUSION/IMAGINATION [Level 4]'.

- However, in some persons, the experience of the mountains goes far deeper even than imagination. They might experience bodily sensations on looking at the mountain, such as lightness or floating. This is the level of 'SENSATION [Level 5]'.

- In a very small number, the experience of seeing the mountain goes even deeper than feeling sensations. Here the person feels the 'ENERGY [Level 6]' of the mountain within him and reverberates with it. At this level it is as if the person perceiving the mountain and the mountain that is perceived are one. A person experiencing at this deep level might simply jump up and down, so basic is the experience.

The Fifth or Sixth levels are typical of an infant or a very small child responding to any external situation. He does not bother to name, feel, or imagine: he just experiences the energy of the moment and flows with it.

These levels also apply to the experience of any event or phenomenon; for example, the sunrise, a piece of music, or a painting. We respond to music at the level at which it speaks to us. The blues tend to arouse our emotions, while classical music evokes deeper sensations. From those sensations, many delusions may arise but what moves us most is absolute music, which generally does not even have a name.

The same holds true in the case of painting. Painting as an art form can simply depict facts; for example, a titled portrait of an aristocrat, such as 'His Highness the Duke of Gilberd'. Paintings can also convey emotions; for example, the evocative 'Mona Lisa'. Other art is symbolic: scenes of dragons, demons, or angels signifying delusions and scenes which do not occur in reality. And lastly there is abstract art: patterns of color only, involving sensation and energy.

The levels can also be applied to any kind of human activity. For example, science, politics, medicine, art, relationships, or religion.

Let us look at the experience of religion more closely. Each individual experiences religion to varying depths. A person may experience his religion at the same level throughout his life, or his beliefs and practice may evolve over time through different levels; e.g. from the level of name to that of energy. The most superficial experience of religion (at the level of name) is limited to simply identifying oneself as Hindu, Catholic, Muslim, etc. At the factual level this experience is also superficial, being confined to daily prayers, rituals, attending Mass or reading the Holy Book. Taken one level deeper, religion can be an emotional experience with feelings of joy, calm, security, or dependence. A person whose inner story (delusion) is 'lost in the wilderness' might experience religion as that which makes him feel 'found'. To others religion may give the sensation of binding or togetherness, unity, or a sense of belonging. At the deepest level, or in the abstract form, it can be experienced as nothing but spiritual energy.

As with any phenomenon, the experience of disease can also be at various levels:

- A person with a very extensive cancer may have accepted his fate so that he experiences no emotions such as anxiety, fear, or grief, only symptoms related to this problem. For him, the experience of his disease is no more than a fact (Level 2): he has cancer.

- On the other hand a young woman with rheumatoid arthritis may experience a great deal of anxiety about her future. One would say even that her main focus is anxiety about the future rather than arthritis. She experiences arthritis as an anxiety. The pains will be experienced as anxiety; the limitation of movement will be experienced as anxiety. The level at which she experiences her disease is emotional (Level 3).

- Another young woman with a patch of eczema may fear that she will be shunned by society because of it. For her, symptoms like itching and scaling even though present will not be as bothersome as this (imaginary) fear of being shunned. For her, the eczema is experienced as a delusion (Level 4).

- A man with bronchial asthma may experience the sensation of being bound tightly in his chest and this sensation will be seen throughout his body and on the mental plane also. His experience of his disease is at the level of sensation (Level 5).

- In a child with recurrent cold and cough, one may observe the child simply running about the place, moving constantly and rapidly. He is oblivious of his disease of cold and cough. Rather, all he experiences and expresses is this energy pattern that compels him to keep running. His level of experience is that of energy (Level 6).

Let us examine each level in more detail, so as to understand them better and see them more clearly on a day-to-day basis.

Level 1: NAME

The first level is the experience of a situation as just

- Name

- Classification
- Differentiation
- Reference

By giving an identity and putting it into a slot, we avoid confusion concerning its identification in the future when we look at another object that appears similar. The experience of a situation at this level ends with the naming or classifying of a situation or person or thing.

For example:

- 'This is a computer.'
- This is 'Kate'.

In medicine this would equate to making a diagnosis like: "This is asthma" or "This is a case of depression". Once the experience has been labeled, the person is closed to experiencing anything deeper.

Level 2: FACT

At a somewhat deeper level one can experience a situation as a set of facts (Level 2). For example, with a computer, one can experience it as a series of facts such as features, specifications, price, manufacturer, etc.

Similarly with Kate – she can be experienced as facts such as height, weight, age, where she lives, occupation, language and all knowable facts relating to her. Regarding a situation, one can choose to look only at all the objective facts of the situation like the where, when, and what of it.

Level 3: FEELING

However, the desire to know these facts about a person or situation arises from a deeper level, the emotional level. We want to know a person and facts about him because we feel emotions for him like love, suspicion, hatred, etc.

An experience at the level of fact involves intellect and thought, whereas at the emotional level the facts are dwelt upon with the feelings rather than the intellect. If a situation is experienced at the level of fact, then this experience will be confined to all the relevant objective characteristics, like the where, when and what of the situation. There will be some emotions associated with such an experience, but the emotions will not be the predominant or the ruling factor. The emotional level is the base for facts. If the facts are money, accounts, things to do with finance, these may stem from a fear of poverty. If the facts are family, friends, other relationships, they may find their basis in emotions like hurt and disappointment.

Sometimes an experience moves us so deeply that we perceive it at an emotional level and are oblivious of the objective facts of the situation. For example, we look at a car and say, "Wow!" We are so mesmerized by it that we experience a desire to own it, to possess it. We just want it and fail to look at the facts, such as price and engine specification. Our response is all at the emotional level.

This level of experience is the most common one in the human world, especially among adults. Adults tend to say: "I have a problem with [this person or that person, in the family, or at work]." Each situation in life is reacted to on the basis of the emotions felt, such as anger, irritability, confusion, etc. The way we speak and react, the fears we have – are all manifestations of these emotions. These emotions have their origin somewhere far deeper than at the level we are consciously aware of. In fact the origin of our emotions lies at the level of imagination. We will not feel a certain emotion in a particular situation if we did not see that situation in a particular way. For example, we will not feel grief in a situation unless we perceive that situation to be one of loss. Such perception is often not objective, but a subjective view of reality: namely imagination.

Emotion stems from delusion. The image or false situation stirs up certain emotions within us. In my experience there are three basic emotions, viz. anger, fear and grief. The other emotions are either opposites (calmness, security and joy) or variants of these.

Human beings view problems at an emotional level; they feel sad or happy in relationships, angry about the prevailing global situation, scared about the future etc. They view the external world in terms of situations and each of these situations is associated with an emotion. Our speech, actions, reactions and fears, all reflect these emotions.

Emotions are experienced through the mind. Also they are individual specific. This means that while the experience of a situation can be shared by all of humanity, the emotion associated with it will vary from one individual to another. Thus the current problem of global terror may be viewed by some people with tremendous fear, by others with a strong feeling of anger, and by still others with a lot of sadness. All human beings are capable of feeling all emotions, but with regard to a specific situation the emotions aroused are also specific to individuals.

Level 4: DELUSION

If we look deeper we see that emotions stem from a delusion or imagination which is beyond likes and dislikes, happiness and sorrow. These imaginations or associations tend to evoke images which in turn give rise to certain emotions in us. So although our eyes see a certain thing, our mind may imagine it to be something else (i.e. a distorted perception of reality).

For example, we experience fear when we perceive danger, especially from some situation or object or person that we are sensitive to. No matter how safe an object may be in reality, if the eyes see it and the mind decodes it as dangerous, a complete chain reaction of feelings, sensations and reactions arises. The imagination evokes this fearful response. Our distortion of reality, our false perception will be exactly the same each time it happens throughout our lives. Similarly, emotions of happiness, security, and love stay with us because we perceive them as fulfilling certain needs in us, which are based on a delusion. On exploring the basis of the experience of a delusion, we find that this experience is not only mental but is also experienced as a physical sensation.

Let us consider the situation of a student who does not like a particular teacher. She dislikes this teacher (emotions) because she imagines her as a 'Hitler' who only wants to torture her (delusion). Every time she sees the teacher she feels a pain in her abdomen, which she describes as "like a punch." Just at the sight of the teacher she feels punched (sensation) although the teacher has done no such thing in reality.

A person who is enslaved may feel oppressed and desire freedom. But if he continues to feel enslaved even after being set free there is a problem in his perception of his outer reality. One could say that the situation of being enslaved, being extremely stressful or difficult for him, has left a permanent impression on his mind and now holds true for his entire life, so that instead of viewing his situation as it is, his mind still conjures up the image of captivity. In most cases we find that there is no stress situation in the person's past that warrants his delusion. Yet the nature of delusions is such that all human beings can relate to them. It seems as if somewhere deep inside a person's mind is a data bank that houses the memory of the multitude of situations that the human race has been exposed to throughout its history. In this way, at the level of delusion a person is linked to the collective human psyche. Sensation is non-human-specific: a human being can have a sensation similar to what a plant or animal or mineral would experience. Delusion, on the other hand, is human specific: a human being can permanently perceive his situation as one that other human beings have been through.

Delusions have been expressed in mythology, fairytales, literature, art, movies, and all other forms of creative human activity that involve the imagination. While expressing our personal delusions we often feel akin to other human beings who have actually lived these situations in history, in movies, mythology, novels, etc. Delusions take us beyond our personal experience so that we are connected with all of humanity. Thus everyone, in any part of the world, can sympathize with the experiences of the slaves in America or the Jews in Nazi Germany or the outcastes in Indian society or the victims of the Hiroshima bombing. These are experiences that are not limited to just one person or group of people, but are experienced by all of humanity. So although the plane of delusion is personal and private, yet this turmoil is common to all and is found in the human consciousness.

Delusions are thus beyond time and are common to the human history. They repeatedly manifest themselves in different eras and through different people in human history. From the beginning of human civilization the same human situations are repeated although there may be some variations in expression. Collective human experiences are beyond the banners of cultures, societies and time. They are even beyond language and beyond the boundaries of nationality.

Level 5: SENSATION

Although the delusion is manifest in the mind, it is not intellectual; it does not arise out of thought process, nor does it stem from emotions like fear, anxiety, hatred and joy. Examined deeper, delusion is a part of a much deeper experience, the sensation that encompasses the mind and the body. This is the general level and as the delusion arises from this deeper level, the experience of it can be "felt in our very bones".

Thus delusion stems from the sensation and expresses itself through emotions. The level of emotions (Level 3) is thus one layer above that of delusion (Level 4).

Let's take an example. A person with a back problem continually says: "I need some support to my back. That is the only thing that gives me relief." Regarding his emotional needs he says: "My friends give me support, I can lean on them." He refers to his religion, god, or guru as his source of "moral support." His experience of needing support resonates at every level within him. It is experienced not only in his body but has a deeper basis within his entire being, manifesting itself as a need for support emotionally, mentally, and spiritually. His basic sensation of "I need support" is felt at a level deeper than, but common to, both mind and body. This is the level of sensation, Level 5.

As a medical practitioner, I have patients coming to me with different illnesses. Their symptoms, their chief complaint, may be primarily in the physical or mental sphere. Whatever their chief complaint, their core sensation will always be clearly and most vividly expressed in these their main symptoms. The way the patient describes the chief complaint, often his physical ailment, is an exact description of the deepest sensation that he experiences all over, in general and in his mind state, a sensation that lies at the core of his being. When I explore the mind state of a patient, I find the same sensation expressed there as in the physical symptoms, and vice versa. In this way this core sensation is confirmed at both mental and physical levels. What is much more significant here is that this sensation is a general symptom rather than a local (mental or physical) one. Since the sensation is felt or experienced at both the levels, the level of sensation is deeper than that of delusion. This sensation that links the mind and body must exist prior to its appearance in both these localities. It is therefore central or vital. Hence the term Vital Sensation.

In health, the sensations come from being in the moment. In an unhealthy state, at the very core of everything that the person does, feels, experiences is an abnormal energy pattern and an abnormal fixed sensation, and these are found at every point in his life. He is unable to experience anything beyond the abnormal sensation that has become innate to his organism. This abnormal sensation can be called the 'vital sensation'. If his vital sensation is along the axis of caught and released, he will experience a pleasant piece of music as a release and the news of an unexpected tragedy will trigger in him the sensation of being caught. Love will be experienced as a release and the loss of that affection as being caught. An achievement will also be experienced as a release, and failure as being caught. This vital sensation and abnormal energy pattern will restrain him from experiencing things in the moment.

It appears that the vital sensation is not specific to human beings. It is what we share with other substances and beings on this earth. Whereas energy is universal, sensation is terrestrial. For example, a person's experiences maybe confined to the vital sensation of 'pressure', and in nature we can see certain elements, like metals, being subject to pressure, and plants and animals too can be sensitive to pressure. When a person is in health he may experience pressure as a result of changes in his physical or emotional environment, but as mentioned above this sensation lasts only as long as there is change, and with a different situation another appropriate sensation comes up. But in the case of disease, the sensation of pressure that is experienced is similar to the pressure experienced by a mineral or a plant or an animal, rather than the transient and appropriate experience of pressure of a healthy human being. The level of sensation therefore connects us to all things on the earth, and at this level the understanding of a human being becomes connected to botany, zoology, chemistry, metallurgy, geology, physics and various natural sciences.

The idea of 'sensation' is not something entirely new to me. At one stage I wanted to experiment with the effects of music on listeners. I played a melody (an Indian raga) to an audience and asked them to record the effects of the music on them at the physical and mental levels. I repeated this process with the same melody on five continents. I could see that some of those listeners noted emotions, others described vivid pictures, still others experienced sensations, while a few simply described patterns. I understand now that for those who experienced sensations, the music had an effect going beyond the mind or the body: it affected their very inner being, their nerves, and this effect was far more intense than a response on the emotional level. A similar phenomenon can be seen in the Walt Disney movie Fantasia. In the introduction a group of artists are asked to depict the images that come to them on listening to a particular piece of classical western music. Initially these images depict real forms, then slowly delusions, and finally, abstractions where one can see only shapes, sounds, form, and movement.

These abstractions, inspired by the music, are beyond body and mind, beyond emotions, beyond even specifically human experiences and situations. It is as if the music, through the sense of hearing, touches and activates the very core sensations. This made me conclude that music need not always be an emotional experience, but like all other experiences can be a 'vital' one.

The level which is deeper to both mind and body, and therefore common to both, I call the 'vital level'. I used to think that the center of the 'mental (emotional/ delusional) state' was the deepest point that we could reach, but I realized that the 'vital' (sensation) level is a step deeper than the 'mental state'. For example, when a person says that he feels jealous or suspicious in describing emotions or thought processes, we can ask him to describe how he feels when experiencing suspicion. He may answer that when he feels suspicion his inner experience is that of being attacked. In this way a delusional situatious is perceived behind the emotion. Having identified the deeper level of delusion from which the feeling of suspicion arises, it is possible to then go further and ask him how he feels when he experiences that attack. We then go a level deeper still, to the intersection or cross point where the mind and body meet. Here he may have the feeling that something is breaking or burning or twisting. This is the common point between body and mind (the vital sensation); **here he will describe his mental and**

physical phenomena in the same terms. This is a very deep level and if we reach this point there is a much deeper awareness.

We need to see what is it in the local symptoms or in the emotional symptoms of the person that surpasses the local or the emotional and is seen to be an expression of his whole being. So the effort here is to see what it is in a particular local that surpasses the local and becomes global. That is to say, what is it that transcends that situation and applies to the person as a whole, and over time? That is the common part of everything in the person, local and general, physical and mental, past and present. It is true of the whole person for all time, and in all aspects, mind and body.

This is the 'Sensation'. Only the sensation can transcend the mind and body. That is the basic core. Once we get there, we will see that every phenomenon in space and time in that person will boil down to the same thing.

The core sensation is like a deep, unspoken (but constantly intimated) thread, running through every sphere of the individual's life and activity.

Let's take, for instance, a lady of sixty-five years who came to me with a swelling of the wrist joint due to a ganglion. She experienced severe pain. On further questioning, she described a sense of constriction in the wrist pain which became tighter and tighter. As she went on to describe other areas of her life, she mentioned her discomfort in her own home ever since her son had married. In the presence of her daughter-in-law, she said, she felt really constricted, almost chained – to the point of feeling completely suffocated and at the brink of it all. On my enquiring in to her hobbies and interests, she said she loved to work for the handicapped. I asked her to describe the experience of working for the handicapped and she said it gave her an amazing sense of freedom.

She said: "I can do what I want. The boundaries between me and the other person drop and I feel so expanded. It's not me anymore – it is us." So her areas of interest give us a feeling that is exactly the opposite of that she experienced in her physical complaint and in her family life.

At this point she has clearly indicated her key sensitivity as being along the axis of "constricted/suffocated" at one pole, and "freedom/expanded/no boundaries between self and the other" at the other pole. Now one has the freedom to go into other areas, especially those that are seemingly disconnected, and see how they all connect to this common sensation.

With this new understanding, I realized that delusion is not only mental but can exist in the physical sphere too. In fact, I could see that the mental state is merely one expression of the vital sensation. Once I realized this and started looking for this common sensation or vital symptom in the physical sphere, I saw that this sensation is apparent right from the outset. Every level of perception and experience within the person resonates with this same underlying vital sensation. It is being expressed consistently and continuously throughout the person's whole being. It is expressed most vividly, and therefore is most easily accessed, in the person's chief complaint. Each person can identify the symptom pattern, or chief complaint, that troubles him or her the most. This chief complaint is a manifestation of the inner energy disturbance, the inner dissonance, of that person. In effect, the chief complaint is where the other song, the other energy pattern, is singing the loudest and so can be most clearly heard and identified.

Level 6: ENERGY

Finally, let us explore the origin of this vital sensation that is at a still deeper level. We cannot explore this deep level of Sensation by thinking about it intellectually. Rather, we must allow ourselves to experience it within our own body, and to observe the ways in which others express their experience of it (usually with their body language). Once we start exploring this level of sensation, we begin to notice certain recurrent body gestures. A gesture is a specific movement in a specific direction with a specific energy (force). For example, when we want to describe a pain in our abdomen which is of a twisting and stretching type, our hands will start moving in a specific direction in a specific gesture which is characteristic of our personal (individualistic) energy pattern. This Energy pattern is one of our deepest experiences, and it is from this level that the vital sensation arises. One level begets the next: from sensation arises delusion, from delusion stem emotions, through emotions come across facts, and facts form the basis of clarification or name.

It is helpful at this point to note as we go down from Name to Energy level how the realm of each successive level enlarges. Name is specific to one person only. Facts (e.g., blue eyes and blonde hair) apply to a group. The realm of more complex Emotions, most would agree, is limited to one person in a given situation, whereas the realm of Delusion extends to include the whole humanity, past and present. The realm of Sensation (e.g., the sensation of pressure, contraction, expansion, heavy, light) is experienced by animals, plants, and minerals. The natural world is made up of these three kingdoms. Sensation is therefore a terrestrial phenomenon while Energy is cosmic.

How do we recognize this energy?

Energy is represented by:

(a) movement

(b) sound

(c) color

- Movement in itself has speed and direction.
- Sound includes music.
- Color includes art.

Each individual experiences and lives his or her own energy pattern. This underlying energy is 'the song that sings us', just as the Bushmen of the Kalahari describe, *"There is a dream dreaming us."* We are the expression of our individual energy pattern, but its conscious perception is beyond the mind and body, as the energy level is so much deeper than both.

Let us take as an example, the experience of listening to music. Music itself is pure energy. Haven't we all had the experience that a certain kind of music moves us, bringing tears to our eyes? We may label these tears emotional, but in fact they often emanate from a much deeper level within us. When a musical chord is struck, vibrations or patterns are created which resonate within us. Those that match the particular energy pattern within our body move us, causing tears. These vibrations are not only picked up by the nerves in the ear and experienced as pleasant sounds, but can also be transmitted everywhere else in the body and experienced as pleasant sensations. (The famous percussionist, Evelyn Glennie, is completely deaf from childhood. She listens with her entire body to the music she creates. Her body is her ear.)

Energy is universal and nonmaterial, i.e. it encompasses all realms of the universe and not just the earth. All things, living and nonliving, possess energy in some form. Energy can manifest itself in the form of different patterns. Although all these patterns are part of a common universal energy pool, each one has its own peculiar shape, direction, speed, form, etc. Energy is thus both universal and particular. Each plant, animal or mineral has its own particular and specific energy pattern. These particular energy patterns are also part of universal energy. All energy patterns exist in balance with each other and the universe. Each energy pattern is therefore specific, but not separate. The energy of any substance is that which is common to that substance and which resonates with that of the entire universe.

As the energy level is universal, it is difficult to differentiate the particular kingdom that it belongs to or represents, whether that of plants, animals, or minerals. The kingdom the particular energy pattern represents and expresses becomes particularized only at the level of Sensation. Differentiation of kingdoms can therefore be perceived at that level but not at that of Energy. A specific energy pattern could manifest itself in the form of any of the three kingdoms.

The material and non-material worlds, the living and non-living worlds all resonate with energy. There are various energy patterns and it appears that these patterns are shared between substances. Thus any energy pattern is not specific to any one substance; there may be other substances or organisms that possess similar energy patterns. It may be that a substance from the mineral kingdom shares a common energy pattern with a member of the plant kingdom and also an animal, and with even perhaps something else in the universe. Energy therefore seems to connect us to the rest of the universe, and to other things and beings on this planet. It is what we have in common with the rest of the universe. It connects substances and organisms rather than differentiating them.

Energy itself is non-material, but it is the propelling force for everything material. Energy itself lacks sensation though it is the basis for sensation, and an experience at the level of energy is therefore difficult to describe.

When the effect of music was tested on volunteers, some of them visualized patterns or flashes of light; in my understanding these must represent energy, or the pre-auditory manifestation of music. The somatization of energy is sensation.

Experiences at the energy level (Level 6) are often witnessed in little children. In this age group we find that emotions are short-lived and inconsistent; they change easily from one situation to another, from one moment to the next. Thus the experiences of a child go beyond the levels of emotion and delusion, into the realms of sensation and energy. It seems that we are born at the deepest level, that of energy, and as we grow older we go from experiencing the world as energy to dwelling at the level of sensation, then delusion, feeling, fact and name. Children, therefore, seem to be far more in touch with their internal energy pattern than adults with all their reasoning and intellect. As we get older we lose touch with this internal energy and become less and less aware of it, and more and more live in levels more superficial such as emotions and fact.

Level 7: THE SEVENTH

Finally, let us explore the origin of Energy itself, or more accurately the fundamental origin or basis of all the levels, that deepest level which forms the background of all the other levels. Even deeper than the energy is the experience that provides the base of a given energy pattern. This is the Seventh level. I deliberately chose not to give this level a particular name. The Seventh, or deepest level, can be compared to a blank canvas on which some pattern or picture can take form. Though it has no energy in itself, it still is individual and specific to the energy pattern that is going to manifest itself on the canvas.

Probably this Seventh level is spontaneously experienced at the moment of birth and death as a blankness from which the form arises and into which it dissolves.

Thus the Seventh level is the connecting link or the continuum. It is that part of you that is there from birth to death, on which your energy pattern, your sensation and various delusions, emotions and pathologies play. The energy pattern first, during conception, is manifested onto the formless Seventh level, then the sensations manifested in a child, the imaginations experienced as a teenager, the emotions of a young adult, the more factual life of a middle-aged person, the name (as in name of the disease or pathological diagnoses) characteristic of old age – and then finally even the name dissolves into formless, onto the canvas of the Seventh level again.

One could also compare this level to the emptiness within a pot just before it holds water, in a state of readiness to receive the water. It is also similar to the silence between two notes of music: this silence is the backdrop against which the previous note was played and the next one is about to be heard. It can be compared to the dark night sky just before and after a display of fireworks.

The Seventh level is thus the blankness on which the energy pattern is manifest. One could also define it as the blankness that will play host to the energy pattern. Perhaps the experience of it could be in the gap between two breaths, or during deep sleep which is characterized by blankness, and it is against this blankness that the dream unfolds. It is perhaps also evident at the moment just before conception, where creation has happened against a background of nothingness. Similarly it may be evident in the time just after death, where there had been a life force or energy just a few moments ago. In this moment just after death the name also disappears. In the spectrum of the levels, the Seventh level can be said to lie in the gap between the first level (Name) and the sixth level (Energy). It is the link between the Name and Energy levels, thus making the spectrum cyclical rather than linear.

The Seventh level is constant, continuous and equal at all times whereas the other levels rise and fall. It is also the part that is not unhealthy, that does not have the other song. The other song is the energy pattern that is imprinted on you. The Seventh level is the non sick part. It is the observer of the Song. It is the blank slate on which the pattern is written. It is a state of deep hypnosis, meditation or deep coma which is beyond the six levels of experience where the person is blank and silent and able to observe, experience and describe the other levels. It is the silent witness beyond name, words, facts, emotions, delusions, sensations, energy.

Levels and ages of Man

Each of us generally experiences reality at a given level at a given time in our lives. One can say that as we grow older and as our vitality diminishes we experience the world increasingly at a more superficial level. This is a general statement with many exceptions. I know so many people well advanced in years who retain the youthful level of imagination and who are in touch with their deepest sensation. Such people are often comparatively very healthy.

It is interesting to see what kind of entertainment generally appeals to a particular age group and, correspondingly, how the levels operate here too.

To a newborn infant in the first couple of months of life, the only things that appeal as entertainment have to do with energy. Energy in the form of sound, color, and movement, like a rattle.

As children grow older entertainment is mostly in the form of sensations. Swings, slides, roller coasters and merry go rounds are what they like. Being thrown up in the air and caught. Here there is energy but energy becomes the source of sensation. Energy and sensation are very closely interlinked.

Then as they get still older what appeals is imagination. So they watch movies like Superman, Batman, and Harry Potter – with characters that are imaginary. It is also at this age that their ambition is to become a fireman, policeman, or a movie star.

Even older, into their middle age, what appeals are soap operas and movies with a lot of emotion.

As they get still older their entertainment consists of activities like reading newspapers and magazines about what is happening in the world. They are more concerned with the 'what' of things. The news channel on television becomes their favorite form of entertainment.

As they age even more their chief entertainment consists of asking people their names or just attempting to know what is what . If you name a thing they are happy. That is all that they want to know. At that age nothing more interests them.

The Levels bespeak universal phenomenon and thus can be applied to all areas of human life and experience.

Time and the Levels

Time is change.

When there is change, it happens in Time.

When many things change, it seems as if time passes very quickly.

- Like when your children grow up.
- Or when you are on a trip.

When things do not change, time stands still, years pass by and it seems like just yesterday.

- Like when you have worked on the same job for 25 years.

Time depends on Levels

- If you are in the fact level, things change soon. Time passes quickly.

  Like when you see your hair graying, or your skin in wrinkles, you feel Oh! time has passed by so soon.

- If you are in the emotion level, it is slower.

  Like when you are angry, or joyous , you relate more easily to the past and the distance between past and present is shortened, making time seem to move slower.

- As you go to delusion it gets even slower.

  Like when you watch a movie or are daydreaming or are having a romantic interlude, you are in delusion, minutes seem hours. Time has stopped.

- At the sensation level you become less aware of the passage of time. You are in your element. Past, present and future do not seem to be well differentiated.

Imagine a situation where you are in an aircraft, there is a problem and the turbulence is taking the plane up and down and side to side. You are gripping your seat and are palpitating. Time loses its significance.

Also at this level, your deepest experience is the same as you had in childhood. Your deepest fears and sensations make a continuum across your life and you are essentially in the same situation as in your childhood and at other times in life. There seem to be no changes at this level. Time does not matter.

- At level 6, you live your energy pattern. Your mind is off for the moment. There is very little recognition of time.

Imagine going down a roller coaster ride upside down. What happens to time at that moment?

- At level 7, at the level which does not change, time ceases to be.

  As in meditation. Or deep sleep. Time does not exist.

A Map To The Inner World

Through careful observation, we come to
the paradoxical conclusion that,
'each human being lives
two lives simultaneously'.

The dictionary defines paradox as, "that which is apparently absurd (or contradictory) but is, or maybe, really true". Life is full of paradoxes. Scientists advance in their understanding only by accepting the truth of their observations, however seemingly contradictory, and seeking an explanation for them. Modern physicists were forced by their observations to accept the paradox that light can behave as a wave form in certain experiments, and as particles in other types of experiments. Although wave and particle appear contradictory to us, both are true of the nature of light.

Although the statement each of us lives two lives simultaneously initially appears contradictory, a careful observation of human nature shows it to be true. To quickly recapitulate the earlier observations, one is our life as a human being where energy sings the human song. On delving deeper, we find a completely different world inside which seems to sing the 'Other Song' altogether, another melody. This other melody is not innately human but is a reflection of a pattern that we have borrowed from nature – be it from a plant, a mineral, or an animal. Therefore this energy pattern is appropriate to nature, not to us. We have borrowed it to cope with our perception of reality.

The natural world consists of the animal, the plant, and the mineral kingdoms. The energy of each of these kingdoms is very different, as outlined below. As humans, we borrow an energy pattern (from one of these kingdoms) which corresponds to our inner way of perceiving and reacting. Depending on which kingdom is the 'source' of the 'Other Song' within a given individual, human beings can be mapped into one of these three kingdoms. There is an innate difference in the basic problem issue of persons belonging to each of these three kingdoms.

Thus the basic problem in a person whose 'Other Song' is from:

- The plant kingdom is that of heightened sensitivity,
- That from the animal kingdom is survival, competition, and victim / aggressor issues, and
- The mineral kingdom is a feeling of deficiency in his own make-up, his own structure, or a fear of losing a part of his structure.

THE RECOGNITION OF THE 'PLANT SONG'

The basic quality of a plant is 'Sensitivity'.

It is a living organism rooted to the soil, unable to move. To survive it needs to be sensitive to changes in the external environment and also capable of adapting to these unavoidable changes. Plants are extremely sensitive to all the changes in their internal as well as external environment. Changes in the soil constituents alter the growth rate of a plant. We all know that plants grow in the direction of sunlight. Experiments have shown that even the slightest change in the atmosphere, including barometric changes, have tangible effects on plants. A plant is always a true reflection of its environment. For example, the nettle, grown in a shaded area, will be tall as it reaches towards the light, with wide delicate leaves spread out to absorb maximum light. The same growing in a bright sunny place will look very different; it will be

shorter with much smaller tougher leaves in response to the greater sunlight. All observation confirms the acute sensitivity and reactivity of the plant family to all factors in their immediate environment.

The book 'The Secret Life of Plants' by Tompkins and Bird highlights this incredible quality of plants. In experiments they were able to establish that plants have sensitivity many times more than humans. They could even read and react to the intentions of the human approaching them. They could be sensitive to what was happening to someone who cared for them even though the event was happening in another city.

These features are also descriptive of a person whose 'Other Song' (or 'non-human song') is similar to the energy of a plant. He is of a sensitive nature. He is influenced by many things and is continuously adjusting and adapting to them. Emotionally, he gets affected very easily and he is expressive of his state, both through speech and gesture. His hands often move in all directions as he expresses himself.

The expressions he uses are:

"I am affected by this", "I am sensitive to this",
"This hurts me", "I can't bear it", "This touches me."

These expressions show him to be a sensitive and emotional person. His feelings are most important to him, and he has a constant fear of being hurt or offended, or of hurting or offending others. Since he fluctuates so much, he can have abrupt mood changes.

The professions he tends to choose are ones which encourage an expression of his deep sensitivity. For instance he may be a nurse, doctor, artist, etc. These are only some examples to indicate his type of preferences.

As I carried out further research in understanding plants, I realized that each plant family has its own individual sensitivity, more aptly called 'a sensation' that ran through all the plants of that particular botanical family. Conclusively, a person who's 'Other Song' was that of a plant also manifested this 'sensation' at a very core level. This (core) sensation finds expression in various aspects of an individual's life. It runs through the physical symptoms, the imaginations, the fears and dreams of each person. The same underlying sensation is apparent and is experienced in all aspects of an individual's life. All speak the same language. The Other Song sings through every level of their being.

Take for example, the plant family, Cactaceae. The Cactus is a plant well known for its ability to contract in the absence of water and expand in the presence of water. In Homoeopathic remedy testing of Cactus, the same sensation was expressed by the testers. I found the sensation of contraction and expansion runs through all patients who borrow their 'Other Song' from plants belonging to the Cactus family. Human beings whose inner energy pattern, or sensation, is that of 'Contraction and Expansion' share this characteristic with the Cactus. This (core) sensation of contraction and expansion will find expression in their physical complaints as well as their emotions and thinking, as the level of Sensation is deeper than mental or physical.

Bringing together the knowledge base of botanical observation (of plants) with that of Homoeopathic observation (of people), leads one to understand that the same energy pattern, the same song, exists and finds expression both in the plant family and in certain individuals. Homoeopathy is a system which treats by giving a remedy that produces similar symptoms to those of the patient. It is based on testing remedies on healthy volunteers in order to bring out the innate effect of various natural substances. Homoeopathic observations thus provide a helpful knowledge base showing the patterns of energy and sensation inherent in the various substances and phenomena in the universe. In such a Homoeopathic testing of the yam family, (Dioscoreaceae) many subjects experienced a, 'twisting pain'. Investigation of the botanical characteristics of the plants of the yam family shows a marked tendency towards twisting of stems and branches. The patient's sensation clearly is: Twisting, Stretching, Winding, Turning, Churning or Cramping. Again this sensation is seen and expressed at all levels in those people whose inner turmoil corresponds to this particular energy pattern.

It is essential to note that all sensations can also be experienced and expressed as their exact opposites. For example, the sensation in the Euphorbiaceae or gum plant family is that of 'Bound, Tight or Taut'. This sensation has a spectrum of expression which ranges from 'Bound and Tied' at one extreme to 'Released and Loose' at the other. (This is another example of postulate two 'The opposite of anything is equally true' described in the next chapter The Three Postulates.)

Some Examples Of Plant Family Sensations

FAMILY	SENSATION	PASSIVE REACTION	ACTIVE REACTION
ANACARDIACEAE (Cashew family)	• Caught • Stiff • Tight • Tension • Stuck • Cramps • Pressing	• Paralyzed • Immobile	• Motion amel • Agg. in house • Agg. sitting • First motion agg • Restlessness • Sedentary agg • You are stuck and want to move continuously
CACTACEAE (Cactus)	• Constricted • Made smaller • Shrunk • Contracted • Bound, trapped, pressed	• Trapped	• Expansion, becoming bigger boundless and released
COMPOSITAE (Daisy family)	• Injured • Hurt or insulted • Shocked • Burnt or scalded • Fear to be touched, hurt approached	• Numb • Anesthetic • Stupor • Catalepsy	• Touching • Hurting others • Cruel • Violent • Strikes • Insulting
EUPHORBIACEAE (Euphorbias)	• Tied and untied • Bound and unbound	• Tied and cannot do anything about it	• Desire to break free

(agg: aggravation; amel: amelioration.)

We have made a detailed study of the common sensation in more than thirty different plant families. This knowledge is of great benefit to homoeopaths to identify the exact family for a patient belonging to the plant kingdom.

After I studied all the plants from one family, I concluded that each plant from that family had the same sensation but that the pace and depth of experiencing that sensation differed. Depending on the intensity with which the sensation is experienced, the person's reaction, or coping mechanism, varies. We shall discuss these variations in 'Ways of Coping' in subsequent chapters.

THE RECOGNITION OF 'THE ANIMAL SONG'

The fundamental issue in animals is one of 'Survival'.

Competition is the rule in the animal kingdom. The theme of survival of the fittest holds true for all living creatures, including algae, fungi, plants, etc, but it is most evident in the animal world.

Survival is seen as an issue of comparison and competition. It is a question of one versus the other, the stronger versus the weaker. Everything is seen in this light.

A person who's 'Other Song' is similar to the energy of an animal, often draws attention to himself by his clothing and behavior. The most fundamental need and an important component of his basic competitive nature is to attract attention. The clothes he wears achieve this because of the color, design or fashion chosen. That does not mean that such an individual is always flashily dressed. The basic need is to attract attention and this may be gained by wearing dull clothes to a party. He is thus dressed differently from others and this difference is somehow noticeable.

Even his behavior can be attention seeking. He is lively, vivacious, and can be extremely animated and excited in his speech. At times he can also be quite abrupt in both action and speech. Since he is very expressive and communicates easily, he seems to have an extraordinary ability to make contact with others. A part of him needs to be in animated contact with those around him.

Another aspect of a person whose 'Other Song' is from the animal kingdom is that he is very alert. He maintains eye contact, always on the lookout for a reaction from the opposite person, and he is himself very quick to react.

It is possible that a person with an 'animal song' may not demonstrate any of the above features. He could be quiet, dressed inconspicuously, and may not show competitive behavior. Such a person may have these qualities too deeply to be seen outside. Yet, he may show it vicariously by being attracted to or fascinated by others who live these qualities externally – or he may express these in his dreams, in his hobbies or in his non-human expressions.

With these features of wanting to attract attention, wanting to excel others, coupled with alertness and rapid responses, he is lured by competitive careers in the area of marketing, advertising, etc. The corporate strategies of big business give ideal vent to his competitive spirit and aggression. He can be very jealous of any competitor and may resort to any means including deceit to achieve his ends. He can be ruthless and malicious, especially when it comes to achieving his own personal goals. In so doing he is acting out of his 'Other Song', his own fixed way of seeing the world. To compete and achieve is a matter of personal survival. He perceives himself (and consequently everyone else in his world) as either predator or prey. This is the truth of the animal kingdom, which he lives and expresses. He believes in survival of the fittest, and in order to survive he must ruthlessly compete or risk annihilation.

His fears, understandably, are of being neglected or looked down upon, of failure in competition, or a loss in his own strength and attractiveness. Situations where he experiences such failure and loss are experienced by him as a threat to his very survival. These situations touch his deepest sensitivity, and thus can be triggers for the precipitation of physical illness.

His talk centers on stories of 'high and low', always tending to personify himself as aggressor or victim, the hero or the deeply wronged. Such views give vent to his inner feelings of strength versus weakness. These feelings are manifest in every area of his life. He experiences life as a process of either being the dominating, strong one, or of being the weak one who is dominated and persecuted by another. For him, at the deepest level, these are the only two possible roles in life. All this makes aggression a marked feature. He has a fear of being attacked and may respond by aggression. The issue is of self and other, the dominance of one person over another. This is seen when he use phrases like: "Somebody is doing this to me," "They are teasing or bullying me," or "I am being victimized, harassed, nagged, abused, forced, tortured," etc.

Another important issue for a person who borrows the 'Other Song' from the animal kingdom is that of 'Hierarchy'. He feels others are either superior or inferior to him. He uses expressions such as: "Somebody is above me, I am under someone" or, conversely, "Somebody is below me." He feels dominated and dictated to.

The fundamental issue is that of survival. He literally experiences a threat to his very life. He has a strong awareness of, and therefore fear of death at the hands of another. This is often expressed as a fear of being attacked, a feeling of being pursued. His reaction to this fundamental threat is the basic instinctive one of "Fight or Flight." Either he feels strong enough to stand his ground and fight, or he feels his inner weakness and seeks to flee and hide in order to survive. His circumstances can make him feel caged, trapped, bound, chained, and captured. He may speak of being shackled, imprisoned, with a strong desire to escape and be free.

The animal song in a human being

A person whose ' Other Song' is from the animal world will be sensitive to issues which relate to his own attractiveness, his personal ability to compete successfully, and the corresponding risk of being victimized if perceived as weak. It is interesting to observe that he experiences his physical complaints deeply in these same three areas. He feels that illness either makes him less attractive, less powerful and able to compete, or that it may result in his being persecuted by others. He feels dominated or almost ruled by his own illness and thus feels victimized.

His personality holds two strongly conflicting traits, which he constantly experiences within himself. On the one hand, his Victim-Aggressor 'Other Song' causes him to experience and express a nonhuman degree of jealousy, competition, deceit, aggressiveness, and maliciousness. This he expresses fiercely whenever he feels under threat. On the other hand there is a part of him which is particularly and vividly filled with humanity, warmth, caring, playfulness, loyalty and communication. He suffers as he strives to live and integrate these two warring themes, or sets of impulses, within himself. This inner battle can go to the extent of the human part within him developing a deep sense of contempt for the 'non human part' (i.e., that part of him which is singing the animal song).

This split in his personality is clearly expressed in his statements, such as:

"Humans are so cruel," "I feel split,"
" I jump at them," "I am not good."

Such statements are indicative of how he perceives himself. The split is expressed externally as a conflict between self and other, but this external battling is only an expression of the deep split within the self. This split runs through his whole being. He begins to hate himself.

It is often

"I versus myself," "I am disgusted with myself," "I hate myself."

His deep need to be attractive has a lot to do with sexuality. Again, the fundamental issue is survival, not just of self, but of the group. This issue is fundamental to the whole animal kingdom, and therefore issues of sexual attraction are strong in people whose 'Other Song' is borrowed from that kingdom.

His desires and cravings are more for food from the animal kingdom like milk, meat, fish, and seafood in general.

His dreams show many of the features discussed above. He has dreams of animals in general, of snakes, and particularly experiences dreams of being in pursuit or being chased or being attacked. He would be fascinated or repulsed by animals in general and especially by the particular one whose other song is within him.

Given below are the qualities, words, energy of people who belong to the various classes within the animal kingdom. These features have been repeatedly confirmed in practice. Also to be noted is that a person belonging to a particular class (say insect) will not have one, but a whole constellation of words or features of that class.

Some sub-kingdoms

We see that a common theme of the 'animal kingdom song' is that of 'Survival'. This often expresses as a victim-aggressor situation. However there are many sub-kingdoms within the animal kingdom, and this predominating theme of survival finds very different expression in each of these. The differences of expression of this basic theme in each animal sub-kingdom are subtle, but clearly discernible. It is almost as if the same melody is being played, but on a whole range of different instruments. It is important that we recognize first the melody (survival, in the case of the animal kingdom), and then the exact instrument playing that melody (the sub-kingdom). In all statements below I am again combining the knowledge base of two hitherto seemingly unrelated sciences; in this case, that of Zoology and Homoeopathy. A further insight into the sub-kingdoms will enable us to relate more specifically to the source of the 'Other Song' that is playing in us.

I cannot deal with all classes of animals here, nor can I talk in detail of any of them. However, to give some idea, I shall describe a few of them. These descriptions do not come from vague abstractions, guesses, or theories. They are distilled from a careful study of the animals' survival strategies and from the symptoms recorded in healthy human volunteers who have taken the potencies of remedies prepared from these animal extracts in order to note the effects. We have made detailed study of each class, but here we have only given sketchy descriptions just to give a general idea.

Let's examine **mammals**. There are qualities of mammals, predatory and prey-like. As predators they feel like aggressors, their power extending over their specific territory. This territory is defined, and they have problems if another encroaches on their territory in any way. In this position of the aggressor they have power, strength, vigilance, alertness, and are forever ready to pounce on anyone

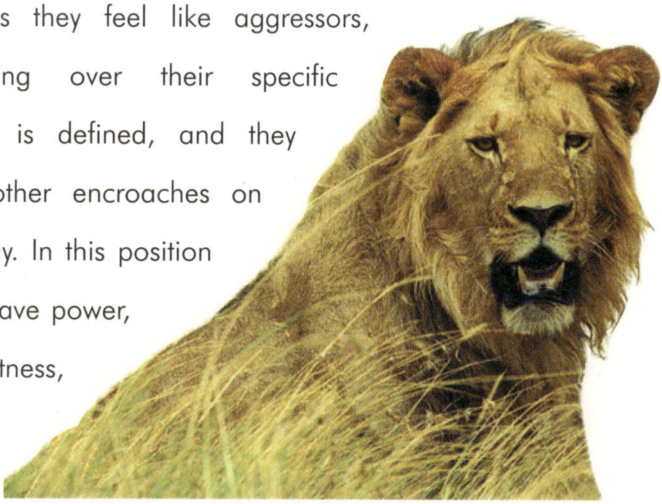

who irritates them, who 'invades their space'. As prey they have the opposite reaction. They experience fear when attacked, and in response they freeze or flee. Another important aspect of mammal behavior is the need to belong to the herd, to conform, yet at the same time, to try and find a position of superiority within the herd, 'to be the top dog' so to speak.

People with the 'mammal song' within express this perception and action and pattern their lives according to this survival mode. At a deep (sensation) level they express these very words, gestures and perception of the situation.

Case of a 35 year old woman with rheumatoid arthritis.

We find that asking the patient about pain in the joints does not lead further. What she keeps emphasizing is that she is unable to do many things due to the pain. So loss of her ability is more significant to her than the sensation.

What does this loss of ability mean for her?

She says it makes her totally dependent on others.

Spontaneously, she says she likes to make her own decisions and does not like to compromise. When asked about compromise she says she does not hide her feelings, that she is truthful. There is no prima facie connection between the concepts compromise and truth, yet in her state these two are connected. To not compromise means to not hide the feelings, to be truthful.

When asked about not hiding feelings, or being truthful, she says that she does not want to please others. Here she shows the connection between hiding things and pleasing others: "you hide things to please others."

One of the main stressful situations in her life was the way her in-laws treated her. She felt that since she came from an economically lower family than theirs they always showed her down, comparing her with the other daughter-in-law who came from a wealthier family.

She felt mistreated, but she felt that she had to accept the situation since she was dependent on the family. Thus she came back to the feeling of dependence which she experiences as a result of her arthritis.

We started with dependence and we have come back there. Now we see what dependence means. It boils down to inequality. Now we can see the kingdom clearly, from the chief complaint itself. The issues are inequality, comparison, hierarchy, exploitation, dominance, etc. This is animal kingdom.

She expressed the same experience in all other situations in her life. In an incident in her office that she had described in a portion of her case not reproduced here, she felt that it was very important to be loyal, even if she was not being treated equally.

Here we see that her deepest consistent experience is one of being in a hierarchy, where she is not equal to the others, yet her dependence on the group for her security forces her to accept and live with this situation. This is the typical survival strategy of mammals.

Another animal sub-kingdom, that of **reptiles** experiences and expresses the survival theme differently. They have a certain sense of cunning in them. Their strategy has always been to know the weakness of the opponent, and that is the key to how they express their aggression, how they attack the other. It is important for their survival to adopt such an aggressor strategy because their inner victim feeling is one of being choked; their inner perception is that their opponent will suffocate and strangulate them. The neck seems to be the weak spot in the reptile. If you get their neck, you have rendered them defenseless. What is interesting to observe is that they fear being attacked from behind; i.e. where they are least guarded and more at ease (quite similar to the way in which they themselves hit upon others, in their weak spot).

The snakes have as a main survival strategy the need to remain hidden or inconspicuous. They often lie in wait, and attack when least expected – such an attack is often fatal. This hiding, waiting for the moment, and surprise attack is reflected in human society in many forms such as the underworld, espionage, terrorism, etc.

The hiding is also reflected in a person with a 'snake song' by the quality of his hiding his real self and outwardly living a completely different life. This duality, often remarked in the lives of many prominent people such as politicians, religious leaders, or prominent figures from show business, could be an expression of the 'snake song' in human beings. Those who do not actually lead such lives, but who have the 'snake song' within are often fascinated with, attracted or repulsed, or strongly reactive to the above themes – be it in movies, novels, or in the lives of others.

This is the case of a thirty-year-old man who consulted me in January of 1993. He is a construction contractor; his job involves travelling into remote places and constructing railways. He was accompanied by his brother and mother for the first interview. He sat at the edge of the chair and his feet were restless.

He could not breathe properly and was slowly progressing into heart failure due to a disease of the heart muscles called cardiomyopathy.

He has a tremendous sensitivity to injustice. He feels that if a person has done his job properly, he should be paid justly. He likes to be honest. He gets anxious when taking up a new job. He gets anxious about his family and feels responsible for them. He is very irritable, yet calms down quickly. When he gets angry, he hits. He can be very malicious. The thing that makes him angriest is a situation in which one person is being beaten up by three or four people. It makes him very angry; he feels it should be one-to-one. He will get off the train and get into the fight and help that one person who is being beaten.

Once he was to give an interview to acquire a contract. He went for the interview and found that the contract had been given away unfairly. The person who had been awarded the contract and the people in charge of it were hand in glove. He was alone, and all of them were looking at him. They tried to "harass" him and asked him to get out. He could not do anything. When he went outside he picked up an iron rod and smashed up one of their cars. They saw him from the window and he called them to come out, saying: "I will show you!" They came out and tried to chase him, but he had the iron rod in his hand and he ran after them. Two days later they came to a compromise and the contract was awarded to him!

In the patient's words, "On seeing anything unfair, I used to become very angry. If someone threatened another person, I would interfere. I still do get angry, but not as much as before. Before I would fight and defend weaker people; now I do not involve myself. But sometimes these problems happen even now. Six months ago, I was involved in some construction work at a village, and the local people started to steal and damage my machinery and equipment. I went to the police station and fought with them a lot. I told the man who was responsible for the damage all kinds of things. I threatened him in the police station itself, and the whole station was quiet. My temper was so high that if he had said even one word I would have done something. Those people had done wrong things, and I could not stand it. My whole body was shivering like I should do something. I cannot control myself where there is so much anger. Previously I would get angry on minor things; now it happens only with major things. It happens especially with matters involving my prestige; where people's respect towards me is involved, I get very angry. For example if someone says he cannot do anything, he is not dangerous. What can he do? Initially when they provoked my workers, I asked them to ignore it. I told them not to fight, and had their injuries attended to. Slowly they started increasing their atrocities. They did more and more damage. They started to think that I cannot retaliate so they did more damage. Now I know that in such a situation I should not retaliate. I am alone and they are a whole village. I am isolated. But at that time I have no control. I went and beat up the guy very badly. When they exceeded the limit, I beat him up. He went to the police and complained. The whole village was there. I told him that if he opened his mouth in that place, I would cut his hands off. I was shivering with anger. The man never opened his mouth, and after that they left me completely in peace. The police advised me not to say things like that. I told them that if he had opened his mouth, I would have done what I said. (Smiles) I said that when he is not even a man why I should talk to him. I had to give him an open challenge. This was one-and-a-half to two years ago.

Four months ago there was a little problem in another city. They had given me a contract. I had done most of the work, but they refused to pay me. What they were trying to do was to get other contractors to come and finish the work. I was there with my brother and one of my workers. Seventy of them came to get us out and start their work. The three of us stood in front of the machinery. I said: "You are seventy and we are three. We are no match for you. I will tell you one thing: the first guy, who puts his hands on my machine, he will not have hands. After that you can do anything to us." No one dared to do anything. There was total compromise after that. I cannot bear it if the person in front of me thinks I am scared. That is a question of prestige. If he thinks I am scared, he will only do more damage. He will do more and more. Now he steals, but the next time he will come and take it from me, if he thinks I am scared. I cannot make enemies of the village. I have to go to them, but at the same time they must have respect for me. They must not think I am scared. I give them my car for weddings. I help them. But when it comes to a question of prestige, I lose control. They tried to oppress me. They troubled everyone else after that, but they never troubled me."

The main feature in his inner experience is the threat of violence. People try and attack him and he threatens to strike back. The other important feature is the tremendous sensitivity to injustice. He cannot bear to see someone being treated unfairly, which is also how he perceives his own treatment by others. When he was not given the contract, he was very angry because he had not been given a fair chance, and he threatened to do violence. The anger, violence, threatening, malice, and especially the perception of a very unequal fight (one victim against many aggressors) all this suggest a snake remedy. This patient also seems egoistic from the way he underplays the story of four months ago to which he refers as a "little problem". Then when he is asked the details it is much more intense.

A remedy from the snake group helped him a lot, both physically and psychologically. His heart functions returned to normal over a period of time and he remains well for more than fifteen years now.

Arachnida **(spiders)** have a slyness, a cunningness in them. They tend to trap the prey or anybody who intrudes on their space and territory. The reason they use this strategy is because at a deeper level they perceive themselves as small in size and power. Those with a 'spider song' within them voice and show this survival pattern through human expressions. Perceiving themselves as small and weaker than their opponent, they use deceit and trickery to get one up on the other. Often they feel trapped, tricked and used by others; and they can use any trick to quickly get out of this situation. These are the people who can trick, cheat, fake, play practical jokes and always think of a crooked and indirect way to face any issue. These people are also very alert to sounds, to music and to rhythm, and they respond to fast music.

A boy of six years was brought to me for recurrent abscesses and boils on his legs and feet, and with fever. Every 3 months he needed antibiotics.

The child was restless and would not sit in one place and he made motions with his arm all the time. He was playing this game in my clinic. He had three different colored pieces of paper and the red one would fire on the other (green and blue) ones and then one would get up and fire on the others. He was doing this continuously. I asked him the meaning of this game. He said, "These are three fighter planes and the one plane is firing on the other and that one is dying and that one is firing back and the other is going down. My plane is the red one and it will always survive and kill the others."

The other part of the story was that he had had a dream: He is going somewhere with his friends and there is a big bad witch who traps the kids and takes hold of them and puts them into a net and they cannot come out and they know they will be consumed and eaten. And he woke up with a fright. I asked the mother about his behavior. She described that he was extremely aggressive but never in her presence. In her presence he was the most saintly person. The moment mother went away he would hit the maid servant. I asked her, "How does he hit the maid servant?" She replied, "I do not know, I have never seen it." I asked her to call the maid servant and ask her. The maid said that he chases her, jumps on her and pins her to the ground, and after that he sits on her and he hits her.

We can see that the boy did to the maid exactly what he perceived being done to him (by the witch). The pattern is one of trapping the victim and then to hurt or harm or kill.

This is a typical pattern of spiders.

It is interesting that after receiving a homoeopathic remedy from the spider group the physical problems of the boy healed very quickly, and have not recurred for several years now. But also his entire behaviour underwent a very significant change for the better.

The **insects** are small, with short life spans. Usually very busy, (think of the ant and the bee) they are concerned with the immediate and basic survival needs – food and reproduction. Their kind of attack is a sudden sting. Their death is abrupt too, and often violent. People with the 'insect song' within them will have several of these perceptions and patterns.

(For Illustration of the 'insect song' the reader can refer to a case of honeybee mentioned on page no. 317.)

The **birds,** a further sub-kingdom, feel trapped and caged when kept away from their natural environment of the sky. The opposite of this trapped feeling is their experience of flight, freedom and openness, with no confinement in any dimension. People with the 'bird song' experience this as their deepest sensation. They express it through several words and gestures.

A woman aged 65 came in with depression. She also had arthritis and migraine. The main stress for her was the behavior of her husband who was very active and ambitious in his business despite his age being 75. This man who was quite wealthy, didn't really need to expand his business yet worked night and day to develop it further. Her children had all grown up and were well settled and self-sufficient. And they had all left the country. This lady wanted to spend her life pursuing altruistic goals. She wanted to work with handicapped and less privileged children. She also wanted time to walk by the seaside, enjoy music, and meditate. But her husband's business compulsions and his asking for her participation frustrated her and caused the depression. I asked her about her experience to be in this situation. She said, "Since I am married to him I must be with him and now I look after him like a mother. This takes a toll on me. (She weeps continuously.) How much can I crucify myself?"

Further, she says, "This is my own fight with myself and I feel a sense of bondage, a limiting of my freedom. I feel enslaved. In this situation I feel trapped and suffocated."

We can already see here the animal song of the fight between the one and the other and the struggle between me and myself.

I asked her to describe the experience of being trapped and suffocated a bit more. She said, "The feeling is I am not a free bird. I cannot fly to see the sky which I would like to do. I feel as if my wings have been cut and I am at the mercy of others."

Here she reflects the story of the bird which is trapped and bound by its commitment to its offspring and waits for the day when it can have fulfilled this commitment so that it can soar the skies again.

The **mollusks**, have a survival strategy where they withdraw into a shell. The people with the 'mollusk song' will see themselves as soft and vulnerable and so they will secrete a hard shell around themselves where they can retreat. They pay a price for the security thus obtained; the price is immobility, being stuck in one position and not being able to participate in the world outside. The words, gestures and images they use at a deep, sensation level reflect this survival strategy.

A case of an eighteen-year-old girl with recurrent headache.

(**R** : Dr. Rajan Sankaran

P : Patient

Hg : Hand gesture.)

R : What's the problem?

P : Since a-month-and-a-half I have been getting this terrible headache. It mostly starts from my right side and as the day proceeds it just spreads. And sometimes I feel a crushing pain in the side of my nose. If it is here then there is a kind of obstruction (hg: of pushing to one side) and it gets better when I switch off the light. Walking and certain jolts increase it. And my mummy suffers with the same kind of pains. So that's it.

R : Tell a bit more about the headache.

P : It's like an **obstruction** (Hg: of circling, with one hand, the right eye) in the eye. Sometimes I feel it is little swollen, not red. But this whole area would get kind of compressed. The frequency was much more when I had exams going on. Now I am relatively free but it happens in the evening or anytime. But somehow I know that the headache is going to happen, that slight lingering and then it starts, heaviness.

(Author: Local Sensations – terrible, crushing and obstruction. Of all these sensations, the hand gesture is there in obstruction.)

R : A bit more about the type of headache you have.

P : It's not a throbbing pain (hg: of holding space like a ball), it's just a compression and the degrees vary, if it's an over stressed day then it irritates me. But during exams I cannot even sit and concentrate on my books. It's a just a compression (hg: holding a space ball with right hand). Even my eye and all, this whole area is majorly compressed (similar gesture). It's not a throbbing pain; I can feel a pressure on the eye, the side of my nose and all this area. And if I press that, it definitely gets better.

(Author: More sensations: Compression, majorly compressed.)

R : When you say, 'compression' what do you mean exactly?

P : Like I explained to you, it's not a throbbing pain (hg: of throbbing), I can feel a pressure, the whole thing, on the eye and the side of my nose and all this area. And if I press that it definitely gets better.

R : So, describe this pressure a little bit more.

P : As when I apply it, to make it better?

R : No. no. You said 'compression and pressure'; just describe that.

P : I feel my eye is half open. Maybe it doesn't look like that. But I feel it is all compressed/shrunk (said in Hindi, with a hand gesture of closing an open palm). It is not like a thumping pain or a throbbing pain (hg: palm opening and closing with energy). It is towards the inside (hg: grasping and pulling backwards). And it definitely becomes much more if I give my attention to it. I think, okay, I am getting a headache. Then it increases. But, you know this whole area would be (hg: palm grasping repeatedly), I would just feel, compressed, that's the only word I can use to describe it.

(Author: Not a throbbing pain or a thumping pain (hand gesture). Denial. It is 'compression.' With 'compression' is a hand gesture. It is shrunk/ inside.

The sensation cannot be fully described in words. We have to look at the gesture, not listening to the words. The word 'compressed' doesn't fully capture it. You have to see the energy.)

R : You are making some movement with your hand like this.

P : There is (hg: of closing palm/hand and drawing it backwards) compression.

(Author: This is one of the main gestures in the case.)

R : Describe that hand movement little bit more.

P : It's not like throbbing (opening and closing palm), but it is inside (closing palm and pulling it backwards). A lot of people have this thumping pain. This thak, thak, thak, going on inside. No, it is nothing of that sort. It just pains. I am having it right now. This area is, it's just paining. I am so used to it, for so long. So there is no word to describe it. Right now it is here but it is very faint, but it is just hurting. There is no way to describe. This uncomfortable feeling is there. And as the day proceeds, then it will just keep coming more. It will pain a lot. Yeah, pain is the right word. Paining a lot, hurting.

R : So, describe this movement of your hand. Just show that movement again.

P : It is (same hg of closing palm and drawing it backwards).

R : Yes. I want you to describe this. Just forget about the pain for the moment. Just describe this movement.

P : The whole thing is (palm closes and pulls backward). Some people say they have a hammering (hg: hammering). It is not like that. It is just that someone is not allowing me to use this part. It is...

R : Just this movement. Just do that movement again.

P : (hg: palm closes and pulls backwards) Compression.

(Author: So far we see the energy pattern through the hand gesture. The hammer on the head is part of the story, since she is spontaneously denying it. We see hand gestures coming with 'hammering' and "Someone is not allowing me to use this part." It is that someone is doing something to someone. This gives us a hint towards the Animal Kingdom. When this energy is seen, what is important is to disconnect her from the pain and go into the sensation. We can do this by focusing on the gesture or the word that has energy. It is where we go away from familiar ground, going into the complete unknown with the patient. It seems so foolish, so silly, such complete nonsense. But we need to have trust in that, to know for sure that this is it. It takes time to have that confidence.)

R : Yes, describe this movement. Only that movement of your hand.

P : It's like again (same gesture) compression. Everything is just compressed inside, and then I am not able to access that part. Everything is just (same Hg) inside. It is compressed and closed. Then it just absolutely does not allow me to...then I cannot use it.

(Author: Asking about the energy pattern (hand gesture) will give us the sensation {kingdom, subkingdom and source}. Some words related to the source are: **Compressed, shrunk, inside, closed and not able to access that part.**)

R : You are doing very well. May be what I need to understand is your experience. So, don't worry about what you are talking. What you are doing is absolutely fine. It is not that you are answering me wrong or incorrectly, but by asking I can understand it deeper and deeper.

P : Much better.

(Author: Reassurance is needed at the beginning of nonsense.)

R : So a little bit more about this movement of the hand.

P : What should I say?

R : Just describe it. Just do it once again and describe it. Do that movement.

(Author: We don't ask what the movement means or any interpretation of it, or what it reminds her of. We only ask her to describe it.)

P : (hand gesture of closing palm and drawing it backwards)

R : Just whatever comes to you, you tell me about that movement.

P : It's only, it is just a way to show how the headache happens.

R : Forget the headache, forget 'compression' forget 'pressure' forget everything. Just describe to me this movement. Whatever you can say about it and whatever comes to you, you tell me about that movement.

(Author: Again, this helps the patient to disconnect and be with the sensation.)

P : It is (hg) pulling in (hg).

R : Tell about 'pulling in'.

P : It is like when it gets (Hg) pulled, then it kind of goes into (Hg) a closure and you cannot access it. It's just that, how can I explain this?

(Author: At this point we see that she doesn't mention compression or hammering but she mentions a third new sensation: 'pulling in'. The presence of different sensations, apparently unrelated, points to Animal Kingdom. In the Animal, one sensation is not a variation of the other. They are related in that they are part of a process, a sequence of action. It is no longer a sensation but it becomes a story.

Pulled in, shrunk, compressed, closed. If you focus on any one action of the sequence of the action, you will get the entire sequence. When asked about 'pulled,' she says, it is pulled in, closure, cannot access. This is the part of the sequence, now we have to see what was before that. What is it that causes 'pulled in, closure and cannot access'? What came before and what comes after it? Then the entire story of that animal will be revealed.)

R : You are doing extremely well. So, describe to me this thing, "pulling in, goes into a closure, you can't access it." Describe this phenomenon.

(Author: Use all the things she said, without emphasizing something that she didn't emphasize.)

P : Pertaining to the headache?

R : No. Headache is gone now.

P : Okay.

R : Just this much. "Pulling in, goes into a closure and you can't access it."

P : Pertaining to something abstract?

R : Whatever comes to you?

P : I don't know, but my theory is that anything is withheld (grasping and pulling backward) or it just goes out of reach. That is why you cannot access it. And this gesture is withholding or retaining it back.

R : Tell about this 'withholding' and this what you described, "It is withheld and it goes out of reach." Just describe this a little bit more.

P : As in, how do I explain it further?

R : This gesture will help you. This is like withholding, out of reach. I am trying to understand this. "Cannot get access." So, I am trying to understand this bit more.

P : It's like just...(closing and pulling back), you know, 'gone inside a shell' would be most appropriate.

(Author: Withholding is: Out of reach, gone inside a shell. So the sensations are compressed, shrunk, pulling in, go out of reach, close. These are a reaction to hammering, crushing. It is soft and delicate inside. It feels the threat of being hammered or crushed. So it develops a hard shell, and goes/stays inside that.)

R : Describe for me this 'gone into a shell.'

P : When something goes in, when a creature goes inside the shell, there is no way that you can access the creature. It's gone out of reach. That is exactly what happens. It is just (same hg) withheld, gone.

(Author: The main survival response of the animal decides the sub-kingdom. In this case, it is Mollusk.)

R : So, describe me this creature going into a shell.

(Author: 'Withheld' is only a part of the process. There is a threat, so it withholds and goes out of reach. To ask about the creature is to ask about the whole process, not just a part of it.)

P : I don't know. I've said as much as I could.

R : Whatever comes to you, when you say, "A creature goes into a shell." Describe that creature or describe that experience or whatever comes to you.

P : I guess, I have always been an introvert. So for me also, I have a little (hg: closing palm) shell. So, similarly, like all introvert people, they are just...it's not that I don't like meeting people but I have certain people with whom I like to interact, who are like me. That's about it. If you put me in a crowd, it's not that I would get lost. I will find my likes and that's it. Then I don't like to mingle with the rest. And, when I am not at all fond of anyone then that's when even I would also go into my shell and then I am quiet and reserved.

(Author: Having merely come to the source, when we ask about the shell, then the patient sees it in her life. She says, "I have a shell. I'm an introvert." Our idea is to find out why the shell, or in other words, what is the threat? This is the point at which there is the shift to herself, the global. It's not the headache anymore, it is I. Suddenly the local becomes the global. It is the turning point in many cases. It defines the patient herself, not just her complaint. It happens when the local flows into the global, and you see that it is the same thing. In the essence of the headache is the essence of the whole being. What is true of the part is true of the whole. It is a sign that you have reached the centre of the circle. Till then you are not sure. The description of the complaint equates with the description of my being. As long as the description is not the same, I have not reached the centre. This is as true as the fact that any cell of the body will have the same set of DNA. This is why you can ask about anything, and eventually it will reach there.)

Understanding of the case:

The experience of the headache is a terrible, crushing, obstruction. There is a hand gesture with 'obstruction.' Then she uses the word 'compression,' but her hand gesture shows a movement. Animals move, and they use moving hand gestures. She uses the words "shrunk" and "inside". It goes in and cannot be accessed.

The sensation in the chief complaint is the ruling sensation of the case. So far we can see the energy pattern through the hand gestures. From here we can get the sensation (kingdom, sub kingdom and source). She shows a whole movement pattern, which is complex.

"Hammering on my head. Someone not allowing me to use this part." At this point you see that **someone is doing something to someone**. This is the animal kingdom. This is the beginning of nonsense. Reassurance is needed at that point, that she is doing well.

At that point I tell her to forget the headache and everything, as this helps her to dissociate.

She says it is "pulling in". This inclusion of three different sensations point to animal kingdom. She uses 'hammering', 'shrunk', 'compressed'.

If you focus on one action, it will bring out the entire sequence. When asked about pulled, she says it's closed and pulled in. This is part of a sequence, and we need to know what is before that and what is after that; what caused her to pull in and close. It is withholding. Pulled into a shell. The shell brings together all the sensations.

The main survival response of the animal decides the subkingdom, namely: Mollusk.

Why the shell? What is the threat that creates the shell in the first place? She says she cannot trust. This is emotion, and from here we need to go to delusion and sensation.

What can happen if you trust? "You hear and read so much in the newspapers about murder, robbery, rape, broken relationship." What are you most sensitive to? "Someone breaking my trust." It would shatter her. Shatter is important. It is non-human-specific. The experience of breaking is sudden. The experience of the shell is confined. It's such a jumble. It is a sticky situation. It has caught you and you are stuck there, caught. She talks about being caught and fixed in a sticky situation, which is the non-human thing. This is the illogical, strange, individual thing.

Fears as a child? Claustrophobia, walls coming closer. She describes it as an oyster shell.

Why do you withdraw? Because it's better to go through suppression than trust and be hurt. The risk of being modern is to be exposed and hurt. She relates to the Oyster. It is bi-valved, stuck and fixed.

THE RECOGNITION OF 'THE MINERAL SONG'

The fundamental issue in minerals is the 'formation, maintenance, and loss of structure'.

Periodic Table of Elements

Columns

	1	2	3	4	5	6	7	8	9	10	11	12	13	14	15	16	17	18
Row 1	H																	He
Row 2	Li	Be											B	C	N	O	F	Ne
Row 3	Na	Mg											Al	Si	P	S	Cl	Ar
Row 4	K	Ca	Sc	Ti	V	Cr	Mn	Fe	Co	Ni	Cu	Zn	Ga	Ge	As	Se	Br	Kr
Row 5	Rb	Sr	Y	Zr	Nb	Mo	Tc	Ru	Rh	Pd	Ag	Cd	In	Sn	Sb	Te	I	Xe
Row 6	Cs	Ba		Hf	Ta	W	Re	Os	Ir	Pt	Au	Hg	Tl	Pb	Bi	Po	At	Rn
Row 7	Fr	Ra		Rf	Db	Sg	Bh	Hs	Mt	Ds	Rg	Uub	Uut	Uuq	Uup	Uuh	Uus	Uuo
				La	Ce	Pr	Nd	Pm	Sm	Eu	Gd	Tb	Dy	Ho	Er	Tm	Yb	Lu
				Ac	Th	Pa	U	Np	Pu	Am	Cm	Bk	Cf	Es	Fm	Md	No	Lr

The central features of the mineral kingdom are its structure and organization. These are the features that help scientists understand this kingdom so well. The structure of minerals is ordered and predictable in many ways, allowing an exact classification of all elements into the Periodic Table. It is this structured organization, inherent in all minerals, which makes chemistry an exact science. We see how the periodic table tells the tale of formation from Hydrogen, which is the simplest of the elements, to heavier elements like Sodium, Calcium, Iron, Silver, Gold and finally the disintegration of structure in elements like Radium and Uranium.

In persons whose other song is derived from the mineral kingdom, the issues of capacity, strength, resistance, stability, solidity etc. which are the innate features of minerals are reflected in human form as capability, toughness, performance, security etc. The core issue for these people is how much they are developed in their own selves or how to maintain the stability of their structure, be it their health, relationships, family, finances, talents, power or position in the organization.

We find these features of structure and organization in persons whose 'Other Song' coincides with the energy of a mineral. The first impression one gets on seeing such a person is that he is very well organized. Even the clothes that he wears are characteristic: symmetrical patterns, stripes, checks or plain.

His speech is planned, giving a sense of exactness and precision. His hands tend to be either folded across his chest or resting comfortably without much movement. His voice and tone are quite flat without many fluctuations in the pitch. He presents his story or complaints (at a doctor's clinic) in a very systematic manner, often beginning with the previous follow up and then speaking of subsequent events almost chronologically: "I came to you last on...for the first 6 days, the pain in my..." I have observed that very often such a patient notes down his symptoms in carefully written points, and describes each symptom completely (in as much detail as he thinks necessary) before going on to the next symptom. He perceives and therefore describes things in an ordered manner. For instance, once treatment starts, he describe his progress at follow-ups in terms of percentages: "I am 25% better." His hand-writing is usually well structured, straight (not rounded), and angled. He speaks precisely and to the point.

All these characteristics are due to a certain attitude of the mind and a structured thought process. Consequently, such an individual chooses professions that demand these qualities. He becomes an engineer, accountant, computer consultant, and business manager. He can be a high performer and makes a mark in his chosen field in a steady, stable, and reliable manner. Whatever his/her role, be it as a mother looking after her children and home, or as a manager of a large corporation, these same characteristics of order and efficiency will be apparent.

He gives prime importance to structure in all spheres of his life: family, relationships, profession. His performance in all areas relates to this inner sense of structure, or lack of it. He is concerned about the security (of structure – relationship) that he has and that he can provide. The role of structure in human life is in building a society, in forming a family, and in developing an organization.

If this is his 'other song' then the human being will view all his problems through the prism of structure.

His main issues are therefore deficiency in, or loss of, structure. A perceived threat to or failure in structure of any kind could precipitate the problem. For example, a fragile or a broken relationship, the loss of a job, other financial losses, or any failure in performance.

He talks of:

"My home – family – relationship," "My work-efficiency,"
"My bank balance, health."

These are the important areas in his life and all his stresses are experienced in these spheres. His fears, too, are centered on these areas of sensitivity. He is anxious about being unable to perform well and therefore failing in his work. He fears that the relationships that he has built up so carefully, and on which he relies, may break. The thought of losing the possessions or status he has acquired (in response to his inner needs) is a constant worry to him.

All his efforts are channeled towards the building up and maintenance of structure. In order to do this he has to be strong, systematic and calculating. This in brief, describes his nature. He is not easily changed, being very consistent in his nature and reactions. His reactions are uniform, hardly varying in different situations.

His dreams reflect his fears and mainly revolve around his performance at work, threats to his health, sudden financial losses, relationships breaking, and domestic losses such as fights within the family or his house burning down. As these are very definite and fixed areas, the dreams tend to be repetitive.

A person whose ' Other Song' is from the mineral kingdom talks about his symptoms in terms of structure at the deepest level. He will use words that apply to minerals, such as pressure, density, solid, light, heavy, cold, build, form, dissolve, empty, etc. In effect this deep inner sense of structure is his sensation.

For example, Mrs. A says she has a headache. The headache is very intense. It is pulling and sharp. She describes several different sensations relating to her headache, but does not come to one clear underlying sensation.

We therefore ask her: "What effect does this headache have on you?"
She says: "It makes me feel very dependent on others; it is as if I am handicapped."

We attempt to understand this further and ask: "What is being handicapped? How do you experience handicapped?"
She replies: "It is as if my legs are missing."

The mineral person will not be able to go beyond that. Her deepest expression and experience at the level of sensation is that her structure is incomplete. You cannot get beyond that.

She says, "Earlier I would cross the street on my own. Now I need my sister to hold me. I am not able to do my activity."
I ask her to tell me more about the headache and how it affects her.

She says that it kept her away from her nephew's wedding. "We are very attached and I do not want to be away."

Once again, the deepest effect of the headache on her life is on her sense of structure, her relationships, and her ability to function within the family. All have to do with structure. Each time we ask for a sensation, we get something related to structure.

Then, as our conversation continues, something interesting happens.
She says: "I have a fear now. The headache causes fear."(She is unable to go further.)

I ask: "What dreams do you get?"
She answers: "I get no dreams, but I have a tremendous fear of ghosts. I cannot stay alone especially at night, so I pray."

I ask her to describe "ghost."
She replies: "For me a ghost is just the fear of being alone. I cannot describe a ghost or tell you the sensation, but I just cannot be alone. I am like a child. I have not developed the ability to be by myself. I need other people. I need my husband, my children, and my family."

We can see her basic issue is the sensation that she lacks the structure needed for her security. She needs others to fill in due to this perceived feeling of lack within herself.

Within the mineral kingdom, her main issue is security. She lacks a secure structure in herself. Her husband and children and family are her security. In that sense she is childish. When I ask her about the fear, she describes the need for security. It is not the ghost that is important but what the threat of the ghost signifies in her. What is lacking in her is the security, the structure. It is not a feeling of being a victim as in the animal person; rather it is a feeling of lacking sufficient structure and security within oneself.

For a person whose 'other song' is from the animal kingdom, the fear of the ghost would be a fear of death, a question of survival. The description of a ghost here would be that of a monster. The monster might have sharp claws, huge teeth, blood pouring from its mouth, and "it will come and get me." For an animal song, the ghost (the fear) is the aggressor "out there" and the person is the terrified victim of the approaching aggressor.

For a person whose 'other song' is from the plant kingdom, the description of a ghost will be different again. It might be something like: "Oh! It is terrible, I will be caught, and bound." His deepest expression will come down to an inner sensation such as tied and bound, with an opposite sensation of released and free. So for a plant song the experience of 'ghost' at the deepest level is one clear inner sensation of a certain type and intensity.

The periodic table of elements is a map of all the elements, the building blocks from which everything on earth is made. All these elements exist in a structured relationship to each other and so can be placed exactly in the above table. The elements in each column share certain characteristics of chemical composition and reaction, as do the elements in each horizontal Row. It is a table which makes chemical sense and which is used to classify and understand the elements that make up the entire mineral kingdom.

Hydrogen, the first element in the periodic table has the simplest structure of all, consisting of one central proton and one orbiting electron in its single outer shell. Going across a Row, the number of electrons increases by one with each element, the chemical properties of the elements showing a corresponding progressive change across each Row. All elements seek stability of structure, and react with other elements in order to achieve that. An element is stable when it possesses a complete set of electrons in its outer orbit.

In the first Row (Hydrogen and Helium), the first outer shell is complete when it contains two electrons, but all subsequent outer shells require an octate of electrons in them in order for that element to be stable.

With each new row another outer shell is added; thus all the elements in the first column (vertically on the far left side of the table: Hydrogen, Lithium, Sodium, Potassium, Rubidium, Cesium, and Francium) contain only one electron in their (new) outer shell. These elements are therefore very unstable and react readily with other elements in order to attain the shared stability of eight electrons in their outer shell.

In contrast, the Noble gases in the last column of the table (vertically on the far right side of the table: Helium, Neon, Argon, Krypton, Xenon, and Radon) all contain eight electrons in their outer shell, and are called "noble"(or pure) because they are non reactive and inert chemically. They are already stable, in themselves.

Thus each row in the periodic table maps and represents a journey towards stability of structure.

It is not important to understand the concept of valence shells that underlies the discussion in the above paragraphs. What is important to see is that the entire periodic table – all the elements that surround us and make us – is about seeking the wholeness, seeking structure, longing for stability. Just like the person whose remedy is from the mineral kingdom.

As one progresses across the entire periodic table, from Hydrogen (with an atomic mass of 1.0) to Radon (with an atomic mass of 222), the elements become progressively heavier and more complex. Eventually this complexity and heaviness of structure sows the seeds of its own destruction. The atoms become so heavy that their inner structure can no longer hold together, and physical disintegration occurs, as in the radioactive gas Radon. Although Radon is inert and non-reactive chemically (due to its complete outer shell), it is unstable physically (due to the great number of central neutrons and protons, with six shells of orbiting electrons). Its central structure breaks down and it undergoes radioactive decay.

Thus the ordered structure of the whole Periodic Table represents and maps a journey from simple, light beginnings (First Row), through progressive development, properties and possibilities (middle Rows), to increasing heaviness and complexity, which ultimately results in disintegration and decay (Sixth and Seventh Rows).

This same pattern of conception of the new, its subsequent continuing growth and establishment, its further progression into disintegration and decay, is mirrored in every event and at every level throughout our world.

By combining this knowledge base of chemistry with careful observation of people who have benefited from mineral remedies in Homoeopathy, it becomes possible to understand that the structure and development of the elements (as shown in the Periodic Table) is a universal pattern which is mirrored in the structure and development of mankind. Indeed, on looking closely, we see that all development, be it that of a person, a relationship, or an organization – occurs according to this fundamental pattern.

The stages of development of a human, an individual human life begins at conception and grows through pregnancy until the moment of birth. The child then separates from the mother and starts to develop his own identity. Once this is established he is able to leave home. He adopts a trade and learns to fend for himself. He may then develop new creative ventures, and as his sense of security and confidence increases, he may go on to take more responsibility for society, assuming leadership roles in various forms. As he matures, he fulfils these roles. Slowly as he grows into old age, he finds his strength waning, and he has to start letting go. Initially, he lets go of his chosen tasks in life, until eventually he has to let go of life itself.

The formation of an organization follows a similar trend. Any organization originates as an idea or concept within a 'parent structure.' This original concept gathers strength and form until it reaches the point where it is sufficiently organized to separate from the parent organization and establish itself as a separate entity, an individual organization in its own right. This separate organization then explores different avenues of growth, branching into other areas and developing quantitatively and qualitatively. Then comes a phase of stability, a plateau. The period of growth and stability varies, but eventually there always comes a slow disintegration and diminishing of the organization's power, strength and capacity. Finally it ceases to be. Thus the growth of an organization is no different from the growth of a human organism.

The development of a relationship, or family unit, also takes a similar course. Every relationship begins as a concept or a mutual feeling between two people who would like to be together. As their relationship grows they reach the stage where they separate from their individual families in order to have a separate unit of their own. Once they are established as a separate unit, their primary aim is to achieve stability and security. Then comes the phase where they want to branch out and have children. This brings a sense of responsibility. The family grows; the children are nurtured and grow up. Then comes the time for the children to leave home and the family is scattered, as the old gives way to the new.

This is how development and growth happen in general. But it so happens that some of us get stuck at a particular point on the journey. Somewhere along the way (irrespective of what our current age may be), we have halted our onward development. We remain at a fixed point.

If our ' other song' is from the Mineral Kingdom, an understanding of the various issues of the rows and columns of the Periodic Table yields a helpful indication of the point at which we are stuck and its extent.

The periodic table has 'Rows' which are horizontally across and 'Columns' which are vertically down. Both rows and columns have particular themes, or issues. (Once again, these statements are based on knowledge of the sciences of Chemistry and Homoeopathy.)

The Rows and Issues

There are seven horizontal rows going across the periodic table. Each of these Rows can be understood as representing a stage in the development of a human being. Each element in each row represents a corresponding specific energy state in human life. If a person becomes stuck at one of these stages, we can recognize the 'song singing' in him as corresponding to the energy of an element at a specific place in the periodic table. In the context of this framework of understanding, I refer below to 'elements' (minerals of the periodic table) and 'human stages of perceiving' (states of being) in an interchangeable manner.

In each row from the fourth to the sixth, the specific theme of that Row develops progressively, as we move across the periodic table from left to right. Elements on the left have the perception of a "lack" in the issue relevant to that row. Traveling towards the middle of the periodic table there is a sense of gradually achieving and becoming more established regarding this particular issue. From the middle of the Row, across to the right side of the table, once again the feeling is one of loss of structure or capability with respect to the particular theme of that row.

The First Row corresponds to the stage of conception.

This is the stage of coming into existence. The question faced by an individual stuck in this stage is: "Do I exist or don't I exist?" "Am I, or am I not?"

The person whose other song corresponds to an element from this row has he feeling of doubt whether he actually exists. He has the feeling he has no mass, no matter. One person put it like this, "I feel like a baby without a body."

There is also a feeling of isolation, separation and no connection with the form, with self or with anyone and hence they look for some connection to make them feel that they exist. Without this connection they feel disconnected, empty and a void.

Another person put it thus, "It's as if I put my body aside. I had to blast this bubble. I was just a gaseous bubble, a shapeless volume, I was made of gas. That's how I was living, a child in a dream, in a nonexistent bubble. A child without a body, an inexistent bubble of energy encysted in and imprisoned in an uninhabited body. I realized that I experienced myself as having less worth than everybody else; minute, tiny, microscopic and bodiless."

The Second Row corresponds to the stage of separation.

Here the individual perceives himself as a fetus, or in the process of being born. His perception of life is like the labor process. Birth signifies the progressive process of separation and coming into one's own. The question in this stage is "Am I separate or am I still part of the mother?"

These people are extremely naïve and very simple. They have no concerns about their appearance or nourishment or security or performance or leadership. Their main concern is whether they are in the womb (or the protective shell or covering) or they are outside it. Do they have the capability to live by themselves or do they still need to be a part of the parental figure?

The main quality of the womb is the stability and uniformity of the environment within, protected from all the shocks and the stimuli of the outside. A person whose song is of an element from the left side of this row looks for such a stable and uniform environment in his life and seeks people who can provide it for him. An imminent loss of such people is a cause for panic. Similarly any sudden shock in the (stable) environment, like news of a natural disaster such as earthquake and floods also cause great panic.

On the other hand a person whose song is from an element on the right side of this row experiences the need to get out of this stable environment, which he experiences as a suffocative and claustrophobic situation.

(For a case illustration refer page 243.)

The Third Row has to do with the development of identity.

Here the issue of separation is in the past. Separation has been achieved. You exist as an entity on your own, but what is your identity? The question now is "I am, but who am I?" Also in this row is the progressive development from dependence to independence in the areas of care, nourishment and choice.

In the Third row, elements to the left, like sodium and magnesium, perceive a lack of identity in themselves. This inner perception is often expressed as 'living someone else's life,' 'not having my own choices,' "I do not know who I am or what I want," and, as a result, being completely dependent on the choices of others. In effect they have dissolved their own identity into that of another person.

In contrast, elements on the right side of the Third Row i.e. Phosphorus, Sulphur, Chlorine have a more developed sense of their own identity, since the ego and sense of self becomes clearer as we move across the Row to the right. The child's own identity develops and as his ego or sense of self becomes more established and complete, he feels at first different from then superior and finally antagonistic to the parent with whom he had earlier identified. This Row is also concerned with care and nourishment. Elements to the left of the Third Row feel dependent on others for care and nourishment whereas elements towards the right side of the Row have dealt with this need, become free of it, and so have a significant degree of self-sufficiency.

It is the stage of development in a child of approximate age 3-6 years where they begin to develop and assert their choices, to develop and demand the ability to do things for themselves and to become conscious of themselves and of other peoples' impressions about them.

It is also the stage where the child needs warmth, nourishment, care and emotional support. Frequently children start to develop fears of unknown and unfamiliar things and start realizing the difference between the known (familiar) and the unknown (unfamiliar) and between right and wrong.

People whose other song is of an element from this row experience the world as if they were such a child. They can experience great emotional dependence on someone, an attachment, a need for such a bonding. There is an implicit trust or a need for someone whom they can trust implicitly. This is to do with very basic, simple and complete trust, like 'You can trust him with your life'. Like the child's trust on their mother, that she will never ever let him down. The feeling is, 'He and I are not different. He is mine and therefore I'll not be let down in any way.' Such a situation often ends in broken trust and disappointment.

The person can say that the other person has disappointed, betrayed, or let her down. So at that level, namely, the level of Delusion, it does seem as if she perceives that the problem is with the other person and may even sound like the victim song of the animal kingdom. But when examined at an experiential or sensory level, it will be seen that her main sensitivity concerns the need for and, therefore, the making of a relationship and, on the other side, the need to be independent and therefore break the relationship. Dependence and independence are basically themes of structure. The structure of the relationship is the sensitive point, but this will be revealed only at the deeper level. This is also true of the other kingdoms, that the differentiation needs to be made only at the deepest, namely the global, or the sensation level.

The feeling is, 'Who is going to take care of me? Who is going to understand me, know me (my identity) for who I am? Who is going to share my joys and sorrows? How will I live without the person who cares for me?' Any situation where they feel that this care and nourishment will be taken away from them makes them very anxious. For example they get extremely affected by any problem between parents or with friends or a spouse on whom they depend for care and nourishment.

Appearance seems to be a very important issue in this row of identity. Since their own sense of self is not fully established they tend to judge themselves by the way they appear to other people.

A 23-year-old girl came with a skin problem called lichen planus. What she had were dark spots all over her lower limbs with much itching. This condition which is known to be brought on by stress is one that is quite difficult to treat. However what was even more of a problem was the state of mind of this girl. She was unmarried and was staying with her parents and every day there would be intense quarrels between her and her parents. These quarrels would become very intense and the patient would get abusive. Her life had come to a standstill. She was desperate and sometimes even had suicidal thoughts. The parents were naturally very concerned. In the interview process she talked of striking, throwing things, wanting to hit back, to kill, feelings of being neglected, dirty, trapped and excluded. I started her questioning by asking her about her description of the skin problem. She said there were two types of skin spots, with different characteristics, and both of them co-existed at the same time, in the same place. I was intrigued by this description of the skin problem, and asked her to describe this phenomenon more. And she said that they were completely opposite and remotely similar. That they were completely opposite like cheese and chalk. At this point the description of it was so strange that it had to come from her other song. I asked her to say more and she generalized by saying that it is the same situation where she lives with her parents, where each one is completely different from each other. And she felt that the others try to control her. She feels she had to listen to them because, "I am not able to think for myself." And so she has two of her inside herself. And there is a constant struggle inside her. This is so intense that she wants to hit herself against the wall or to destroy herself.

The essence of her perception is one of her own non-development. Since her own sense of identity and choice are not clearly established, and she is not able to think for herself therefore there is a conflict within her whether she should listen to herself or to others. This conflict is so confusing that she is frustrated enough to want to destroy herself. The issue of non-development of herself is a mineral-kingdom issue. In this girl it is particularly manifested in the area of development of one's identity and choice which is an issue of the elements of the third row of the periodic table. (Along with her own awareness of her problem through the interview process, homoeopathic remedy (Alumina) from the third row healed her both in skin and mind.)

The Fourth Row is related to issues of security.

The issue in row 4 is of solidity, stability and security, which is in terms of money/finances, relationships, house, job and health. It represents the development of one's security or mass or strength, with which one develops the ability to defend oneself.

Once the identity is established, the next step is the development of solidity or defensive capability. Elements toward the left side of the row show a deficiency of solidity or defensive capability; movement across the row to the right finds these elements slowly starting to develop solidity or defensive capability, which then starts to become lost by the elements on the row's right side.

This process of accumulating mass from the outside is the most important theme in row 4. This development of security or mass or strength can be expressed in human beings by:

- Development of physical strength
- Development of bones and muscles
- Development of finances, having money, insurances, etc.
- Health
- Job
- Relationships
- Security
- House
- Insurance
- Safety

Here the feeling is, "I have an identity, I am me. What I need now is security." People whose inner song emanates from this row are concerned about the security of their job, their finances, and their health. They are particularly sensitive to any threat to their own health or the health of those they depend on.

Refrains that recur in the lives of individuals stuck in the fourth row often have to do with robbers, soldiers, and policemen. Either the individual perceives himself as weak and vulnerable to robbery (left side of fourth row) or he perceives himself as strong and able to protect others from being robbed (right side of fourth row). Although these two presentations may look different, it is clear that the underlying theme is the same: security.

Stability and security also have to do with the ability to do routine tasks, to do your job, to fulfill your function, to earn your livelihood. To sustain through their routine tasks they need endurance, but then over a period of time, because of the constant wear and tear, they develop fatigue. It then becomes very important for them to endure (or bear or persist or last or continue) through their jobs despite fatigue.

Also, in order to keep their job secured they need to be very efficient and honest and follow ethics and principles. Guilt in row 4 arises from a feeling of having failed in their duty or being inefficient in their job or not being responsible enough in doing the tasks assigned to them. It's more a feeling of being blamed and reproached for not having carried out their duties and responsibilities. Losing their job would mean losing their security and stability.

The Fifth Row has to do with stepping out into the new and being creative in one's life.

The individual is now at the stage where his separate identity is developed and he is secure. From this secure base he can start exploring the new, trying out fresh ideas, seeking a new profession, risking an adventure. Individuals stuck at some stage in this row (especially if on the left side of the row) doubt their capacity to face new situations, to solve problems, to create, to invent, to innovate .They need back-up support when they encounter difficulties. They therefore seek a guide, a person who has experience in whatever field they are stepping into.

The chief theme of the Fifth row is creativity. Whether the individual chooses to work in the field of Art, Science, or Literature, it is the creativity of his work that will matter most to him. Elements on the left side of this row, such as Strontium, have a constantly felt need for a guide or advisor to give them back-up. Strontium feels ill equipped to tackle anything new, and will only do so with the support of someone who will instruct what to do and how to do it. Progressing across the row of elements to the right, the sense of confidence in their own innate creativity develops, until towards the right side of the row, they need to maintain their success in their creative abilities and fear its loss.

The capacity to face the new and to create is completely lacking in the left hand side of the row. We are referring to the ability to solve problems which are not routine, which are new and need innovative thinking to solve.

To improvise, to invent, to innovate, to improve, to ideate, to investigate.... this is what the people whose song is in this row are concerned about. It develops gradually so that elements in the middle of the row are successful as performers and towards the right hand side they start losing the capability to perform. To begin with they don't know what they want to do, but they gradually find out (as their capability increases). When they identify their goal they become more and more **specialized** in that area of creativity. Being specialized is a very important function of their capability in this row. For example, for a sitar player (musical instrument), playing the sitar is the only thing he knows how to do very well; he can't do anything else. He is so attuned to do that, that if you asked him to do accounts, he would go crazy. The more specialized he is, the more anxious he becomes. What would happen if he develops cramps in his arms or if he makes a mistake in front of important people? His entire reputation and ability to perform is gone. As you go from the left hand side of the row to the middle, the specialization gets more and more fine, but at the same time the anxiety to perform increases because it's a bigger potential fall each time.

Individuals who are stuck in this row are particularly sensitive to criticism from others and are anxious about how others perceive them. Since they have a great desire for the appreciation of others they put great effort into their performance. As a result, they are often gifted speakers, authors, scientists, ministers, strategists, planners, etc. Elements placed centrally in the Fifth Row, such as Palladium and Argentum, are the performers, artists, and scientists who are always doing something new in their field. Their creativity lies in their self-expression; it is the theme, the adventure of their life.

A sixty-year-old man saw me with kidney failure following a cardiac surgery.
I asked him about himself.

(**R** : Dr. Rajan Sankaran
P : Patient.)

P : The body should be active. Otherwise one becomes dull. I keep engaged in some activity.

R : Tell me more about your hobbies and interests.
P : I am not highly intellectual, though I like some good, serious reading. I walk in the morning, and do yoga in the evenings. I am very very cautious about my diet.

R : Tell me about your job.
P : I run a factory. It is a one-man show. I have a lot of commitments. I don't like doing repetitive jobs. I design things. Every job is a challenge. I like to take up things which are not fully specified.

R : Say more about this.

P : The customer wants a particular job to be done. I sit and talk with them, give an idea about it. I have to convey the idea in such a way that should appeal to them. However, some jobs are more difficult than anticipated. I have to keep consulting others for small areas. I ask other people for their ideas.

R : What things do you get tense about?

P : Unknown things. When problems are encountered. When we are under pressure because of the delivery schedule. Or when I have to redesign the whole thing.

R : Say a little bit more about challenge.

P : It is to do anything that you have not done before. You have to do it for the first time. Then you consult people, study, refer to books, and then find the solution. I like creative work and don't like it when it is routine. And then once you are set on a path, and are halfway through it, you can't deviate from it.

R : Say more about this.

P : When there are deadlines, you can't give up. You have to accept losses. We are committed. You cannot go back on your words. Trust is a very important thing. I struggled for one full year, and I just can't give up. Once I commit to a job, I'm a slave to it. Sometimes I feel frustrated, but I don't think I am a total failure.

R : Tell me about your dreams.

P : Nothing anxious. Sometimes I get ideas in my sleep. Then I go back to the table and work on them. Once I get an idea, I have to tie the knot.

Design, creativity is Fifth Row. He doesn't like repetitive jobs and routine. He likes to take up things that are not fully specified and gets ideas about them. But then he needs to ask other's advice. Every job is a challenge. Commitment, you cannot go back on your words. You can't give up.

His other song is: "Perseverance in going into something new."

With a homoeopathic remedy (Ruthenium) from the fifth row of the periodic table the patient's kidney condition improved significantly.

The Sixth Row has to do with responsibility and power.

In row 6 the issue is about taking up responsibility, the need for power and the need to withstand high pressure. The feeling is, 'I have an identity (row 3), I can protect myself (row 4), I am creative (row 5), but now I have to take leadership and responsibility.'

Elements to the left of the Sixth row, like Barium, have the feeling that they should take on this level of responsibility, but sense also that they completely lack the wherewithal to do so. They are very dependent on others for even the smallest things, and are acutely aware of their own inability, their own 'lack'. Since they are unable to take responsibility for their own actions, they always look to others to make important decisions on their behalf.

Progressing across the Sixth row, centrally placed elements such as Aurum and Platinum represent the complete development of the themes of responsibility and leadership. Here we find the people who perceive themselves as having the responsibility equivalent to leaders of nations and heads of organizations. They feel a tremendous pressure to fulfill this (inner-sensed) ability and duty, to shoulder heavy responsibility. On achieving the high position they desire, they experience a corresponding sense of power. On the right side of this row, they experience a progressive loss of power despite their desperate attempts to maintain it.

Mr. R.F., a 45-year-old man, consulted me in 1998 for an acute abdominal pain.

He said:

"Since the last one-and-a-half months I have a stomachache. I get a gripping pain and a terrible burning sensation in the upper abdomen. " A number of investigations have been done and he has been going from one doctor to another for relief. They cannot come to a diagnosis, he is suspected to have ulcer, tuberculosis and cancer by various specialists. His manner of description is very structured. He gives attention to the details of the correct sequence of events.

He continues:

"But when the pain starts, for example, right now it is there, you lose... if somebody asks your name you do not know... that kind of pain it is. You lose your capacity totally!"

Not only does it tell us the intensity of the pain, but also his reaction to the pain is such that he will not even know his own name if someone were to ask him.

He then describes his nature:

"My wife and child have never seen me in a good mood around the house. All the time I feel tense for some or the other reason. Even some small thing in the office irritates me. If something is not done as per the way I feel it should have been done, it irritates me. If some thing has to be done and repeatedly it is not done, it irritates me. I have a daughter and so her development and upbringing also keep on worrying me. The office is also highly competitive: handling projects, construction of factories, etc. I am temperamental and all the time I feel depressed."

I ask him what is the stress. He says:

"All the time tight schedules for project completion. Sometimes they are unrealistic tight schedules. They pay higher than the market. But they all admit openly, including the chairman, that as long as you are performing it is fine, take your money but if you do not perform say goodbye. There is no job security whatsoever. Even if you have performed for five years, for the sixth year that has no credit. You have to constantly perform. There is also tough competition in whatever you are doing, for coming up in the organization."

Though competition is an animal kingdom word,it is not the word by itself that dictates the kingdom, but rather the experience. His experience of the situation is of pressure, heavy pressure, and this gives a clue to the mineral kingdom. There is constant pressure on him. His survival in his job depends on his performance. In order to rise in his job he has to deal with this sort of constant, ever-increasing pressure.

The issue here is of responsibility. His major anxiety gives us the clue that now he has little confidence in his ability to handle the responsibility.

He talks of a very stressful situation in his life:

"My father's long illness also made me a little tense.He was staying with us. All the time you are living under tension as to what will happen to him. He ultimately died of a cardiac arrest. He had diabetes since 30 years. I was the one responsible for taking his sugar levels."

Later he says:

"If anything happens to someone in the family, we forget everything My sister's children, my brother's children... if anyone tells me today that something has happened to one of them, I will leave any work aside and run there. I feel committed, responsible in a way. The same thing applies for my mother and father, both. For the last one year I was very disturbed because we thought that we had killed our father. I could see him dying but could not do anything. I feel so guilty as if I have had the biggest insult in my life. I have accepted my defeat.. I cannot come out of it for the last one year. I feel as if my negligence has killed him. I should have taken at least a second or third medical opinion."

He feels he has totally failed in his responsibility. There is no chance to redeem it.

The important features of the case are:

- Constant very high performance pressure
- Very strong sense of responsibility

These points towards the 6th row.

The issue of responsibility is seen clearly from:

- His feeling is that he is responsible for his father's health and even a slight slip up spelled doom; everything is finished.
- He feels responsible for his family, their health, getting his sisters married and his daughter's upbringing.
- He also holds a high position in his company.
- He dreams of falling from a high place.

He feels that things are out of control, feels helpless, that in spite of his doing everything his father dies.

So there are issues,

- High responsibility
- Lost his capacity
- He has failed

One can see many words of that indicate the failure side of this row, namely a metal from the later columns of the periodic table ;

- Destroy
- Destruction
- Damage
- Ruin
- Wreckage
- Failure
- Setback

One can also see that the coping mechanism here is of the impossible type.

P.S.: He was given potencies of Plumbum (lead), from the 6th row (and 14th column) which quickly healed his ailment, and also helped significantly in a crisis situation in his health many hears later.

The Seventh Row represents disintegration.

This is the stage of development where the height of power has been attained, but now it is the time for the disintegration and dissolution of that power.

Whatever builds up must also at some point disintegrate and decay. Just as the elements themselves (Uranium and Plutonium) have become so heavy and powerful that they can no longer hold their inner structure together, individuals at this stage also experience a fragmentation and dissolution of their previously complex and powerful role and status.

Summary

All the elements of the mineral world fit perfectly into their given place in the periodic table. The periodic table, the basic pattern of the worlds of Chemistry and Physics, makes manifest a fundamental developmental process, which is echoed throughout our world. The process portrayed so clearly in the mineral world is that of a gradual progression towards increasing complexity, a middle period of a plateau of stability, followed by a subsequent inexorable decline into disintegration and decay. It is remarkable to observe that this same fundamental pattern is echoed in all growth processes throughout our world. It is as if the elements, the basic building blocks of our world, show us through their structure the deepest realities of our human existence. The 'mineral story' truly echoes in the 'human story.'

The natural development of human beings fits into seven stages, the seven ages of man, corresponding to the seven rows of the periodic table.

Stage (row) 1	Conception
Stage (row) 2	Fetal life and Birth process
Stage (row) 3	Infancy and early childhood
Stage (row) 4	Later childhood
Stage (row) 5	Teenage
Stage (row) 6	Adulthood
Stage (row) 7	Senility and Death

Problems or stresses arise when a person, for whatever reason and at whatever actual age, becomes 'stuck' or fixed at one of the stages, or Rows. When this happens all the person's issues will revolve around the theme of that particular Row, to the exclusion of all else. His whole inner being sings the song of that Row. He is unable to be fully present and free in the moment because he so strongly senses an inner 'lack in' or 'loss of' his fundamental structure. This is his delusion (about his inner structure). This is the inner song which colors all his perceptions and experiences. This is the filter through which he experiences life. His inner reality and outer reality do not converge, since they are not congruent, and this produces stress in him. He is constantly living a tension, a pressure, experiencing a problem which he believes he lacks the capacity to solve.

Humor and the Kingdoms

If we look at jokes, these are very expressive of the Other Song within each one. They are a socially acceptable and even appreciated way of expressing the Other Song. Jokes are in the level of Delusion (Level 4) and therefore very close to the Sensation level (Level 5).

"Everything human is pathetic. The secret source of humor itself is not joy but sorrow. There is no humor in heaven."

Mark Twain

Take the example of this joke from Australia:

An aborigine and a white man were in the same prison cell. The aborigine asked the white man what he was there for. The white guy says, "I am here for 6 months for shooting my mom-in-law, and I am lucky I missed, otherwise they would have given me one year. What are you here for?" The aborigine says, " They gave me five years for driving my motorbike without headlights on, and boy! am I lucky that it was in the daytime...."

The sheer discrimination, the comparison of the animal song, comes through.

Heard this one?

Jacob, a clothing manufacturer, returns from a trip to Italy. "How was your trip?" asks his partner. "Terrific" replies Jacob. "Did you get to see the Pope?". "Certainly." "And, what did you think?" "I figure a thirty-nine short."

Quite a mineral song. Like this one :

> The afternoon was drawing to a close, and guests were getting ready to depart. "Mrs. Solomon," said one of the ladies, I just wanted to tell you your cookies were so delicious I ate four of them."
>
> "You ate five", replied the hostess, "But who's counting?"

And this one? Does it not beautifully depict the dependence of the mineral song?

> The married daughter calls: "Hello, Ma?"
>
> "Shirley darling, what's the problem?"
>
> "Oh Ma, I don't know where to begin. Both the kids are sick with the flu. The Frigidaire has just broken down. The sink is leaking. In two hours all my friends are coming here for lunch. What am I going to do ?"
>
> "Shirley darling , don't worry. I am going to get on a bus and go into the city. Then I will take the train and get off and walk two miles to your place. I'll take care of the kids. I'll cook a nice lunch for your friends and I'll make dinner for Barry."
>
> "Barry , who's Barry?"
>
> "Barry – your husband!"
>
> "But, Ma, my husband's name is Steve. Is this 546-3030?"
>
> "No, this is 546-3040."
>
> (Pause.) "Does this mean you're not coming?"

One can see that humor, and its appreciation is very individual and will express or resonate with the inner song of the person who narrates or appreciates it.

The Other Song and Health

For man to feel one with minerals, animals and plants is not always a sign of sickness. In health too he has elements of all the three kingdoms within him. He has the strength of the metal, the bonding of the salts, the fluidity of water, the beauty of a flower, the fruitfulness of a tree, the sexuality of an animal , the flight of a bird. In fact he incorporates all these aspects into his life, art, poetry, and in his everyday speech, symbols and similes. Further, the presence of all these qualities in him results in his desire to revel in nature in its multifarious splendor.

I was at the Jim Corbett national tiger reserve in north India. Every day hundreds of visitors line up to go on a safari hoping to catch a sight of the tiger in the wild. The park has over a thousand square kilometers and has just over a hundred tigers, so sighting is not common. We went on four safaris and missed seeing it. But still visitors go several times and spend a lot of time and money to see the tiger for a few seconds.

Man's attitude towards animals , be it awe, fondness, sympathy, fascination, hatred or disgust expresses itself in a myriad forms. In India the throne is called 'Lion's Seat', reflecting the regal status of the lion in the animal kingdom. We have several stories, cartoons, ads, names, products, symbols, designs, perfumes, fashion products, based on animal themes. The bulls and the bears of the stock market, the hawks and doves of international politics and the sharks in the business world are only some examples of the presence of animal consciousness in human life. Metaphors like 'he bugs me' or 'he hounds me' or 'she is creepy' or 'I am a free bird' reflect the animal song as well.

Equally interesting is man's fascination with rocks, crystals, mountains, and also man-made structures like buildings, bridges, castles and forts- all speak of man's connection with the mineral world. The Grand Canyon, the Great Wall of China, the Himalayas and the Niagara falls draw many visitors, like the tiger in the Corbett reserve. Many mineral metaphors are in use too like 'rock hard foundations' 'steel resolve' 'iron will' 'golden era' 'platinum jubilee' 'political heavyweight' 'fragile relationship' 'strong bond' and '(his passing) left a vacuum'.

Plants attract man's attention too, and not only those with a green thumb. The Californian redwood trees, the cacti, the various flowers, the palms and various other plants are appreciated for their beauty, for the greenery they provide. Metaphors related to plant kingdom include among several others 'shaking like a leaf', 'painting a rosy picture', 'branching out', 'take root', 'to flower', 'to sow seeds of', 'to reap the fruit', 'to bring to fruition', 'to stem from' and 'to nip in the bud'.

Man's sensitivity to the other kingdoms reflects what is within him. Each individual will be particularly sensitive to the kingdom to which his other song belongs.

In fact these qualities help him in different aspects of his life. The mineral part of him is the one that helps him work, make his accounts, innovate, lead, form relationships and build structures and nations. The plant part of him helps him to appreciate beauty, be sensitive to art, music, to the feelings of others. It adds the color, the fragrance, the warmth and the heartiness to the structure. The animal part is the one that keeps him ahead of others, that keeps him in the group that adds the spice and the winning spirit.

One can see these aspects of man drawn upon especially in advertisements (commercials). An ad for a bank or an insurance company will focus on mineral aspects like growth, security, relationships, etc. An ad for a paint company would focus on plant aspects like sunshine, color, warmth, etc. An ad for a perfume will emphasize animal aspects like attractiveness and sexuality.

Animal advertisement: Perfume (or fashion, entertainment, etc.) has mainly to do with attractiveness, competitiveness and attention – getting which are animal qualities. An advertisement for these products has to target the animal side in us. It focuses on sexuality, attractiveness and is attention – getting.

Mineral advertisement[1]: Insurance and investment is about safeguarding and building your assets (Structure). Therefore the advertisement for it must appeal to the mineral part of you. In the above advertisement we see several mineral qualities and words like safeguarding, worth, trust. It shows volume and the worth of this company. It shows the performance in terms of rating. It also talks in terms of statistics. The picture of a man with childish features holding a piggy bank symbolizes an innate desire to put your money in a place that you can trust. Here you can see the features of the third and the fourth row of the periodic table namely issues of trust (Row 3) and issues of money and security (Row 4).

ET - Mumbai

[1] Reproduced with the kind permission ICICI Prudential.

Plant advertisement: An advertisement for a paint company (or certain food products like coffee, spas, furnishing, etc) usually focuses on our plant side, with emphasis on color, nature, light, aroma, touch, etc i.e. our sensory part. This has to be so since these products have to do not with structure (mineral) or with survival (animal), but with our sensitivity (plant).

So it is not the presence of the animal , mineral or plant quality in man that is sickness. Sickness is a fixation in any one aspect and the lack of freedom in an individual to be any different even if external reality calls for a different type of response.

The Three Postulates

Of whatever you say,

And whenever you do, Mean whatever you may,

The Opposite Is Equally True!

The philosophy expressed in this book is based on certain postulates, all of which have been derived from many years of medical practice.

The First Postulate:

"Sensation and action are equal and opposite."

This means that we react to situations according to the way we perceive them. Our actions tend to mirror our perception and feeling of what is happening and being done to us.

For example, if one perceives an insult, mental or physical, then one tends to react by insulting. Or if a person feels that he is being injured, he will want to injure in return, in proportion to the perceived degree of his own injury. He may not necessarily translate this inner feeling into action, but this way of reacting will be his natural tendency.

The opposite of this is also true. For example if you want to injure someone, it means that somewhere you perceive, consciously or sub-consciously, that you yourself are being injured. To take this to its most extreme: a person who perceives serious threat in his surroundings, to the extent that he feels he might be killed, will respond to this mortal threat by being ready to kill others. This is often the case in individuals with homicidal tendencies. They are prepared to take the lives of others because their inner perception is that their own life is about to be taken.

Such predictable opposites in sensation and action can be observed in many people. This postulate, that 'Sensation and Action are equal and opposite', is extremely useful in the process of understanding another person. Often a person reveals only one side of this equation of sensation and action in the way he himself reacts to a situation. Using this concept, we can infer how he perceives himself within that situation. We thus reach a much deeper understanding of his individual way of experiencing life. Alternatively, he may only describe how he perceives and senses his situation, rarely translating these feelings into outward actions. Again, we can understand how he would like to react, even if he refrains from actually doing so.

Sensation and action are two sides of the same coin; one is inherent in the other. When there is sensation, there must be a tendency to an equal action in the opposite direction. When there is an action or tendency to action, there must be an equal and opposite sensation.

As a medical practitioner, I find that this principle is of great help to me when listening to patients. It alerts me as to what to expect in various subconscious expressions they may use. If a patient says, "I feel like killing somebody", one is automatically on the alert for his inner sensation to be, "under threat of being killed". This sensation is likely to be expressed in his dreams, interests, and hobbies. Sometimes one can even find the sensation in his main problem (physical or mental). For example, the person may say, "My throat pain is killing me!"

The Second Postulate:

"The opposite of whatever is said is equally true."

Of whatever you say, And whenever you do,

Mean whatever you may, The Opposite Is Equally True !

This postulate has to do with sensitivity. Sensitivity is the most important thing to be understood in any person, and sensitivity always denotes opposites. For example, if a person is sensitive to wet weather, he will prefer dry weather. If he is sensitive to criticism, he will relish praise. If a person has a strong sensitivity to music and harmony, he will not be able to bear discordant music. In contrast, another person without a musical ear might be unaffected by either; he simply does not have that sensitivity.

When a person spontaneously raises an issue without being directly asked, it means that this issue in some way relates to his particular sensitivity. This sensitivity can work in two ways. If a person expresses a tremendous lack of confidence about speaking in public, this means he is very sensitive to the issue of public speaking. However, though lacking confidence to perform in public, he also has the potential to become a very good speaker because of this same sensitivity. Thus his sensitivity both makes him afraid and, at the same time, gives him the possibility of becoming an excellent public speaker. It is true that our chief virtue also holds the seed of our major vice, and vice versa.

You may wonder how a lack of self-confidence in public speaking could be the opposite of a great potential to be a good public speaker. What I mean is that every person who says that he does not have the confidence to speak in public also expresses the desire, in the same breath, to be a public speaker. What underlies the lack of self-confidence and the desire to be a successful speaker is the person's proclivity in that direction; his sensitivity to that ability. Hence, all these are expressing sensitivity to the same area i.e. public speaking: having the confidence to be a good speaker, having the potential to be one, lacking the confidence to be one, or the feeling of lacking the ability to be one. Whether it is expressed in positive or negative terms, what requires focus is the sensitivity of the person. Once this concept is understood, the manner of its expression matters little.

All opposites are two sides of the same coin. The coin is the issue, the whole sensitivity. Fear cannot exist except in relation to its opposite, courage. When a person says, "I am afraid to talk in public", he also means: "I want to speak in public, and given a chance, I may be very confident speaking in public."

Let us take another example: a person whose sensitivity revolves around moral issues. He says that he is sensitive to cheating and wrong-doing. This most obviously means that he is affected when other people do these things and that he will not do them himself. However, it can also mean that he is capable of cheating and doing wrong things himself, the very things which he is speaking against. It is only because such sensitivity exists in him, that he is able to speak about these issues. Sensitivity therefore can always work both ways. Consequently, with regard to sensitivity, **"The opposite is equally true of whatever is said."**

This postulate goes hand in hand with the first postulate that **"Sensation and action are equal and opposite."** So the person who says, "I am sensitive to certain issues" is also the person who is capable of doing those things. In a wider context, when a person talks about something, the very need to have to emphasize that topic can only exist in the background of its opposite. If an object is white it will not be visible on a white background but can only be seen on a black background. In the same way love is most apparent against the background of hate, and beauty in comparison to its opposite, ugliness.

Thus the president of a particular country who emphatically claims: "The economy of our country is doing very well," or "Our relations with neighboring countries are very good", may actually be betraying the fact that the opposite is actually the truth. When something is very obvious and does not exist in the opposite, it is usually not said at all. There is simply no need to refer to it.

It is the same story in any situation. When a person emphasizes peace, violence must also be an issue with him. When a person talks about his positive qualities, boasting of great courage, this means that he is also fearful. This fearfulness will be expressed subconsciously, in his dreams, hobbies, childhood memories, etc. If he says that he has no fear of death that means that he is most certainly afraid of it. Whenever someone strongly and spontaneously denies something, the opposite is equally and always true. If the opposite is not true, it is usually not emphasized at all.

The Second Postulate then goes hand in hand with the First Postulate.

The Third Postulate:

"There is no one or nothing out there other than yourself."

This is both a development and an application of the first two postulates. Let me explain this further.

All of us function according to our individual sensitivities. Each person can perceive only what he is sensitive to and ignores the rest. If he perceives particular qualities in others, he does so only because he himself is sensitive to these. For example, if he perceives others as being contemptuous, it is because his sensitivity lies in the area of contempt.

Let us take the example of a person who perceives himself as insulted. Now this person can perceive insult only because he is sensitive to insult. His sensitivity being in this area, he cannot perceive anything other than that. He will then react in an equal and opposite manner to the insult. He will react by insulting, or at least his impulse will be the wish to reciprocate in equal measure. As a result, there is really no difference between what the other person is doing and what he himself does in return. They are both being equally insulting, just in the opposite directions. He sees an aspect of himself (the sensitivity to insult) in the other person and reacts to that. This means that within him lies exactly the same person that he sees (the one who insults). This is his sensitivity and he perceives only this and reacts only to this. Everything else lies outside his field of perception. He sees only that aspect of others which relates to his own particular sensitivity.

Thus the outside world simply becomes a mirror for our own inner issues, our own individual sensitivities, and if these are particularly strong in us, only these parts of another person or situation can be perceived by us. All other aspects of the external world fade into insignificance or, in actual fact, are not even perceived in the first place. So, in effect, there is no one out there but our self, since our own sensitivity is all that we are capable of perceiving.

The same is true for everything around us. For example, if a person is immensely impressed by the Himalayas, whatever he says about the mountain is going to be an adjective that resonates with his own inner sensitivity. If he says that they are incredibly beautiful, it is very likely that his sensitivity lies in the area of beauty. If, on the other hand, he says they are powerful, it is very likely that his sensitivity lies in the area of power. The adjectives he uses and the meaning they have for him, or their connotation, are related to his self-perception. The adjective "powerful" might indicate an inner experience of power or its opposite: helplessness. The adjective "beautiful" might indicate an inner experience of beauty or ugliness. So when we see the Himalayas, we always see ourselves or an aspect of ourselves. When we see any other person, we see ourselves.

There is hardly anything around us that is not actually a perception of our own self. So when we talk about the world coming to an end, we are basically talking about when we are going to end. We can only perceive the end of the world as the end of ourselves. We see something that is going to end, so in us there must be the awareness or fear of our own selves ending.

I found a strong confirmation of this idea in an experiment I conducted with some volunteers in my student group. I asked all of them to write five words describing the Taj Mahal. I asked them to use words that were objective, i.e. as would be used by a journalist, in order to minimize individual subjectivity. What was interesting was that no two descriptions matched. For example, one wrote, "romantic, beautiful, sentimental." Another described it as "grand, royal," and so forth. The third person talked about engineering, structures, and its shape.

When I examined the words that each person had written, I found they gave a very accurate picture of the one who wrote them. This meant that each one had a different perception of the Taj Mahal, based on his own sensitivity, his own way of seeing the world. So the question that arises is, "Does the Taj Mahal really exist?"

The same thing holds true when we talk of concepts like *justice, love, peace,* etc. At a superficial level there will be some commonality in how different people define these. But, when examined deeper, you will see how each one experiences each of these concepts in his own individual way. And how that experience is not limited to "Justice" or "Love" but is the consistent experience of that person in all situations. For example one individual may talk of his experience of love as one of expansion and another may talk of it as a strong passionate attraction. It is when you hear these completely different experiences in connection to one concept e.g. "*love*", that you begin to wonder whether there is such a thing as "Love" or "Justice", etc, and begin to see that the only reality for each one is his own unique experience – his 'other song'. It also becomes obvious that when two people are talking to each other each one is talking from his own experience; it almost amounts to each one talking to himself in the presence of the other!

In the past, if a person talked of a certain situation or relationship in his life which strongly affected him, I would first try to establish whether this situation actually existed or not. Having ascertained that, I would then try to understand what he felt in that situation, question it, and so seek to understand his own perception of reality. However, I gradually came to see that when a person describes other people or situations, he is always describing his own sensitivity, as highlighted in that particular situation. In this way, the postulate that **"there is no one out there but yourself"** proved very helpful in understanding people.

Often I have entire families coming to me for treatment. There is one particular family where I am treating a woman, her two daughters, and two daughters-in-law. The daughters and daughters-in-law visit individually, and on such occasions have described this lady to me. Each one's description of her is so completely different that a third person would find it difficult to believe that they are talking of the same person. I understood from this that each one is in fact describing her own sensitivity when talking of her mother or mother-in-law. So instead of asking them their feelings regarding her, I simply started noting down their description, and thus came to a fairly accurate understanding not of the person being described, but rather of the person doing the describing. In effect we are all, each one of us, constantly painting our own self-portrait in whatever we do or say.

Another example demonstrating the same point is the case of a woman of 40 years who consulted me for symptoms of ulcerative colitis. She was on heavy medication, and she said that all this had started after the death of her husband. I asked her about her life with her husband. She said it was pure hell. She said that her husband had been the most suspicious, possessive, and jealous person. He had always been insanely jealous of her talking to any other man. Her expressions and gestures while describing her husband were just as vehement, forceful and violent as she had so vividly described him to be. She could have described her husband in a completely different way. She could have described her husband as cruel, torturing her, persecuting her; or she could have described him as foolish, stupid, and so forth. But this was not the way she had experienced him. The way she described him helped me see that her sensitivity was in the area of jealousy ,suspicion and rage. Thus we can understand a person's sensitivities even when they are not speaking of themselves.

Understanding all this has been a very spiritually uplifting experience for me personally. It becomes clear that all that you find fault with or criticize is nothing but your own sensitivity. This awareness calms you down. The world exists only the way one perceives it; one perceives only oneself. And knowing oneself is the root of wisdom.

Our Coping Mechanisms

As I began my journey as a physician, I sought to deepen my understanding not only of my patients but of all human behavior. Different individuals react very differently to the same situation, and I sought to detect what lay behind such differences in their ways of coping. I realized that the state of a person's mind is an attitude towards a perceived situation. Each individual perceives and reacts to the same external situation in a unique and different way. His state of mind is but an expression of his perception of reality.

For example, a man fleeing panic stricken from a lion is responding in an entirely appropriate manner to a life-threatening situation. However, if he sees a cat and reacts in a similar manner, this reaction does not suit the reality of the external situation. In effect, he is reacting as though he had seen a lion. The survival mechanism is inappropriate to the situation. He is acting out of a deluded perception of a situation that does not exist in the present moment.

Once I arrived at this idea, I took it a step ahead. If the state of mind is based on a delusion, a false perception of reality, then what are the different ways in which a situation can be perceived? Clearly there are as many different ways of perceiving and reacting as there are individuals, since each person's way of perceiving is unique. But is it possible to categorize, albeit broadly, these myriad ways of seeing and experiencing? I observed that not only is such a categorization possible, it is also extremely helpful.

The survival response that an individual chooses depends on both the external situation and the individual's own perception of his internal capacity. Reaction to a threatening situation also varies with age.

Some examples:

- If a snarling dog approaches a child, the child will probably panic and flee.
- An adult may throw a stone and try to scare it away.
- A middle-aged person might sit where he is and wave a stick to keep it at a distance, making a constant effort so that it does not come near.

- The infirm aged person would not be able to mount any type of active reaction, might not be able to react at all, might feel entirely helpless, give up, and wait for the dog to get him.

Depending on the depth, degree and the intensity of the survival response, we can classify ten basic ways of perceiving and reacting to a given situation. While individual responses vary, a given individual tends to react in the same way to all stressful situations in his life.

These are the types of reaction mirroring the glasses through which he sees all life:

1. The Panic Type
2. The Crisis Type
3. The Possible Type
4. The Persecuted Type
5. The Doubtful Type
6. The Fixed Type
7. The Chaotic Type
8. The Claustrophobic Type
9. The Isolated Type
10. The Impossible Type

Each reaction is influenced by an individual's perception of the situation. The response of a completely healthy person (i.e., one without any delusion) is flexible and appropriate to the situation. His reaction is determined by the external reality, not by his own fixed perception of that reality. If a bomb goes off he experiences acute alarm and flees; if a small fire starts in his house he picks up the fire extinguisher and puts it out. If he is unfortunate and, say, loses a leg in an accident, a loss which has to simply be accepted and adjusted to, he accepts the situation and adapts his life accordingly, with no need felt to hide his handicap. Even if the situation were hopeless – for example, he knows he is about to die due to a serious illness – he accepts even that and so is free to be himself within it. Due to his open way of seeing, he is free to make the best of any situation. These are all examples of complete and healthy flexibility of reaction.

However, most of us tend to 'tune in' and stay with one particular way of reacting to all stressful situations in our life. It then becomes our habitual mode. Although we may have flexibility of response in mild situations, in more stressful situations we all tend to revert to our habitual mode of reacting; our default strategy remains remarkably constant throughout life. For instance, we could probably predict fairly accurately how each one of our close friends would react in a given emergency.

Though I have mentioned a particular stage of life exemplary for each type, this does not mean that a particular stage of life is synonymous with a particular type, or that individuals progress from one type to another as they age. A person usually remains fixed in a particular type throughout his life. Thus it is common for example to find a young man fixed in "the impossible type" or an elderly person in a "possible type".

The majority of people can be classified into the 10 broad types listed earlier and elaborated upon in the rest of this chapter.

THE PANIC TYPE

"I must escape and run because my very life depends on it."

What characterizes the Panic Type is that they perceive acute, sudden danger in most situations. They therefore react instinctively, sharply, intensely, and violently. They readily experience alarm, then panic, followed by total terror. Here, feelings about one's own self are not in the forefront. It is as if the situation itself is so overwhelming that it doesn't matter who is facing it. The reaction will be the same: Let me just escape and run because my life depends on it.

Stage of life *exemplary of the Panic type's attitude*
It resembles the reaction seen in babies. At this early stage in life there is an instinctive reflex reaction to any external threat. Therefore, even in adults, this type of reaction carries the stamp of childishness.

An adult whose reactions are of the Panic Type will rapidly become acutely anxious, but can be as rapidly reassured and made to feel safe by being held in the arms of a protective figure in his life. In general, the Panic Type is excited, excitable and hyperactive. He can sometimes go to the other extreme of being completely shut off and insensitive. His dreams, too, are full of excitement and contain examples of acutely threatening situations. His reactions are excessively loud, whether with laughter or abnormal bursts of courage and cheerfulness. In general, Panic types function at a very high voltage.

Dreams *representative of the Panic type's perceived situation*

Dreams of Panic types often personify the terror and alarm that they innately feel. Example dreams of panic types include natural and man-made calamities—such as earthquakes or aircraft crashes—in which victims typically might experience alarm and panic followed by total terror and have to run for their lives.

The Game *that mirrors the Panic type's pattern of action*

The game that symbolizes this type of acute alarm response is peek-a-boo. Here the parent or familiar person momentarily hides his face behind his hands, then peeks out again at the child. For a moment the infant loses sight of his parent or familiar person and his face shows momentary alarm. But the very next moment he catches sight of the parent again and feels safe. Similarly, young children get a thrill out of being thrown up into the air then caught. Here, for a moment, the child is out of the secure grasp of the parent. This is momentarily both fearful and thrilling for him. Then he is caught and feels safe again. All is well.

THE CRISIS TYPE

"The situation is suddenly critical, but if I make an urgent, intense effort I can regain my security."

The Crisis Type has the feeling of a sudden, unexpected crisis which, if handled correctly, can be overcome. The reaction to any crisis is therefore one of immediate and intense struggle. The Crisis Type readily perceives this acute threat, but unlike the Panic Type, perceives himself as having the inner capacity to save the situation, through intense, concentrated effort on his own part. He feels he must rapidly regain his previous position of comfort and security, since there is always the inherent threat of sinking further during the time of crisis. Once the crisis is past, all is well with him again.

For example, if there is a bomb blast, the reaction to it is acute and instinctive; the situation is life threatening and warrants acute panic and immediate response i.e. escape. In contrast, if one's house is on fire, the response needed is one of intense struggle, a concentrated swift effort to put out the fire and resolve the crisis. Similarly, if a person owns shares and the stock market suddenly crashes, he will feel the threat of a sudden acute drop in his financial security. However, an intense, concentrated effort can result in the recovery of his fortune. Once the loss is recovered, the need for the effort ceases because a position of security and comfort has been regained.

Stage of life *exemplary of the Crisis type's attitude*

These reactions are typically seen in childhood. The attitude here is one of impatience. The person has to regain lost ground over a short period of time. He is therefore impatient, demanding, wanting things immediately, and grabbing things only for himself.

Dreams *representative of the Crisis type's perceived situation*

Dreams that typically signify the feelings of 'crisis management' would be an emergency room situation where the person is constantly facing an unexpected crisis which if handled correctly can be completely overcome.

The Game *that mirrors the Crisis type's pattern of action*

A game that personifies this attitude is hide-and-seek. The child has to put in an intense effort to find the hidden person. There is always the thrill, the threat that he may not find him. However, once he finds the person, all is okay and he is comfortable once more.

THE POSSIBLE TYPE

"The situation can be worrying for me, but never hopeless.
Life is a steady ongoing struggle."

The Possible Type has highs and lows. The struggle is like a tug-of-war with the outside world. Sometimes the balance is on his side and he feels high; at other times the balance is on the other side and he feels low. This is an active person. The struggle is an active process which becomes apparent especially at times of stress.

There is a lack of confidence in facing the situation, a feeling that he may not be able to do it. This causes anxiety which becomes marked when he is actually confronted with the situation. It is also present, but to a much less degree, when he is not facing a situation. He then has a kind of anticipatory anxiety, though he is not so distressed. This causes a kind of internal restlessness, insecurity, dissatisfaction, sensitivity and anxiety about the future. But there is always hope however bad the situation is.

In a nutshell, the feeling is that of a difficult situation where one has to struggle in order to succeed. There is doubtful anxiety about his ability to do so, but he is hopeful and failure does not mean the end of the world. He must struggle in order to recover or maintain his position.

Stage of life *exemplary of the Possible type's attitude*

The reactions here are almost like those of teenagers. This is the time they have to face the world and stand on their own feet. It is like a teenager learning to drive. The task is well within his reach. All it needs is some effort and it will be accomplished.

Dreams *representative of the Possible type's perceived situation*

There will be many and varied dreams. Depending on the everyday situation, the dreams will reflect his anxiety about not being able to cope. They will also reflect the ongoing steady struggle that is part of his daily life.

The Game *that mirrors the Possible type's pattern of action*

A game that is popular with young people is football. The goal is very much in sight here (not out of reach), and after a bit of struggle one is able to achieve it. It is not impossible, given that the goal is accessible.

THE DOUBTFUL TYPE

"The situation is difficult. Sometimes I try to overcome it, other times I just accept it."

The life of the Doubtful Type is characterized by alternating periods of struggle, trying (with anxiety over success), and giving up (with despair of success). He will at times gear up to make considerable effort to resolve problem areas in his life. However, he is somehow not motivated to persist with such effort. There will then follow a period when he gives up and just accepts the circumstances of his life, problems and all.

This type of reaction contains elements of both 'The Possible', involving struggle and uncertainty about the success and 'The Fixed' which signifies acceptance of the problem.

Stage of Life *exemplary of the Doubtful type's attitude*

This kind of reaction is typically seen in the age group of mid-twenties to thirties. This is the time when tasks start to seem a bit more difficult and out of reach. The person makes an effort and achieves some amount of success. But the effort is not sustained and he slides down again. The problem recurs and he has to begin again, struggle afresh. The theme here is of unsuccessful efforts. It is the situation of a man who fears the water while attempting to learn to swim. His enthusiasm will sustain his efforts for awhile, before his fears take over at some point and he gives up. Then he is again motivated and renews his efforts, but at some point the fears take over and he is again resigned to not being able to swim. Another example is that of a plump woman in her thirties trying to lose weight. She has accepted being overweight, but there are times when she still feels she should lose some weight. So there is an alternation between periods of dieting and exercise, and periods of dormant resignation.

Dreams *representative of the Doubtful type's perceived situation*

Such people have is "trying to do something" dreams. The doubtful type may dream about going on a journey but failing to reach his destination, or unsuccessfully undertaking a search for a lost item.

The Game *that mirrors the Doubtful type's pattern of action*

The game that typifies this attitude is snakes and ladders (chutes and ladders). One struggles to reach the top of the board, and just as one is getting there, one slides to the bottom and the struggle begins all over again.

THE PERSECUTED TYPE

"I am stuck in a difficult situation,
and from time to time I am attacked."

The Persecuted Type has an underlying feeling of being permanently stuck in a particular situation. Within this fixed situation, from which there is no escape, he experiences intermittent moments of sudden acute threat. He reacts with an acute panic to these moments of sudden threat, but once the threat passes, he reverts to accepting his underlying feeling of being chronically stuck.

One can say that the Persecuted Type has a constant underlying feeling of vulnerability or weakness, which makes him unable to rise above the taunts and control of others and assume his rightful place in society. He never seems able to muster the means of escape from this fixed situation. He experiences periods when he feels more defenseless or helpless than usual and seems to invite increased abuse. These crisis situations may provoke him to an attack of acute anger or retaliation, but he is unable to sustain a posture of standing up for himself and continues to remain oppressed.

This type of reaction is therefore a mixture of the Panic Type and the Fixed Type's reactions. The overall effect of perceiving and reacting to life in this way is to feel both persecuted and unfortunate. He constantly broods: "Why me?" He feels stuck in life, hindered, and obstructed. From these perceptions stem emotions of being unfortunate, being tormented and picked on by other humans, god, or life. He develops a sense of bitterness. Things seem unworthy and never good enough.

His behavior reflects his mindset. As he feels irremediably weak, stuck, hindered and obstructed, he broods and fantasizes about his situation. Although he bitterly laments his fate, he is also accepting of it. However, on top of this come sudden acute attacks of fear. These he reacts to with paroxysmal outbursts of anger and desperation.

Stage of Life *exemplary of the Persecuted type's attitude*

The feeling is one of being stuck in a dependant position, and being powerless and attacked intermittently. In Indian society this feeling can be experienced right from childhood up to middle age, since many Indians, even when married, are living in their parents' house. It is difficult for them to be on their own, but they have to accept their situation since they still depend on their parents. From time to time, there are differences of opinions, arguments, fights, criticism from their parents (who are of another generation). However, the young married couple cannot rebel openly because of their dependant situation. They start to think of moving out on their own, but financially this is not easy. In the meantime they begin to fantasize about what they would do if they had their own space and freedom.

Dreams *representative of the Persecuted type's perceived situation*

The dreams of the Persecuted Type are mostly indicative of the position or place they long for; a kind of fantasy, giving them a joyride of what they want.

The Game *that mirrors the Persecuted type's pattern of action*

The game of blind man's bluff corresponds with this type of situation. The blindfolded person has the fixed handicap of being unable to see, and from time to time, others in the game can hit him on his head or back, trip him, etc.

THE FIXED TYPE

"I am stuck in a difficult but not life threatening situation and I just have to accept it and hide my problem."

The person of the Fixed Type perceives a fixed, irremediable weakness within himself, about which nothing can be done. This weakness is not life threatening, but he feels it must be covered up at all costs. The rest of the world must never see it. He therefore appears somewhat secretive to others, as he is always maintaining a cover, or mask.

This cover or mask can take the form of egotism, fixed and forceful opinions, compulsive acts, the seeking out of distractions, anything to avoid experiencing or revealing his inner problem. His behavior is very closed, with an underlying air of guilt, as something is always being hidden (both from himself and from others). Maintaining the mask is stressful and requires constant effort. However, accepting the inner problem and covering it up is the survival strategy that must be maintained at all costs.

Stage of Life *exemplary of the Fixed type's attitude*

This is the attitude adopted in middle age. This is the time when the person, after having struggled long, begins to feel and accept his limitations and tries to hide them rather than being open about them. It is during this time that the person becomes fixed in his way of doing things and his ideas become rigid. A typical, perhaps frivolous, example of this is a woman whose hair is turning grey. At first she will struggle to correct things in her diet, will consult beauticians, etc., to try and prevent the problem developing. By the time she is middle- aged, she tends to accept the fact that her hair is grey and acts instead to hide the fact - she simply starts to dye her hair so that others do not see it. This fixed way of reacting is reflected in other fixed habits and traits. Even dreams tend to be specific and fixed.

Dreams *representative of the Fixed type's perceived situation*

Here the dreams have elements of secretiveness in them, so that no one knows; dreams of covering oneself or of being exposed. The fixed type's dreams typically involve a scenario in which he must conceal a fact or cover up an action so that no one will know what he has done. Feelings of guilt and fear of discovery permeate his dreams.

The Game *that mirrors the Fixed type's pattern of action*

The game of poker typifies this way of behaving. As a poker player, one must be careful not to reveal one's hand. The truth must be kept hidden from fellow players at all costs.

THE CLAUSTROPHOBIC TYPE

"Time is short and I am hemmed in.
I must break free before it is too late."

The Claustrophobic Type experiences stressful situations in life as oppressive and suffocating. He feels limited and too weak to handle pressure while experiencing it in every field of life — pressure of time, pressure of work, pressure of not enough space around him. The pressure of time is experienced especially keenly. He constantly feels that time is narrowing down on him, that deadlines are close. He reacts to this inner perception that 'time is short' with hectic activity. He races to complete all tasks and burns the candle at both ends, striving to experience as much as possible in the short time available to him. In an attempt to break free from his inner feeling of oppression, he constantly desires change and new experiences, restlessly wanting to taste all of life to the fullest. This type of hectic reaction lies between The Fixed and The Impossible (see page 208).

Stage of Life *exemplary of the Claustrophobic type's attitude*

We can see this type of reaction in the youth. The young feel they have a right to live their own lives - they feel imposed upon, trapped by the "restrictions" laid down by their figures of authority. In order to prove (often to themselves) their independence, they do things which are not approved by society. These young adults want to break free from the bonds of society. They do things that, while not actually antisocial, are on the borderline of what is acceptable to society. They constantly push the existing boundaries, since they experience these boundaries as oppressive. They zoom about on fast motorcycles, going for wild, daredevil stunts, etc. They seek change and excitement and can be bold and rash in their behavior.

At the other end of the generational spectrum there can be a similar type of claustrophobic feeling. As we reach our forties and fifties, we start to feel that old age is narrowing in on us, that there is little time left to live. Simultaneously we realize how much we still wish to accomplish. A certain urgency can enter into our way of doing things, as we increasingly sense we are working against the clock. We feel the urge to travel, to visit the places we have always postponed seeing, and to do everything we have not yet managed to do . Sometimes this is seen as a midlife crisis. The most stereotypical expression of this behavior is the purchase of a convertible sports car.

Dreams *representative of the Claustrophobic type's perceived situation*

The dreams of the Claustrophobic Type tend to reflect a sense of suffocation or claustrophobia in various forms and shades. At other times, the dreams reveal an intense need to break free of such confines. The themes might be of travel, of daring exploits, anything revealing the intense inner need for freedom and for change.

The Game *that mirrors the Claustrophobic type's pattern of action*

The games that typify this type of reaction are races or games with a fixed time schedule or where a record has to be broken. The person must speed up and fit everything into a short span of time. The need to achieve is not only intense but becomes increasingly desperate as the game draws to a close. Race-against-the-clock games such as hot potato produce the sensation of the claustrophobic type. (Hot potato is a game that involves players quickly gathering in a circle and tossing a small object such as a beanbag or tennis ball to each other while music plays. The player who has the "hot potato" last when the music stops is out. Play continues until only one player is left. The game is designed to be fast-paced and high-pressured and is often played by children. The game can also be played without music where there is a designed leader who shouts out "hot!" and the player holding the object is eliminated.)

THE CHAOTIC TYPE

"There is chaos everywhere; control is almost impossible, but it is my responsibility to strive to bring about order."

The Chaotic Type experiences life as chaotic and disorganized. He reacts to this perceived chaos by striving to control life. He recognizes that the task is too great for him, yet he still tries single-handedly. The task is superhuman, beyond his capacity, but he stretches himself in his nearly impossible attempt to create order from chaos.

A person who perceives and reacts to life in this way constantly feels that he is expected to fulfill a great demand. He feels he is not up to the task and would like to conceal this fact. Since the consequences of failure are increasing chaos (to which he is most sensitive), he has to continually strive to survive. Thus his life is a continuous, prolonged, hard struggle which seems endless. Because he is stretching himself, striving to be perfect, yet hiding the fact, there is no rest or freedom from the tension. Everything appears chaotic; therefore everything has to be controlled! When things do not go as planned (as they seldom do), the feeling of disorder increases in magnitude. His struggle and effort increase accordingly. He feels that if he fails to control the burgeoning chaos it will be the end of the world.

In the Crisis Type too, there is a concentrated effort in response to perceived insecurity, but once the effort has been made and the position of comfort regained, the Crisis Type can rest. All is then well for him. The goals of the Chaotic Type are much harder, if not impossible, to achieve. Consequently, rest is not possible for him. The intense effort has to be sustained, as complete order is never achievable. His position is quite desperate as he continually stretches himself beyond his limitations in order to have an outside chance of achieving his goal.

The Crisis Type is like a person participating in a 100-meter race. If he concentrates all his efforts on the race and gives it all he has, there is a very good chance he will win. Then, having achieved the position he desires, he can rest. In contrast, the Chaotic Type is like a person who has to break an international record. The target that he has set for himself is already one that is beyond the reach of an ordinary person. He has to stretch himself beyond his capacity in order to achieve this goal. He knows this goal is nearly beyond him. Even if he achieves it, he will only set himself a further, more extreme target. He is caught between his twin perceptions that (a) Life is a set of nearly impossible tasks, which it is his responsibility to complete and (b) Failure means disaster and chaos. He therefore has to sustain an almost impossible level of effort in order to avert disaster. His ultimate chances of success are slim, but he has no option other than to continue

Stage of Life *exemplary of the Chaotic type's attitude*

The attitude that typifies this type is that of a person of sixty to seventy years. He has been unable to accomplish many of the things he wished to in life. With increasing age it becomes increasingly difficult for him to work with the same vigor and enthusiasm. The task seems increasingly out of his reach. He feels his life is slowly slipping out of his hands, out of his control. He responds to this by stretching himself beyond his capacity, putting in sustained intense effort, despite his years, in the hope he can still manage to achieve some of his goals.

Dreams *representative of the Chaotic type's perceived situation*

The dreams of the chaotic type usually involve some sort of superhuman effort. For example, they could be of doing an almost impossible balancing act, or of walking on a two-edged sword.

The Game *that mirrors the Chaotic type's pattern of action*

The state of being of the Chaotic type is similar to that of a person juggling on a tightrope. Tremendous control and accuracy are called for every instant. The task is complex. Perfection is demanded in both the juggling and the balancing. One wrong move could result in total disaster.

A 30-year-old woman was referred to me for treatment of ulcers and intense pain in her feet. She had an autoimmune condition involving her blood vessels (vasculitis). On being asked about herself she said that her memories begin with childhood where she found that her father used to come home drunk everyday and her mother was in depression and would hardly get out of her bed. And she remembers this from when she was three years old. I asked her what her experience in this situation was. And she said she experienced the situation as being completely chaotic and she felt as if it was upto her to put order into the situation, which seemed a nearly impossible task at her age. I asked her to narrate other vivid memories. One of them was as a nine year old when she was on vacation with her grandparents; she remembered that her grandfather tried to touch her inappropriately. When I asked her how did she experience this, she said once again she felt that she was facing a very difficult situation for her age and that it was upto her to do something about it and she had to use all the strength that she had to push him away. Interestingly she chose a profession which reflected this feeling of facing a very difficult, chaotic situation; she became a nurse in the acute psychiatric ward. The woman was a great stickler for order and perfection. Her whole perception of various situations is one of intense chaos which needs her to put things back in order, a nearly an impossible task. She is typical of the chaotic type.

THE ISOLATED TYPE

"I am disgusted with myself and my situation
and feel completely alone.
Society does not want me,
and I don't want anything to do with it."

In the Isolated Type we find a progression of the claustrophobia. The oppression increases to such a degree that an intense inner feeling of hopelessness and disgust develops. The person reacts to this by isolating himself from the world. He cuts himself off from others since his own state disgusts him. He has an insurmountable, despairing desire for change. He perceives his state as isolated, disgusting, and shameful. He has the intense desire to escape this desperate situation, coupled with the knowledge that such an escape is almost impossible.

The Isolated Type is epitomized by the situation of a leper in society. Leprosy is one of the oldest diseases known to man. In the past there was no cure; the disease, once developed, could not be escaped. Nearly every country in the world experienced the scourge of leprosy at some time. Since ancient times, its occurrence has been attributed to a punishment or a curse from god. Once afflicted, a leper was isolated from the rest of society, an outcast—not only because of the infectious nature of the disease, but also because of its repulsive appearance. Despite the discovery of drugs that cure leprosy, the stigma attached to it remains strong. The state of the leper in human society has always been a piteous and isolated one.

Stage of Life *exemplary of the Isolated type's attitude*

The attitude that typifies this state is that of a seventy-to-eighty-year-old person suffering the diseases of old age. He is no longer able to make himself useful, to care for himself. He finds it difficult to relate to younger people and their values, and therefore cuts himself off. He narrows down his acquaintances to a very few. He feels unwanted by his family (and society in general) as he is cast off into an old-age home. There he feels a sense of hopelessness with no possibility remaining in life other than death.

Dreams *representative of the Isolated type's perceived situation*

The dreams of the Isolated Type reflect these feelings of inner revulsion and despair, a loathing of self and others. The dreams may include themes of being cast out and shunned or of shunning others (action and reaction being equal and opposite). This disgust can also be seen symbolically in dreams of dirt or of feces.

The Game *that mirrors the Isolated type's pattern of action*

The Isolated Type is a human state involving both cruelty and self-loathing. There is a resonance with perversions such as sadism. The sadistic person gets pleasure out of inflicting cruelty and pain on another. (His inner perception is that others are being cruel to him, inflicting pain on him, and he reacts similarly.) An activity such as sadism is also unacceptable to society. It is considered shameful, it is a hidden activity, and if uncovered, results in the isolation from society of those involved.

THE IMPOSSIBLE TYPE

"The situation is impossible, I have no chance of succeeding, only drastic, destructive actions are of any effect."

A person of the Impossible Type perceives life as an almost impossibly dangerous and hopeless situation. He feels that only drastic measures can be of any use in such a dire situation and, therefore, often sets him (and others) on a path of total destruction.

He feels neither the highs nor lows of the Possible, nor the secretiveness of the Fixed. He has an overwhelmingly pessimistic view of life. He feels that moderate means of change are useless. He does not believe it is possible to modify what is wrong. The only option is to radically change or destroy it. This internal feeling of desperation and destruction almost literally eats him up. He can react impulsively, destructively, and out of all proportion to even minor situations. It does not matter whether the situation is one of insult, criticism, or domination; his instant feeling is that the matter has gone far beyond a tolerable limit. Since he sees no point in trying to adjust or accommodate, he instead reacts excessively, violently, and destructively.

A person with this type of reaction harbors a deep and chronic pessimism. This complete hopelessness and despair is interspersed with occasional, sudden, impulsive violence directed at himself or others; a mercurial temper.

He is rigid in this pessimistic outlook and can see no other. This fixity of view applies both to himself and to the external situation. The Impossible Type is therefore aggravated by any contradiction. He is dictatorial, brooks no discussion, and is not amenable to change or conciliation.

This type of reaction occurs when a person is faced with a completely superhuman task, one where no man stands any chance of succeeding. In a desperate effort, he nonetheless tries to change the entirely hopeless situation. The result is usually destruction.

Stage of Life *exemplary of the Impossible type's attitude*

The attitude typified here is that of the age of senescence. There is absolutely no hope now. Their health deteriorates as their bodies and minds fall prey to so many illnesses that even coping with them becomes an impossibility. The only way out is death.

In their attempt to achieve the impossible, some persons of this type can reach very high positions. We can see them as heads of government, people in power, heads of institutions, or leaders in their field. People who see life in this manner feel they have to achieve positions of great, almost awful power, as they perceive only drastic measures as being of any value. In exact contrast, others of this type can become revolutionaries, terrorists who are prepared to commit both homicide and suicide in their desperate attempts to achieve the impossible.

Dreams *representative of the Impossible type's perceived situation*

Their dreams would indicate the hopelessness and failure, and a feeling of the end of life.

The Game *that mirrors the Impossible type's pattern of action*

A person who perceives and responds to life in this way is like a person playing a game where, from the outset, there is no hope of success. It is like an ordinary man playing chess against a state-of-the-art computer. The task is hopeless, the outcome certain and unfavorable.

KEY WORDS OF EACH TYPE

The Panic Type	The Crisis Type	The Possible Type	The Persecuted Type	The Doubtful Type
Acute	Crisis	Effort	Stuck	Trying
Sudden	Intense	Success	Intermittent attack	Giving-up
Violent	Sinking	Optimistic	Persecution	Accepting alternating with effort
Panic	Recover	Struggle	Unfortunate	Irritation
Danger	Child	Possible	Paroxysmal	Discomfort
Reflex	Intense short effort	Hopeful	Contemptuous	
Escape	Sub-acute emergency	Confidence	Disobedient	
Helpless	Homesick	Comfortable	Struggle	
Terror	Intense struggle	Within reach	Confidence	
Insanity	Critical period		Possible	
Infant	Collapse		Migraine	
Fright	Reaching position of comfort		Periodicity	
Alarm	Impatience		Harassed	
Storm	Demanding		Hindered	
Instinctive			Obstructed	
			Tortured	
			Hampered	
			Hopeful	
			Within reach	
			Comfortable	

The Fixed Type	The Chaotic Type	The Claustro-phobic Type	The Isolated Type	The Impossible Type
Fixed	Control	Hectic	Disgust	Destruction
Covered-up	Perfection	Intense activity	Great contempt	Homicide
Guilt	Fastidious	Suffocation	Isolation	Suicide
Hide	Beyond one's capacity	Trapped	Mutilation	Total
Secretive	Superhuman	Closing in	Intense hopelessness	Impossible
Warts	Cancer	Change	Intense oppression	Despair
Neurosis	Great expectation	Freedom	Dirty	Psychosis
Fixed weakness	Chaos	Oppression	Hunted	Devastation
Avoidance	Order	Desire for change	Despair	
Acceptance	Stretching beyond capacity		Outcast	
Middle age	Loss of control		Sadism	
	Self-control		Repulsion	
			Loathing	
			Confine	
			Castaway	
			Seclude	

The Technique Of Reaching The Depth

The non-human song within each of us is the cause of our stress, our turmoil.

To find out what it is, to see it, is the first and most important step to coming out of it. This is not easy, for often (especially in adults) it is deeply hidden, covered up by our normal civilized behaviour which pushes this inner story deep within.

If one wants to discover what the nonhuman song within us is, the song whose voice is speaking through us, singing its own melody; if we want to see that hidden force, that energy that colours our perception—the way we think, we act and react—one must go through a process of inquiry .

It is better that this inquiry be guided by another, one who is qualified and skilled. *Though I shall describe the technique here, I do so with the caution that this is not to be done lightly or casually. Done in a flippant way by someone without the training, it can have an adverse effect.* However, done in a professional manner, it can open inner doors of perception and be a significant step forward in the healing process.

The guide must be one who is empty of prejudice and effort. He must let the seeker lead from the start of the process. Both need to be open to the moment, empty of desire and free to flow with whatever comes up.

I have been using this technique to go along with my patients to their innermost experience, (the Sensation, the Source, the Other Song). I then used this to find the appropriate homoeopathic remedy. However many patients remarked at the end of the interview that the process itself had been revealing and had a healing effect. I therefore feel that it can be used even outside of homoeopathic clinics.

I must say that not everyone is prepared to undergo the process and, without cooperation, it is nearly impossible to get deeper. Therefore it is important that we should explain to the seeker what we are about to do. At the same time the guide must also be ready.

This technique is simple, as simple as getting to know someone.

When we first meet someone, how do we begin the conversation?

- With an introduction, with our NAME and identity.
- Then we get to know more FACTS about him, by observing his appearance and his way of dressing. Further on, we may get to know his age and occupation.
- And if the conversation continues, he will tell us about the various EMOTIONS that move him. He might tell us stories of his past years: situations that have influenced his life, the way he looks at reality.
- A still deeper conversation will get you a sneak preview into his nightmares and fears. When he starts trusting you enough and is comfortable with you, when he has crossed his socially acceptable threshold, he will start talking from the world of imagination (DELUSIONS).
- If we take it a bit further, we will see the KIND AND DEGREE OF REACTIONS that these imaginary situations provoke in him.

When we come to know someone at this deep level, we begin to have a fair idea of his or her fundamental outlook on life. Although we all perceive and experience life uniquely and differently, at a deep level it is possible to discern three broad, fundamental ways in which we do this. Going back to the analogy of the spectacles we see life through, it is as if there are a million different types of lenses for the spectacles, but only three basic frames for these lenses to fit into.

These three fundamental "frames of seeing" are related to:

- **Sensitivity (the Plant song),**
- **Survival (the Animal song),**
- **Structure (the Mineral song).**

Depending on our make up, either we manifest great sensitivity and reactivity to any stress in life; or stress brings about in us a deep sense of external threat related to our very survival; or when faced with difficulties in life, we feel at a deep inner level that something is lacking in our fundamental structure.

When we really know someone, we can know whether he perceives stress in life with a sense of panic and crisis, with a sense of openness and possibility, with a sense of being tortured and persecuted, or with a sense of doubting the outcome. Alternately, he may experience stress with a fixed sense of weakness, with a suffocated and claustrophobic feeling, or with a feeling of desperately needing to control the stress. His problems may make him feel like an outcast and isolated from the world or, if he finds the situation totally impossible, he may fear he will be destroyed by it (and so be ready to destroy others).

The process we adopt in order to reach the deepest core of disturbance is similar to the one we follow while getting to know another person. I found the best place to start is always with whatever symptom or situation is bothering the person most in the present moment. The main complaint can be physical or emotional. It could be a fear, a nightmare or any dream for that matter. If the person has troubling symptoms both emotionally and physically, I found the best way to start was by focusing on the physical symptoms as these reflect best the truth in the present moment. In contrast, we can be easily confused trying to follow and understand the emotional state of another person, our own emotions can interfere, and we can get lost in the "story".

Even the most insignificant physical aspect will ultimately lead to the core sensation. My point only being that everything about you is you: it is the clothes you wear; the place you choose to sit; your profession, friends – it is all a reflection of your deepest experience. Although wherever we begin – be it even the button on the person's – shirt will ultimately lead to the core sensation, it would be strange to start an interview like that! The truth of the moment is most clearly expressed in the main complaint (physical or emotional symptom) and is therefore most accessible there. The complaint that bothers one the most in the moment is the crystallization of one's sensation at that moment.

We can begin by asking, "What is bothering you the most right now?" The person can give you a diagnosis, be it diabetes or migraine, and go on to give clear, physical facts about this diagnosis. From here we go deeper, asking how he experiences these physical symptoms, what the exact sensation is. How does this problem affect his life? Our job as a healer is to guide the person from this level into his "core", the deepest part of his soul, of which his disturbance is an expression.

When we come to this "core area", the fundamental issues for that person become very clear – there is no confusion at this basic level. It is as if we have reached the core of the volcano, of which the eruptions (the physical and emotional symptoms) are only a by-product. If we become embroiled in the emotional state of the person, it is as if we remain too absorbed in the experience of the tremors of the volcano without going deeper to the core from which all symptoms originate.

As we begin focusing on the various details of the physical complaint, we come across an element which has more than just a physical connotation, and that spontaneously connects to the mind state. We then focus on this key area of connection, where we can clearly perceive that both body and mind are expressing the same phenomenon. This leads us to a very deep core level.

Case of a 62-year-old man who came to me with cervical spondylitis. He complained of stiffness in the neck and could not move his neck without difficulty. A few excerpts from the case:

(**R** : Dr. Rajan Sankaran
P : Patient
Pertinent phrases in italics.)

P : I have this stiffness of neck. My attention is more on the stiffness rather than on what I am supposed to do.

(Author: He runs an organization. If he is discussing something he has to stop because of the condition. He feels handicapped and not useful.)

P : The connecting thread of my life is being useful and meaningful. If I can't do this I feel worthless. The arthritis handicaps me and I have nothing to do. Life becomes meaningless. I've achieved so much in life, but at this point life doesn't feel worth living. Everything is good except this feeling of being handicapped.

I search for the meaning of life. This haunts me. I learnt meditation. I honor that which is within. It gives an honor and dignity to life. If I don't honor this I feel there's a war within. I have joined a movement, in which I am involved with since 22 years. I believe in taking nothing for what I do. I believe that nonviolence is the most important thing in life.

Doing nothing, retirement, feels vegetative. I love my body a lot, but I am more in touch with the spirit. I don't want allopathic medication because it's doing violence to my body. I want to grow, and to harm any of the natural feelings is violent. I feel that the war starts with allopathic medication, which is something that I don't want.

I am a trustee for a hospital and have collected several million rupees for the earthquake. I want to usefully manifest myself, to be useful for everything. When I am handicapped I can't reach out. When I reach out I feel connected to life. Deep inside I feel an impersonal connection to life. It's like a river that's cut off, cut off from the river that's everywhere. There is a compulsion from within. I don't know when it will burst or I'll float six inches above the ground. I feel that an enclosure has burst and I feel light and at the same time I feel connected to everything as if there is no other person. I feel the unity so they don't look like other people to me. I feel this when teaching others and I feel overwhelming, tremendous joy from this. I feel joy when I have the sense of 'doer-ship'.

(Author: His talk was very much at an intellectual level. He is well- read and has an inclination towards philosophy. There are many notions that he has derived from such writings e.g. cut off from the river that is everywhere, connections to life, joy, unity, 'doer-ship', etc. but I wanted to get deeper. So I focused on his chief complaint.)

R : Tell me more about the neck problem.

P : I have a strain in my neck and I am not able to work fully. *I am not able to move freely.*

(Author: The patient is describing a sensation of stiffness. Now let us understand this sensation and what effect it has on the patient. How do they both connect?)

R : Describe the stiffness.

P : It gets more and more straightened and I am not able to move the neck both ways.

R : What is the effect on you?

P : I am divided in my work. I'm less efficient. Rather than going ahead in my work it brings attention to my neck. I've stopped working.

R : How do you feel?

P : I feel I should get relieved.

R : How do you get relief?

P : I just rest for a while.

(Author: Then I questioned him about meditation, as I realised that has a deep interest in meditation.)

R : What does meditation mean to you?

P : It means quietness, stillness. It is acknowledgement of interdependence. It is an acknowledgement that everything that I do happens because of many things. I don't exist in isolation. In the past I felt that things happen because I do it, but I realized over time that things happen because of many things. So many factors contribute to make something happen. It produces harmony inside me, a sense of peace.

(Author: What is interesting is that I know in my mind that his main sensation is "I can't move. I can't move in my work because of this. My neck doesn't move and my work doesn't move." But the whole idea here is that every aspect of the case—everything in the patient's life that is important to him—will tie in to his vital sensation. Thus, when we examine meditation, we must go deeper into what meditation means to the patient until we come back to his vital sensation of "not being able to move". Meditation is a kind of compensation. So I take him further in the interview.)

R : Describe peace.

P : I feel a sense of harmony with people, less and less of divisions. I feel like being silent. With speech there is an internal commotion. But I allow that to pass off. Earlier I was reacting to everything. It felt like being *caught*.

R : What was the effect on you?

P: *I wouldn't move from this being stiff. That is, things pulled me in different directions. It was a compulsion of feeling.*

(Author: When he gives this word 'stiffness' he gives a physical picture of an emotional feeling. This is exactly his sensation.)

P: It was as if I was in the middle of traffic, in the middle of a traffic jam.

R: How is that feeling?

P: *The feeling is lack of movement.*

Understanding of the case:
Again, the same thing: cannot move, caught, stiff. He had to meditate over two hours a day in order to avoid this experience.

We can see that this person does not perceive the situation as a competition (animal) nor as a lack or loss in structure (mineral), but rather that he shows a sensitivity to the situation, and as a result any situation will produce in him a sensation of stiffness and caught. This indicates that the patient belongs to the plant kingdom and—in this specific case—to the family of Anacardiaceae (which includes diverse plants such as cashew nut, mango, and poison ivy) which has the same sensitivity and sensation.

Here the job of the guide is to have a completely laid-back attitude, where he always "throws the ball in the other person's court". When the seeker explains an issue, it is important that the guide make no assumption that he has understood; rather, he should continue to look puzzled and so encourage the seeker to go deeper and clarify further. Only by further elaboration and by the seeker journeying to deeper levels of inner experience and describing these will the guide begin to gain a perception of the person's way of perceiving and living his life.

Thus the emphasis throughout is not the seeker's story (i.e., the outer situations or scenes within which the individual leads his life) but his **inner experience of living within that outer story**. It is not that the story is irrelevant – it is highly relevant. It is, rather, that the outer story is not specific enough for us to gain a deep understanding of the seeker's inner core state. On this journey inwards, the guide jumps to no conclusions, makes no assumptions, and always follows the seeker's lead.

This is the most crucial part of the whole process.

In order to faithfully follow the inner journey, the guide must stay very alert while being totally detached. The process of enquiry is gentle, slow, and gradual. The sensation this line of enquiry filters down to is the crystallization of an individual's life. It is the fountainhead where all the vital phenomena are expressed in their raw form. It certainly cannot be neglected. It is the core, the foundation for every facet of a person's way of being. It is the key by which every single aspect of the person's life can be understood. All revolves around this core sensation.

As the seeker is describing his main complaint, one also notices the pace and depth of the way he experiences and responds to this deep inner sensation. This can become clearer by asking the question: "What do you do in response to this sensation?" That is, what is his way of coping with this inner experience?

Once we have understood a person's deepest sensitivity, or sensation, it is relatively easy to observe the manner in which he copes with this sensitivity.

Take the case of a person whose sensitivity or inner sensation appears to be that of being injured (either physically, mentally, or both).

We then need to discern his reactions to this key sensitivity:

- In what way does he respond to his perceptions of imminent injury?
- Does he panic in such situations?
- Does he perceive it as an acute crisis and respond by a concentrated effort to overcome the crisis?
- Does he feel stuck in a position where he is intermittently injured?
- Does he feel hopeful and try to get out of the injuring situation?
- Does he have an attitude of resigned acceptance, so as to conceal his sensitivity?
- Does he react to injury with a desperate, last-ditch effort to escape from it?
- Does it make him stretch himself far beyond his capacity in order to gain control?
- Or does he experience his sensitivity to injury so keenly and desperately, so hopelessly, that he wants to kill someone else or himself?

If a person perceives and experiences injury to the point of destruction, his reaction will have the same depth and desperation, and he will want to injure in turn, or kill. (Postulate 1: Sensation and action are equal and opposite.)

However, if he reacts passively he may become numb and hopeless. If he compensates well for this sensation (i.e., reacts by developing strong, almost opposing sensations) he may become the tough guy, the one who can face even the most severe and destructive type of injury. However, even fully compensated, his sensitivity to injury remains.

We persevere by asking the same question in various ways, until the seeker responds by touching on another, deeper sensation that is more precise and descriptive. In this way we move to deeper levels. The seeker himself needs to have the spirit of perseverance and patience, coupled with complete conviction that something deeper will be made manifest, will be expressed.

Inevitably the question arises:
How does one know that the sensation described is more precise and one step deeper than the one already expressed?

There are two keys that help open this "Pandora's box" of inner exploration.

Actions speak louder than words.

Sensations are deeply and clearly felt but are very hard to express accurately. I realized that often an individual best expresses his inner sensation through the medium of gesture, rather than speech. In effect, his hands are able to communicate and describe what his speech cannot.

Let me illustrate with the case of a young schoolgirl with headaches.

While describing the pain of her headache, she kept making a pushing hand gesture, saying that her head felt as though a part of it was being forced out. She also described feeling very bad when her friends didn't share everything with her. When asked to elaborate how she felt, she initially kept saying, "Bad and sad" and then described a depressed feeling. All the while, her hands where flying in the air, depicting exactly the same hand gesture that she had used when describing her headaches. That is precisely what she felt even with her friends: that they were, through their actions, somehow forcing her out, leaving her alone to the point of exclusion!

Hand gestures also help clear the confusion that can arise when seeking to understand the deepest sensation. For example, one person may give a good verbal description of how her lungs feel when she has an asthmatic attack. She may use words such as "blocked" and "jammed", but all along her hands are telling us another deeper, truer story. While she talks of blocked and jammed, her hands move round and round in a twirling motion, giving the appearance of tying or winding and unwinding something. By gently asking her to describe more exactly the sensation of "blocked and jammed", she finally comes to the deeper sensation of "tied and bound", what her hands had been telling us all along! Thus hand gestures are the best indicator of the truth she is experiencing. With patience and persistence during questioning she is able to arrive at an exact description of the sensation her hand gesture had been constantly illustrating to us. We can then be sure that we have arrived at her deepest sensation.

Hand gestures are subconscious, involuntary and are often not even noticed by the individual making them. This is their truth and their beauty. The gestures unselfconsciously portray an inner reality. It is therefore essential to take time to understand these repetitive gestures. Once we have identified what they denote, our understanding of the person deepens.

A 35-year old lady described her sensation in an asthmatic attack "as if" something was being tightly twisted in her upper chest, "as if" she was being choked or strangled. Her description of this sensation evoked a python strangling its prey. Later on in the case, she spoke of being hurt when her husband admonished her. When asked to describe the feeling of hurt, she used the word sad, while at the same time her hands clenched and went towards her chest – exactly the same gesture she had used while describing the strangled, twisted feeling she experienced with her asthma. What she could not express in words, her hands expressed eloquently, without her even being conscious that this was happening. It is therefore vital that the guide, the observer, is conscious of and is immediately alert to gesture.

The Gesture is often the Key

Thus the gesture becomes that secret door, the hidden passage into the land of the seeker, a way by which, with help, he can get in touch with his inner reality. It is a window to the sensation. Focus on it, and another world opens up. The other song that plays within that world is heard. While the seeker is talking, he or she reaches a point where words are inadequate to describe the experience, and only a gesture is made. At that time, ask the seeker to focus on the hand gesture, "Do it again, focus on it... then tell me whatever comes to you."

A word of caution over here seems mandatory. It is very important that we do not interpret gestures. Interpretation is a mental function while the sensation lies beyond the mind's grasp. The use of the gesture then is going to be the total catalyst for the seeker to spontaneously express the sensation. When the gesture comes up we should not ask ourselves or the seeker what the gesture means. What we need to do is to focus the seeker on the gesture and ask him to observe what spontaneously comes up.

The question about the gesture should be so framed that thinking stops and spontaneity is encouraged. Whatever comes spontaneously comes from a point that is beyond reason, beyond logic and beyond the mind. It will therefore come from the sensation.

If the seeker attempts to explain it, theorise about it—cut him off. "Tell me whatever comes to you" (beyond mind, beyond reasoning; that which is absurd, illogical, but simultaneously arises when the energy is experienced).

The mistake we make is to ask them to explain the gesture.

Don't ask "What does this mean?"

So it's not, "What are you doing?" It's just, "What comes to you" (when this energy pattern is being experienced). Something illogical comes to them; with a laugh or a smile (for example), "When I do this, I feel it is all dispersing! It's stupid!"

At what point should we ask about the gesture, when should we ask them to focus on it?

As we have seen in earlier chapters, there are seven levels of experience: name, fact, emotion, imagination, sensation, energy and the seventh. The seeker may speak at any of the levels at a point in the interview.

If the seeker speaks at the emotional level and makes gestures, it may be inadvisable to pursue this straightaway. If you ask too early, the seeker gets confused. When you go through level 3 and 4 do not stop to ask about the gesture. On the other hand, after asking if they are making a gesture, stay focused, do not get diverted to something else.

You need to pursue the emotional and delusional level to a point where words fail and the seeker needs to use gestures to express his experience. At that point, when you ask about the gesture, then it takes the case to a new level. It takes you into the other (inner) world of the seeker.

The other world is not human.

It is a stranger that lives within us, from another kingdom, who has been part of us, who now talks like he owns the place. A plant, animal or mineral lives within. We need to hear that song, to go to that level of experience.

So the first key to reaching a deep understanding is "hand gesture". The second key is the word or words that crop up repeatedly when the individual describes his main problem. He may use words that seem completely out of context to the situation being described, or he may always accompany a certain word with a strong hand gesture.

To simplify it, I have identified seven main criteria to help identify which (of the many) words a person uses carry special significance. These criteria can best be remembered alphabetically - **M, N, O, P, Q, R, S.**

CRITERIA FOR IDENTIFYING WORDS OF IMPORTANCE:

1) MOVEMENT

A word has importance when it is associated with a hand gesture that has energy, speed, direction and movement.

2) NON-HUMAN-SPECIFIC

Let's take an example to demonstrate this.

(**R** : Dr. Rajan Sankaran

P : Patient.)

A young man of 25 years came to me with chest pain.

I asked him, "What is your problem?"

He answered: "Some kind of sharp pain in my chest."

(Author: Sharp is not human specific. "Sharp" is a reality in the human realm, but also occurs in the animal, plant, and even mineral kingdoms. Sharp can be anything that is pointed and that hurts.)

R : Tell me a little bit more about sharp.

P : This sharp comes and attacks me suddenly; it is an attack of pain.

(Author: **Sharp** and attack are not human specific.)

I asked : "Tell me more about sudden, attack, and sharp."

P : I'm working in this company and my boss is a rude person. His words are so sharp.

(Author: While saying this, the seeker makes a strong gesture. The words are human but the energy is not specific to humans. You hear the energy. Forget the human words.)

So I ask him, "Tell me about this (the guide repeating the seeker's words, asking only about the gesture, while imitating the seeker's way of speaking) when you describe it with your hands (repeating the same gesture). What is this?"

He answers, "My boss treats me the way they used to treat slaves."
The reason we do this is to enter into a new realm, a realm that is not specific to human beings, but one which is wider, more basic, and more inclusive. The passage from the "human specific" to the "non-human specific" is not an easy one. It is rarely a smooth transition to move from one level to a deeper one. The situation he perceives (my boss treats me like a slave) is at the delusional level. To go deeper still– to the sensation level– one needs to focus on hand gestures. If there are no strong hand gestures, one needs then to see if the word "slave" can be associated with a strong image.

I therefore asked him, "What do you mean by slave?"
It is at this point that one must ask the seeker, "Tell me your experience of this particular situation" (mentioned by you). Then the sensation will come,

since sensation is an experience. Sensation is not an emotional feeling, nor is it a delusion. It is deeper than both, being sensed and experienced in the mind and body simultaneously. It is a complete physical, emotional, vital experience that is not human specific at all. Our deepest experience is not human specific, it includes all realms. This deepest sensation cannot be adequately expressed in words. It can be expressed in groups of words, hand gestures, and sound, but is very difficult, indeed, to encompass in words alone.

I asked, "So what is your experience of a slave?"

He answered, "They do horrible things to you. They take sharp things and poke you."

I continued, "How would that be experienced by you?"

He answered, "It is just a sudden sharp pain."

So we see that the same song sounds throughout. In the physical complaint, he says that he has "sharp pains." At the emotional level he says, "I'm affected by pointed remarks." Then from the delusion level (being treated like a slave), he comes to the same sensation. Once we begin to hear the universal, it sounds at all levels.

There is always a personal resistance to going deeper, into a level of self-understanding and self-expression. Words do not readily describe these deep sensations, but it is also as if we have somehow, in the process of living our life, forgotten to trust and express our own deepest sensations.

However, if we persist in our approach, he will directly lead us to the source. By this I mean the other song within him, which is sounding clearly at this deepest level of sensation. Sometimes the individual will actually tell you the name of the source (in the animal, plant, or mineral kingdom) or describe it so accurately that you can clearly hear the melody of the other song his life seems to sing — note for note, melody for melody.

3) OBDURATE

A word is important if it is persistent, in the sense that it remains firmly in the conversation no matter what the subject discussed.

4) PICTURISED

A word is important when it is associated with a strong image or delusion, as in the earlier example when he spoke of slaves: "My boss treats me the way they used to treat slaves."

The guide should see if that slave image holds. He might be just using the word casually, so it is important to seek clarifications. See if he gives you a vivid image and whether in so doing he is actually transported into the situation of a slave. If the word holds deep meaning for him, he should give you the entire movie of a slave. You can guide him into that state where he is actually living and dreaming that situation right there and then. It is a little like past-life regression, like hypnosis. A deeper truth comes through and expresses itself. He takes you to a different time and place, one removed from present-day reality.

At that point, you ask the question, "What is your experience of this situation?" and the underlying sensation will become clear.

5) QUEER

If the word is queer, i.e. used out of context, we pay close attention. We carefully note a word that really does not make sense, a word that would not normally be used in that way. For example, a girl described her throat pain as "My throat pain hits me." Now this word "hits" is out of place and quite strange. What does "hit" truly have to do with throat pain?

6) REPETITIVE

If a word keeps recurring, irrespective of the levels reached, it becomes important. A word that keeps coming up again and again becomes important if, even after going to further questions and subsequent levels, the word still keeps coming up, almost like a recurring hint or shadow.

7) SYNONYM

The ability of the individual to give synonyms of the main word, and illustrate it with various examples, indicates the strength of the energy that the word truly holds for the person.

For example, a young girl who had recently got married expressed her discomfort in her in-laws' house. She said, "I don't feel this house is my house. I am never allowed to do what I want. I am a captive here." Obviously, my next question to her was about captive and the feeling a "captive" experiences. She described the captive as experiencing what a prisoner may feel. "You are all contracted; the only thing is imprisonment, without being tied up in shackles."

These words are to be taken seriously and treated with respect. They allude to her deepest experience. These words come from the source whose melody is the other song or the non- human song that sings inside her. If you honour these words, focus on them, more information on the source whose energy sings in us can be obtained. You may take these words and go to the next level.

Moving Deeper

Thus, in order to move to deeper levels, we have to select words that are odd, repeated, or that are used out of context. Alternately, we can select a certain hand gesture that recurs with vivacity and clarity. These important words or gestures act like footholds on an unknown surface and help us to move on.

These words and gestures of the person need to be carefully tested to see if they truly hold, in much the same way as a rock climber tests a foothold. The climber has to know that he can trust his whole weight to a foothold, before relying on it as a means of ascending to the next level. A rock climber knows a sure foothold not by the look of it, not by the size of it, but by testing out the feel of it (i.e., the experience of it), the knowledge within the body that a seemingly insignificant irregularity in the rock can hold his whole weight for the next move. Similarly the individual's (thoroughly tested) words or gestures can be relied on to lead us to the next level. Indeed, they are the only things that can lead us to the next level of understanding.

Once we have a good idea of what the deepest sensation is, we look for confirmations that this is indeed the key sensation throughout. It is best to seek confirmation in areas of the person's life where he is "uncompensated". As described earlier, we are all past masters at coping with and compensating for are deepest underlying sensation in life. Areas where we are least compensated are our vocation, our relationships, our recreation, hobbies, interests, dreams, fears and above all in our childhood. The same sensation or its opposite will be found here, together with the same intensity of reaction in coping with that sensation. One will return to the same core which is deep, unspoken (but constantly intimated) and runs through every sphere of the individual's life and activity.

Sometimes it may also happen that it is just when all the parts of the seeker's story seem to connect, that you notice a common thread **(the seeker's constant experience**) that strings all the situations and experiences together. But sometimes one might then encounter a portion or a bit that does not seem to fit in with the rest of it. It stands out, unusual and different, and you don't know what to make of it.

Take for example, a person who talks of pressures at work or home. He says he must withstand all this force and pressure. It is important for him to do so, for if he did not, everything would collapse (Here he is talking of his other song from the mineral kingdom. A metal structure needs to be strong enough to withstand great force and pressure. If the structure were not built to withstand all these external agents, it could collapse, fall, and crumble).

As you continue your process of inquiry and you come to the dreams, he mentions falling into a shark cave and trying to come out of it. Here one might be puzzled about the link between a shark cave and resisting force and pressure. This may feel like unknown and uncharted waters. Fear of the unknown could creep up and you may not want to step on it. That is why one needs to put the mind aside and not analyse anything. Instead one needs to step on this bit that does not fit and follow it to the deepest sensation level.

This gives us the freedom to flow in the moment with whatever surfaces. It also becomes the greatest test of the core sensation. If this new, incongruous detail also finally arrives at the same coherent expression we can be sure of the core sensation. If not, one must be very careful. That is the test. In the above case, on being asked for his experience in the shark cave situation, the person said that it was like being put through a period of pressure where he had to use all his skills to emerge unscathed. Thus for this seeker, the element that initially seemed out of place actually proved to be part and parcel of his core sensation: his perception that he constantly needs to withstand pressure.

Let us take another example to clarify this. An elderly person came with a long-standing skin allergy. He experienced a sensation of pricking all over as if by needles. He felt very troubled by this pricking (which he showed with a gesture of poking). When I enquired about his dreams, the man said, "I dream of shit." Such dreams seem prima facie completely unrelated to the sensation of pricking, needles, and poking that he had described earlier.

Here you need to go into the dream of shit. I asked him "Tell a little more of this dream," and he starts laughing. "What more can I say about shit? Everyone knows shit." I persist, "Tell me more." He ponders over this and says, "I should not dream of shit. They say that to dream of shit means impurity." He is from a sect that holds this belief. Being aware of this and wanting to be careful not to assume anything, I want to know what the underlying sensation is, so I persist with "Tell about impurity." "Impurity I should never, ever have. Then you go to hell." Now I follow the hell clue, which will lead us to his core sensation. "Tell about hell." He replies, "I do not want to go to hell; it is so much suffering." I follow him with "Tell about suffering." There is a pause.

I continue, "Speak about suffering." And he spontaneously replies, "There they take these needles and prick and poke you."
He pauses and recognizes that it is the same sensation that he has been speaking of in connection to his skin condition.

The Interpretation of Dreams

Books and theories abound on the interpretation of dreams. Just as they do on the interpretation of any phenomenon. Probably the best way to interpret a dream is to not even dream of interpreting it! A dream is an expression of the other song within. The dreamer should be asked to describe the dream in the maximum possible detail.

He needs to observe and express:

1) The feelings in the dream.

2) The sensory experience in the dream.

3) The energy in the dream: the speed, movement, pace, etc.

4) The type of coping mechanism seen in the dream.

5) Any nonhuman elements in the dream that could connect to the source.

6) The effect of the dream on the dreamer.

The sensory experience, when explored more deeply, will be seen to reveal the experience of the dreamer, which will be the core experience (sensation) in the person and will be seen in all aspects of his being, body and mind, past and present. The dreamer, along with the guide, needs to explore this experience without interpreting it or thinking about it, just observing deeper and deeper, till the centrality of it becomes evident.

The way we look at our dreams is often the same way we look at any other phenomenon; we think about it, analyze it, interpret it, classify it and basically intellectualize it. While this may satisfy our mind, does it really help us learn something about our true nature?

There is another approach, another way of looking, which does not involve the intellect. It is the way of going deeper into the experience of the dream, to become aware of what we experience in that situation. When we do that we come to the inner sensation that transcends the dream and can be seen to be the experience that pervades our whole being.

As an example let us take the case of a young woman who comes with a long-standing recurrent sinusitis.

When asked about the effect of the problem on her she says, "Generally my activities go down very slow. I miss my walk for quite a few days because I am unwell and tired; it takes all the energy out of me. I feel very sleepy all day long. I don't feel like doing anything. So, it is like a heavy day; the activities are reduced because I cannot do much. After that I get these bouts and irritation in the whole head. Sometimes I have to miss work also because of that. I just feel sleepy all the time. Just avoid entertainment and just sleep."

The effect of the problem is: when she goes outside there is a problem and so 'I have to be shut down inside and be sleepy'. She needs to go in and be covered in a quilt.

She reports the following dreams:

"I have been getting these accident dreams, often about plane crashes, about sea before tsunami. For a long time, I have been getting dreams of drowning in the sea, air crashes, dead people, riots, flood and dead bodies. Then I have been getting dreams of stool and everything soiled.

I also dream I am trying to save my loved ones or keep them safe. There is a particular plane crash; my family would be involved and I run to see that everybody in my family is all right. That is very often."

It is interesting to note that she has two types of dreams: disasters and stools. One might be tempted to find a logical explanation for these two types of dreams or attempt to deduce something common in them. Such deductions will remain a theory and will be of little help. The way that will lead us somewhere is to follow the energy, the experience in the dream to the deepest point possible.

In this case we took the dream of disasters to begin with and traced the feelings deeper.

"I have an insecurity problem in the first dream of accidents; I feel that I am going to lose all my loved ones. That my father, mother, my husband, and my sister-all should be safe. I am secured that nothing should have happened. It is more of a scary feeling. At that particular time I feel in the dream I am totally choked. It is just that I can't imagine my life without them."

Here we see that her main experience, her main sensation is, 'I can't exist without them'. We don't see downward movement in the air crash. She did not say it is all going down, this is not the energy. The energy is in losing, that she will lose something. That takes you to the mineral kingdom. The experience is not one of fright or shock but rather of losing something that you need.

We can go deeper than this and ask what it is the experience for her of losing such a person. She says that she is extremely dependent on her close relatives that she needs them around all the time. They are like a security blanket for her and she cannot imagine her existence without them.

Having investigated the first dream to this level, we now turn to the second dream (of stools) and ask her to speak about this. She says, "I feel that I am impure and that I need to wash my legs often and I am feeling sick about it because generally even if a kid is shitting, I can't see. Feel like everything is stuck on my feet. It is sticky and very odd, difficult to remove it off. It is unhygienic, like when mud is on your leg, you feel you slip on it, and you have to scrape it out with some leaf or something. Like germs, it is basically waste of your body; I don't want to touch it because it can give me infection. Even if I am in a public place, people are sweating and touching me and all that makes me sick. Basically don't like anyone touching me except some people, if they touch me I feel consoled and good."

She has this same feeling in all public places. The only place where she likes the touch is from her mother and father and that makes her very comfortable.

I ask her to describe this feeling of comfort. She explains, "I feel sheltered. I am under them; nothing will affect me, if they are there. Like they are protecting me like a house. Nothing is going to affect me if they are around. They are my shelter, probably I can think of a home."

When asked to describe the *shelter* further, she continues, "A protective shield around (Hand gesture), very closed atmosphere (Hand gesture). I feel like I am in a protected glass ball around me. The whole feeling of that dad, mom, husband is like a circle around me."

Later she describes exactly the experience of a fetus in a womb. This experience is the common one to her sinusitis (remember, she cannot come out, has to stay in covered in a quilt), her dream of disaster (where she loses the loved ones, her shelter, the ones without whom she cannot imagine her existence) and the dream of stool (being touched by the outsiders, wanting to be inside a glass ball, protected and insulated).

Thus, if you take any dream deeper to the sensation level, to the level of the inner experience, you will come to the one experience that pervades the whole being. This is not an analysis or interpretation of the dreams but a going deeper into the experience of it.

That is the adventure, the beauty and joy of this technique. When you have two completely dissimilar things and they arrive at the same point, you are completely sure. That is the joy of every case. It is amazing to witness it unfold.

Going to the core

Quite different techniques are required at this stage of listening. At the beginning of our enquiry, we allow the individual complete room to move, prescribing no limits or direction. In this way, the person is free to gradually reveal to us his deepest sensation. Towards the end of the enquiry, once the sensation has become clear, it is necessary to stay focused on that sensation, in order for the person to lead us deeper to their core state, where everything connects. At this point, it becomes necessary to guide the person and to limit their room to retreat into the more superficial areas of their life, which are so much easier to describe. There is a natural tendency for the person to do so at this stage.

If this does happen, our understanding of the seeker's state can falter as we become lost in a renewed multiplicity of external detail. The process is therefore to stop their moving back, but without imparting any other sense of direction. You do not tell the individual where to go; you simply block the ways back to more general levels. Thus the only place for the individual to move is deeper, to a description of his exact state.

This endgame tactic is similar to that employed in chess: towards the end of a game, after the board has been cleared of most pieces, a skilful player can secure a swift conclusion and prevent the game's plodding on interminably by blocking the king's escape back to a more defended position. In just the same way, gentle guiding of the individual at this point can help him reach a deep point of understanding within himself – where the "king" (i.e., the deepest core sensation) surrenders and reveals itself clearly.

Once the core sensation has been revealed, we need to go back to the areas of greatest stress in the person's life, since these are the points where the deepest sensation AND the way the person copes with that sensation are revealed most clearly. It is as if we are trying to see a hazy image, one that we cannot quite make out. More light is needed if we are to see it clearly. Stress is the stimulus which intensifies the image, heightens or "brightens" the sensation, and also brings out the person's individual coping mechanism. When we do this, when we go deeper in these areas, we find again and again that we reach a point where both the sensation and the coping mechanism concur with our earlier perceptions of both. Confirmation is then complete.

So the guide takes the important words and gestures of the seeker, as described above, and gently and gradually together they proceed to deeper levels and clearer understandings. Honestly, one does not need to understand this process, just be with it experientially, in the moment. It is the sum totality of all the phenomena. If we trust the process, trust and focus on the key words and gestures of the person, then the specific, unique "core state" of that person gradually emerges into clarity.

This core "way of being in the world" holds true for the individual in all aspects of his life. Every single element of his story, his reality, and the language of his source "make sense" when understood at this deep level. All becomes clear at the end of this process. It is very moving to share this journey with another, and together gently come to see and feel how everything about him is connected, is part of a discernible pattern. As the guide, one almost sees the other person (in varying degrees, depending on how deep the process goes) wake up to the sheer integrity of his or her whole being. When the shared journey is successful, the individual has a much surer sense of his or her own processes – he is surprised and relieved to discover the manner in which all so clearly connects. This gentle, persistent process of enquiry, in which every single aspect of the person is honoured, can result in a very deep awareness and consequently a sense of integration and empowerment for the concerned individual.

The method will be better understood with the help of an illustration.

A forty-five-year-old male comes in with a severe cough.

(**R** : Dr. Rajan Sankaran

P : Patient.)

R : What is your complaint?

P : Cough four to six times in the day.

R : Describe the cough some more.

P : I blank out with the cough. There is a want of breath. Also, a pulling sensation in the abdomen and throat. It is worse when going out, from a draft of air. That stops me from going out of the house. It comes on suddenly, especially when talking.

(Author: One can see that he has a cough which gets severe from time to time, and at such times he gets a blank out. The cough gets worse when he is outdoors and so he cannot go outside the house. So there are two aspects to the cough:

- Blank out (sensation)
- It comes from time to time, and he can't go out of the house anymore (pace/coping mechanism))

R : Tell me about 'blank out,' describe it.

P : It becomes black before my eyes, as if I am stuck to one point.

R : Stuck to one point meaning . . . ? What is the feeling when stuck to one point?

(Author: I have used only the words of the individual, and keep up this questioning until he leads me to the next question. This could be a more precise feeling, or a visual picture, or something that comes up by association.)

P : It is as if I cannot move.

R : What is the feeling when stuck to one point?

(Author: He reverts to the physical complaint. Now it is our job to keep him on track, so repeat the same question till he goes one step deeper.)

P : It is like you are in the middle of the street and a car is coming at full speed. That is how I feel.

(Author: Now this is a visual picture. It could have been an actual experience from his life. It is a window into the Mental State, one level deeper than the Physical. Question him further and ask about his experience in this situation and one may be able to see a connection with the cough.)

R : How does one feel when one is in the middle of the street and a car comes at you at full speed?

P: It happened to me as a child. I felt the same way.

(Author: We have to get to the sensation in that situation. Ask him now to describe the experience in emotional and physical terms.
We started with the cough and then came to "blank out," then to "black before the eyes," then to "stuck to one point," then to the childhood situation. All this, simply by staying with the chief complaint (cough), and faithfully following the key sensations and images that the person associated with this cough.)

R: What did you feel?
P: The fear is I will be suddenly killed and so I cannot move.

So by simply chasing the chief complaint, one can come to the main feeling or fear, which is that suddenly he is going to be killed, and he is stupefied and unable to move because of this fright.

Now you can see the connection with the cough. The cough comes suddenly from time to time and he cannot go out of the house. It gets black before the eyes and he is stuck to one point as if he is going to be killed. He is frightened and stuck to one point. Fright stupefies him. The cough stupefies. He avoids going out of the house because he will get a cough. He avoids the situation that stupefies him, but he still gets the cough from time to time.

I am reminded of what Sheng-yen said about spiritual practice, which could well apply to this path of inquiry.

"Be soft in your practice. Think of the method as a fine silvery stream, not a raging waterfall. Follow the stream, have faith in its course. It will go its own way, meandering here, trickling there. It will find the grooves, the cracks, the crevices. Just follow it. Never let it out of your sight. It will take you."

This process of inquiry happens at the seventh level of experience. This is the level where one can step back from the other song and watch it from a distance as a witness. This witness level is unchanging and constant and has existed from birth to the present moment. From this level one can describe the experience. Therefore, the seventh level is the most important level for healing. If this level did not exist there would be no way a person would describe his turmoil and become aware or find the healing agent. Incidentally the guide also has to go into his own 7th level to be in the process of inquiry. Only then can he be an unprejudiced observer.

Throughout this whole process, whatever "maps" we as guides carry in our minds, it is important always to remember that the person before us is far greater than any overarching map or theory we may personally hold about them or the world. The individual before us is unique. We will not experience his or her uniqueness fully if our sole underlying intent is to categorize him or her, to put him into a box, however subtle that box may be.

If we seek to do only that, then in effect, we diminish not only his uniqueness but also our own learning. We fit him into our existing understanding, which of necessity is limited. This results in two serious failures: simultaneously we miss the truth before us and also the heaven-sent opportunity to broaden our own understanding, to let in the new and to learn more.

We all need maps in order to somehow "sort" out and order our existing understanding. We are better able to journey through life if we have some sort of agreed framework or map to journey by. As healers, we often utilize our maps in the service of others. But our maps can become more of a hindrance than a help if we treat them as anything other than provisional sketches, schemas, which are constantly evolving as they grow to include all that we meet in the world. Maps represent images of the world but are not the world itself. The person before us, the world around us, is the full reality, of which the map in our head is but a dim, possibly distorting reflection.

It is therefore vital as healers that we use our maps lightly, in order to travel almost empty-handed to the places the seeker can take us, to the landmarks of his own unique reality. This is his own inner land that only he knows, only he experiences, only he can show us. The process of enquiry that I have outlined above is a way of journeying with another person deep into this unique land. As complete strangers to an unknown country, we ask the seeker to take us, in effect, to the highest point of his personal landscape so that we, too, can see and come to understand it.

The highest point of his landscape is his main complaint or symptom, since it is here that his inner energy is most forcefully expressing itself. From this clear vantage point, together we are able to gradually see how all else in his inner land falls into place. When we see some hazy (to us) part that we do not understand, we simply ask the seeker. He knows and lives this land – he is the only one who can—and does—explain and make all clear to us.

This process is not mathematical. No amount of logic will work. The mind is our greatest obstacle to real knowing. The mind may want to analyse- this may be the greatest hindrance in the process. Knowledge is the experience of truth, it is not the result of mathematics or analysis. You can't quite blame the mind, because its function is to classify what you see according to what has been seen. One needs to sidestep the mind to be able to have a glimpse of one's experience – if you want to perceive it clearly.

The guide is like an archaeologist who unravels the entire object buried deep beneath and then marvels at its beauty once it is out! Until then, it is only guesswork until the seeker and the guide reach that point where the seeker's other song is revealed.

Once the seeker has truly shown us the coherence, specific detail, and beauty of his inner land, then our maps are of great aid to help us get our bearings. No man exists in a separate unrelated bubble; we all exist in the context of the natural world. It is important that we recognize where in that natural world we are. Only when we have clearly heard the true melody of the other song singing in the seeker do our maps come in to play. Since we know the place well having been shown it so clearly, we are immediately able to tell whether it fits with ease and exactness into one of our existing maps, or whether we are in uncharted territory and therefore need to extend our maps. It is the same process of human exploration and discovery that has gone on through all time.

Once we discover where we have journeyed, we are able to relate the unique and particular inner song of the individual person to the all-embracing context and truth of the universal. We are able to hear and place the person's other song in the context of the natural world – the mineral, plant, and animal kingdoms–in which we all live.

The process is both exciting and affirming as our understanding grows, not just of the other person and ourselves but also of the whole universe. We come to see the wonder, beauty, and interrelatedness of all that is. We come to see both the self and the other in a true, all-embracing context.

Nonsense Phenomena

In the process of guiding the seeker to deeper levels, upto a point the seeker's story makes sense. Then , as one comes to the delusion level, there could be vivid picturization. For example, he could say "I feel like a slave" or "I feel like I am alone in the wilderness." While it is not likely that the seeker is facing or has ever faced the actual situation that he is on the delusional level describing, these are still human examples and experiences. Tracing this even more deeply by asking, "What is the experience of this?", we get deeper and more individualized. Sense fades and a unique pattern is seen, while strange sensations emerge.

The above question may raise a small barrier or invite resistance on the part of the seeker in our process of enquiry. It is uncomfortable for the seeker to describe this, for it is not a familiar zone. This process is almost like shepherding the seeker into a hypnotic-like state where he is able to verbalize details of his inner turmoil. This area that he now discovers is new to his current awareness and his understanding, but he recognizes it as his own. Words being inadequate to demonstrate this deeper experience, he starts using his hands.

And so in response to being asked "What is the experience of this?" the seeker describes this alone-in-the-wilderness experience as emptiness, solitude, a huge vacuum that sucks downwards. This has nothing to do with the situation. It is irrational, illogical and so complete nonsense. This is a magical moment in the process of enquiry, and it is very important to continue to inquire as if nothing had changed. At this point, the seeker may remark on how crazy it all seems. Or may burst into laughter at the absurdity of what he is saying. This is the point at which we know we are on the right track. The seeker is speaking from source.

At this level of complete nonsense we know we have arrived at the essence of the disturbance of the seeker. Imagine somebody saying (with hand gestures of palms facing each other moving together and moving apart) he feels like his whole being is expanding up to infinity, and then it suddenly contracts into a small ball. This has nothing to do with his being, his body or mind, or him as a person. Yet it is his truth.

Truth is what is, not what is supposed to be, not what makes sense, not what is logical, not what is comprehensible. Truth at its very core does not make any sense. It simply is. Logically, nations should coexist peacefully. It makes sense that we should eat healthy food. Birth, death, illnesses, behaviour, etc., follow no logic, make no sense. So also nature, the weather, the plants, the animals, the minerals. They simply are what they are; we categorize them, we try to find reasons, and they simply do not fit.

It is not logic that should work, but pure observation, deep and complete. The mind is our greatest obstacle to real knowing. Its function is to classify what we see, according to what has been seen. So we have to step beyond the mind to have a direct experience that which we don't already know. Knowledge is the experience of the truth **for that individual**.

Truth is not who you are, what you know, what you think, or what you feel. It is not your story or your situation. Nor is it your dream or your nightmare or what you imagine. It is your experience behind all of this. It is what makes you who you are, influences what you know, leads to the way you think and feel. It is the paper on which your story is written: what made your past and what will make your future.

It has no logical sequence, it just is. This phenomenon cannot even be explained by the mind. Since it eludes sense it is nonsense. Nonsense lies at the core of the ultimate truth. It is the purest language of the turmoil within, although the seeker hesitates to speak about it, or even feel it.

That is why during this process the mind needs to be bypassed (categorizing and analyzing are both tasks of the mind). Then one reaches what is almost a 'no-mind' state. Crossing this barrier one is able to describe further, employing gestures and non-human-specific words as tools. Only after crossing the barrier that lies beyond the mind is the real internal self able to be fully described.

The guide focuses on the primitive thread that identifies the other song of this seeker, keeping the seeker in the present moment, discounting logic and reasoning. Thus we zoom in on the pure experience of it. At this point, the nonsense pours out. The seeker may himself casually comment, "What nonsense am I talking!" At this point, a little encouragement from the guide is always helpful to dissolve any hesitation. It is like being on an aircraft, hesitant to jump off with the parachute: a gentle push is needed.

Sometimes even the guide is confused. For example, when the seeker says that his experience is black, dark, and sticky, this does not make logical sense, yet it describes the seeker's experience at the very source level. The guide, at this point, does not know what the seeker could be talking about. We do not even know to what kingdom this belongs. The black and sticky could be from the mineral, plant or animal kingdom.

The seeker is speaking pure words of the source of his other song. We need to have patience, to inquire further, to see to which kingdom and subkingdom the seeker belongs. Then these strange data can be seen in context; the totality makes perfect sense, since it mirrors one substance from nature.

When we examine further we note which specific thing in nature has the same phenomenon. And slowly towards the end of the process of enquiry the whole nonsense makes complete sense. The whole pattern is so beautifully revealed and it fits so completely and exactly.

To follow the seeker into his nonsense words (since they appear so unrelated to where he started from) is one of the most challenging and rewarding of experiences, both for the guide and the seeker. As my valued colleague and friend Roger Morrison (M.D.), after observing this technique, put it: "In case after case, you followed the thread of the seeker's expression to this nonhuman level. In each case I began by feeling 'What nonsense is this?' and ended by feeling 'What sublime nonsense that was!' He then added, "I had already accepted the concept of non-human and made efforts to pursue it in practice but finally I came to understand that no other information was so specific."

Going into the Experience

We have seen that when the person is in the energy, through the gesture or the NHS[1] word, sometimes he can spontaneously enter into a kind of trance or hypnotic state and speaks from a place beyond himself. He gives various words and images, unconnected to himself. It is as if he has crossed the barrier of his individual self and made a bridge to the source in nature which is singing in him. These experiences, images, words, etc. at this level are often the exact language, qualities and images of the source. In this state one feels as if the person is channelling the source, so exactly does he describe things.

Sometimes, when he does not spontaneously go there, we can attempt a process by which we can encourage this passage. **The most important requirement of this process is creating the space. The space is silence, stillness. The space is time, enough time, patience, no hurry. The space is openness.**

It helps to make the person close the eyes. From a non-human-specific word, gesture or energy we ask that he go into the experience right in that moment. We give a long pause, allowing him to go into the experience. When he tells us emotions and thoughts, we point out that this is from the mind, and ask that he stays with the experience. When he gives images, we encourage him to go into the experience and not stop at the images but go deeper into the experience.

[1] Non-human-specific

And to tell us whatever spontaneously comes up when he is in that experience, whether it is related or unrelated to him or to anything he has said so far.

Our attempt in the questioning is to take the person beyond his own experience, i.e., beyond sensation felt within himself (physically or mentally) into something beyond him, whether it be in the form of human situations or preferably in the form of completely non-human situations, images, colors, movements and qualities. In these expressions we shall hear the pure language of the source. Therefore while paying close attention to the person's sensations, one needs to encourage the patient to take that crucial step from himself to the universe. That is the reason that we often ask the person "go into your experience and in the moment when you are at your deepest level of experience please tell us what comes to you spontaneously". This question invites the person to take the leap into the source or one can say it is the question that invites the source to take a leap in his awareness.

In Other(s') Words

The following excerpt from an article by my colleagues Judyth Reichenberg-Ullman, ND, DHANP, LCSW; and Robert Ullman, ND, DHANP eloquently summarizes the whole process:

"The method is, as with any doctor, to ask what brings the patient to treatment. Once the patient has named the condition or problem and given some initial information about it, the homoeopath begins to focus clearly on the precise words of the patient. Except in cases of relatively uncommunicative patients, the person will begin to use certain words and phrases to describe the chief complaint. Or, more accurately, his or her experience of the chief complaint. There is an expression, "If you give him a rope long enough, he will hang himself." It is much the same here, but let's say, "cure himself". In other words, the more you let a patient talk, in her own words, about what is most compelling, in this case the chief complaint, the more you will zero in on the nature of that patient.

As soon as expressions or phrases begin to emerge, which they generally do, then it is the job of the homoeopath to simply repeat back to the patient, with a querying intonation, those phrases that seem to hold the most energy. More words, phrases, and expressions will follow, eliciting even more clearly the experience of the patient relative to the chief complaint. There is no question of leading the patient. It is a process of listening and inquiring, then listening and inquiring more.

The Case Unfolds

The job of the homoeopath is simply to listen and to follow the energetic lead of the patient. If a word or phrase has definite energy, the patient will use it over and over. Or that particular phrase will evolve into another that better describes the experience. It is a process of closing in more and more, always using only the words of the patient herself.

Now, a few things happen during this process. One is that, as the patient speaks, there are indicators of the kingdom and miasm[2]. Themes arise. If someone needs

[2] Miasm here refers to the type of coping mechanism

an animal medicine, victim-aggressor issues will arise, whether the complaint is a head injury or bipolar disorder. If the patient falls into the category of a plant medicine, the patient's words will reflect a particular area of sensitivity again and again. In the case of a mineral, the words and phrases that predominate will ring of loss or gain of structure and function. This process can take moments, in the case of an acute illness, or hours in some first-office calls.

The trick is to listen, follow the energy, inquire, and listen again. Not to make assumptions about anything. It is one of most attentive listening processes we have ever engaged, yet it can be quite frustrating for some patients. Explaining early on that we will be asking the patient to repeat certain words almost endlessly in an effort to get to know him more deeply helps. We assure them, from Rajan's cue, that it does not mean they are not expressing themselves clearly or that we are not able to understand them. Only that it is a process of going deeper and deeper until we find the best possible medicine to help them. If a patient seems intent on "doing it right", we reassure her that there are no right or wrong answers, that whatever they say is what is right.

Nonsense Leads to Speaking from Source

What happens next, assuming the case is moving along without significant resistance from the patient, is a curious phenomenon. As we continue to simply repeat back the energy-holding words and phrases in an inquiring tone, the patient begins to say things that just don't make any sense. Words come out that seem to have little rational meaning. The descriptions appear to have less and less to do with the chief complaint.

This is a magical moment in the case taking process and it is very important to continue to inquire, as if nothing had changed. The patient, at this point, may remark at how crazy it all seems. Or may burst into laughter at the absurdity of what she is saying. This is the point at which we know we are on the right track. The patient is speaking from source.

What is speaking from source?

It is when the patient, having disconnected from the rational, limited mind, begins to describe the substance from nature, or homoeopathic medicine, that she needs. Rajan says the most angst-producing moment is sitting down with a patient wondering if the magic will occur again. Then, through patience, listening, and inquiring, again it does and once more the patient reveals the medicine that he needs, often even naming it without realizing that is what is happening. The wonder of it all for the homoeopath is not having a clue about what the patient will say next. Just waiting, engaging the process, and trusting that it will unfold.

Since we returned from Bombay in early December and have put this method into practice, we can honestly say it is the most exciting time ever in our practice. It makes so much sense that there is some way that our patients can tell us what they need if we allow them to guide us in the right direction."

The Levels of Experience

The Levels	Question
Name: Diagnosis, nomenclature	So what exactly is happening?
Fact: "What?" a) Fact unqualified b) Fact qualified c) Peculiar signs and symptoms	How do you feel? How does this affect you?
Feeling: a) Feeling unqualified b) Feeling qualified c) Feeling Peculiar	How does if feel like? What comes to your mind? One situation that had a big effect on you? How did that feel like?
Delusion: a) Situation, exciting facts b) How it is experienced/feel c) Dream	What sensation do you experience in that situation? What are you showing by that gesture of your hand?
Sensation: a) Kingdom-plant, animal, mineral b) Subkingdom/family c) Source	Go into the experience and see what comes up spontaneously.
Energy: a) Movement b) Shape c) Colour d) Sound	
The Seventh Blank, consciousness	

Doorway Through Doodles

Doodle: *"A drawing or abstract, irrational, illogical and unconnected to the external reality, produced aimlessly or absentmindedly while doing something."*

Being spontaneous, without a plan, without the mind or intention, it must come from a very deep level–namely, the sensation.

Many of us at some point in our life have got bored during a lecture and found ourselves scribbling in the corner of the page we were supposed to take running notes on or, during a telephone conversation, drawn some form or repetitive shapes on a sheet next to us.

I noticed that when I got tired or sleepy during a conversation I too would automatically (i.e. involuntarily) start drawing repetitive shapes and patterns. After years of doing this one realizes that inevitably there are these 2-3 patterns that keep repeating themselves spontaneously. Very naturally one tends to wonder where these come from and what they mean. I was certain that these were "individual", varying from person to person, and not logical since they were obviously unconnected with external reality. Yet if "I" did them repeatedly they came from "me," from deep within my own self.

This thought led me to my research on this form of expression of our inner reality. I began my quest by reading already existent research on it.

A doodle, as described by the charity National Doodle Day, is "a graphical expression of an unconscious association."[1]

Psychologists across the globe have conducted a lot of research into the interpretation of doodles that is comparable to the interpretation of dreams during the course of treatment. Interpreters of doodles not only look at the

---

1. What Are Doodles? ed. The Neurofibromatosis Association, 2 September 2007 http://www.episepsy.org.uk.

drawing itself but also consider the line pressure with which they are drawn. For example, light lines indicate sensitivity, or a tentative nature–the artist worries about making errors. Medium-weight lines suggest a balanced, confident personality. Heavy marks can indicate resolve, strength, and energy. Aggression produces overly heavy lines, and the paper may be impressed or torn within them.

Interpretation of Doodles

Just as specific dreams are interpreted in specific ways, doodles too have been the subject of interpretation. For example:

1. Circles indicate a self-protectiveness, as well as a pliant nature.
2. Ovals show the exacting nature of a person who demands high performance from himself and others.
3. Irregular, shaded dots indicate that the person is a deep-thinking type who can become restless easily.
4. A separate square or a series of squares represent a concrete, hard working, and practical person.
5. Squares with crisscrossing lines inside signify an ability to cope with the complexities of life and handle them effectively.
6. Three-dimensional forms are symbolic of a probing, intellectual, logical mind.

7. Ladders and steps display a desire to move up in the world. The ladder, especially, shows tremendous ambition.

8. Check marks indicate that the person concentrates on the business at hand and may distrust others. May also correct others and/or self.

9. Triangles signal a strong and well-developed mind. An inverted triangle represents introversion and a need to probe for information.

10. Jagged lines often spell out a mood of resentment or hostility and a critical nature.

11. Curlicues with loops at the top indicate an imaginative, good-natured disposition. Curlicues with loops at the bottom indicate a protective, worrying disposition.

12. Spider webs indicate that the person is constantly seeking to widen his horizons and improve himself—usually with much more complication than is necessary.

A New Look at Doodles

After having read the available information, many questions persisted in my mind as to how a speculation or interpretation could be made about an individual's subconscious mind! Because of the paucity of answers, I decided to explore for myself—experience and experiment with *shapes*.

As I understood it, a doodle is spontaneous, unconscious, unplanned, without mind or method. It is also without an intention, a theme or a message. Since it is irrational and unconnected with external reality, it is non-human in its expression. Moreover doodles, individualized as they are, stemmed from a deeper reality. And yet here I had read so many interpretations of something that only an individual who drew it could himself describe.

For me there are two approaches possible –one is the understanding of someone through the "mind", where we are looking at someone else's subjective pattern through the prism of our intellectual belief system i.e. our own subjective pattern. This makes our interpretations nothing but guess-work, which would mean that my interpretations and analysis of another's reality could be completely different from somebody else's analysis of that same reality.

The other approach is to know directly through experience, by-passing the minds of both seeker and guide. If a "seeker" is keen enough to know "his reality", he is the only one who can help himself with the assistance of a "guide". Such an attempt would eliminate the scope for interpretations and brilliant speculations. He would be in the freedom of the moment to express "the experience of his reality" which is the only truth for him. Knowing through the mind is vastly different than knowing through experience. The experience is the truth; the mental knowing is at best a clever guess work or a projection on the current situation of what was seen elsewhere.

It is therefore for the maker of the pattern to experience it and express this experience in words, gestures, images, sensations etc. This is the truth for him and this is what we need to discover by going with the seeker into the experience.

With this observation providing a foundation for further analysis, I was keen to experiment with these shapes.

I began this process with a group of volunteers where each was asked to make a shape, what ever resonated within. I asked the volunteers to each draw a shape—preferably what they scribbled when they were idle—that was not a drawing that they had learnt or were taught (like a flower, scenery, or a portrait), i.e., nothing with a universal, unambiguous meaning. It was important that they draw it without a thought or a plan. It needed to be abstract. If he/she is used to doodling something repeatedly in his everyday life, he should make that shape. If he/she is not used to doodling then he should just draw any shape that comes spontaneously without using his conscious mind. He/she can draw more than one shape if the desire to draw them comes naturally. If he has drawn more than one shape then he has to choose that shape which has the maximum impact on him, which draws his attention the most.

Then one needed to focus on the doodle, just look at it and experience the effect it produced, and describe it. It was important to explain to them that they needed to describe their experience of drawing and focusing on their doodle. They did not have to describe the doodle or talk about it, interpret it or explain its meaning.

They had to observe and narrate the experience while focusing on the doodle. This experience could be both a physical sensation and a mind experience. They had to talk about what was happening within them and not about the doodle. They needed to let the flow come from within spontaneously and describe the whole phenomenon of this experience, of looking at their "inner art".

The 1st doodle

The first volunteer described his experience as a feeling of uncertainty and confusion felt in the region of the heart; especially a spot in the 4th or 5th rib space close to the sternum. Simultaneously there is a loose and lame feeling in both the upper limbs extending all the way to the hands. Inner trembling felt in the forearms. Heaviness on the right side of the abdomen. Rest of the body seems relaxed. The central wavy line in the pattern seems to connect all the chaos and take it back to its source.

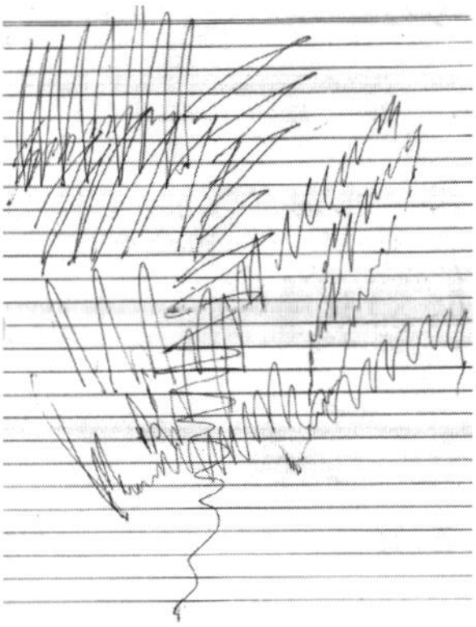

The 2nd doodle

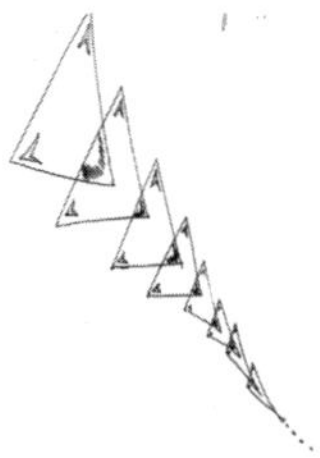

1

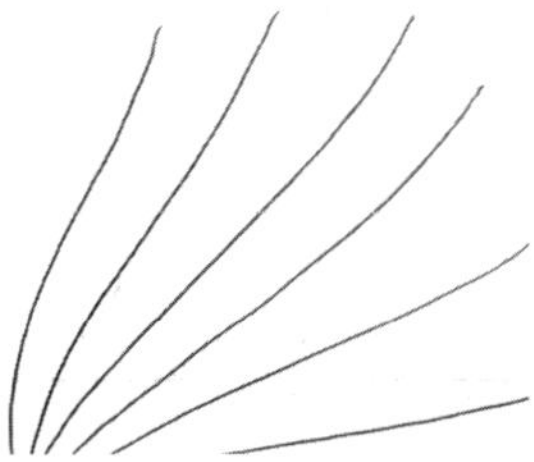

2

3

The second volunteer described her experience:

1st image: "While drawing I drew from the biggest triangle downwards, but on looking I experience it from the dots upwards. It is like a beginning and you go higher and higher each time, with a feeling of expansion, which is a good feeling. It's like a kite flying, as it goes higher and higher up in the sky. With a sensation of 'lightness' and 'freedom.' Though this is the first time I drew such a picture, yet it had the strongest impact on me."

2nd image: "There is a beginning which starts at one point and then spreads/ travels in different directions, still staying connected to its beginning."

3rd image: "This picture I draw often which means a group of birds flying together. Many times it is also a part of a larger picture with a sea, mountains, shore, small hut on the shore, and some palm trees.
The leaves are usually 3-4 together which means growing from a common point and each one still remaining connected to the origin."

The 3rd doodle

The third volunteer described her experience:
"First thing I experienced was I started breathing heavily. The form was giving me some kind of discomfort. Each line moving on and trying to find its way out. From all the points it tries to come out. Something is churning inside

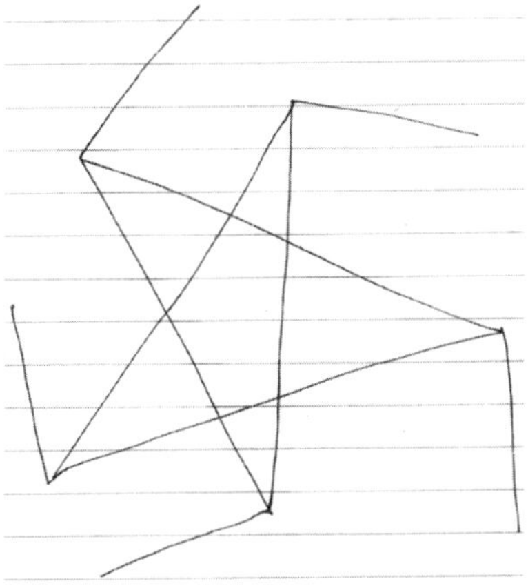

which is very very deep and giving me too much pain. I am trying every means to come out of it but none of the outlets is enough to get me out of that pain completely. The space within is not enough to get me out of the pain which I am experiencing inside and I keep moving in this zigzag pattern. A life unable to free myself from this pain."

Each individual made his own peculiar shape and on looking at it experienced sensations, emotions, and imaginations that were intense, deep, and very familiar to the realm of that person. Interestingly, this experience may be totally unconnected with the drawing.

What we also tried as a variant was to ask the rest of the volunteers to view somebody else's doodles and see what experience emerged. In this case, it sometimes had no effect and sometimes excited the sensation of the observer i.e. it triggered the innate sensitivity. Nevertheless, it was found conclusively that the individual's own doodle produced in him the maximum effect.

There was another interesting observation that I made – those volunteers unused to doodling in their everyday lives experienced even more intensely the effects of focusing on their doodles than did those accustomed to it.

The 4th doodle

The fourth volunteer described her experience:

"When I drew the 1st picture I was blank but not satisfied with it. I wanted to draw something else—this not proper; then I drew the second, but was not fully satisfied; the third, fourth, and finally I drew the last picture, and I felt "Yes, I wanted to draw it like this."

"When I looked at the last picture I felt some pain in my chest on both sides of the upper lobe. I diverted my mind to confirm this. But then I saw the picture,

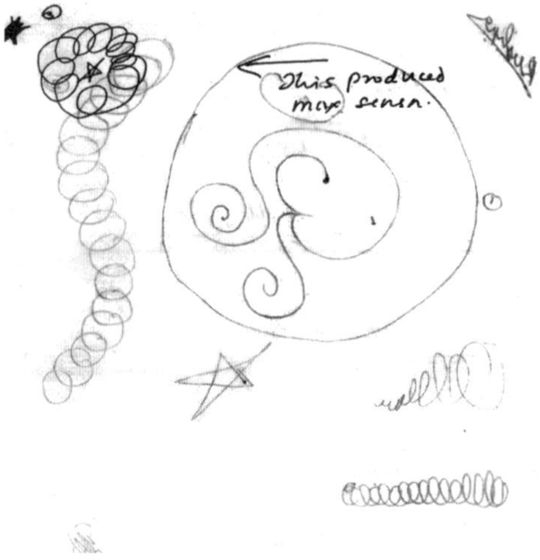

and the same thing came up. I tried this two or three times to confirm what was going on within. I feel myself in the centre of this circle of circles, with lots of circles and curves around me which are continuous. It's not breaking at any point. I am enclosed in these circles and they are holding me."

The 5th doodle

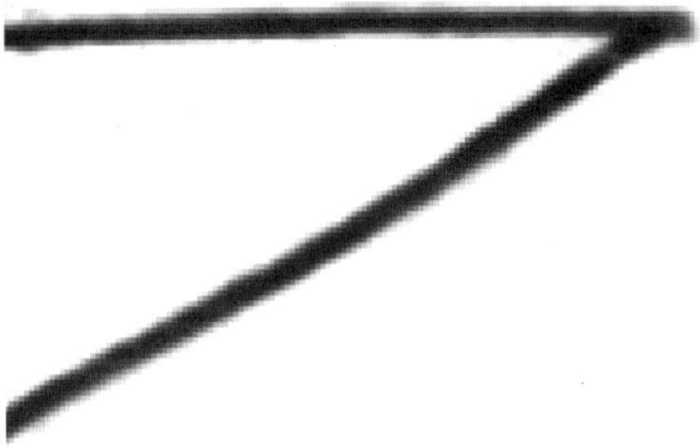

This doodle is an example from a patient whose other song required giving him the remedy made from the lava of a volcano.

"It gives the impression of motion, and 'moving ahead.' Reminds me of a 'sharp,' 'sleek' shape.
The body actually feels 'light' while seeing the image. A sort of 'in-the-clouds' feeling.

I am reminded of the 'free-fall' dreams that I used to have. Also I feel that I am riding in some open vehicle at a good speed. The fresh air is stinging my face and eyes, but it is a very nice feeling.

The image also reminds me of a very familiar feeling 'I could have done better', and in that sense feels incomplete. I am reminded of the Concorde and a very funny feeling of being in the clouds/seeing this image on a background of clouds. The overall feeling is quite 'nice', 'light' and just as if I am putting down the burden."

Just as we confirmed in his case the voice of the other song that very clearly emerged through the doodling process, we repeated it with other patients.

The results were amazingly accurate as to how quickly and yet directly each of them went to their inner turmoil. Irrespective of the situations in life that would affect each of us, this process of doodling highlights that one experience encompassing our sensations, imaginations, and emotions and that pervades our ever changing life and its circumstances.

We clearly saw how the doodle differed in each person and how this piece of individual artwork so beautifully and spontaneously reflected the deep turmoil within the human consciousness. This turmoil was clearly the replica of the notes of the other song. In order to verify our observations and conclusions, we took our experiment to the next level where we asked patients who had improved both physically and emotionally with homoeopathic medication to doodle for us.

A doodle happens best when the mind shuts off, and it is precisely at this point that "sensations" come to the surface (just like what happens in our case taking at deeper levels). I did not attempt to understand, interpret, or analyze the doodle.

In fact, I did not even need to look at the doodle. All I did was to listen to and observe the patient's experience. When I hear sensation words or see hand gestures I pick that up and then take it further. Very often this confirms the findings of the case-taking process.

The next inevitable question was "What happens when two people draw the same doodle?" As we kept verifying our experiment with newer volunteers and more patients who had shown considerable improvement, we came across two patients who drew a three dimensional cuboid:

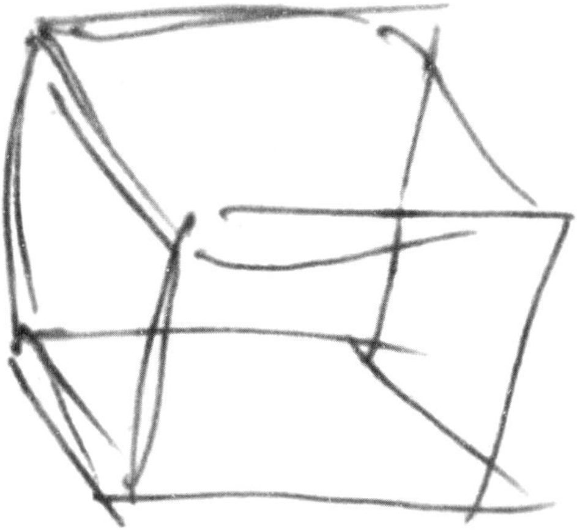

Experience of the first patient who drew a three-dimensional cuboid:	Experience of the second patient who drew a similar three-dimensional cuboid:
"It's like I am challenging myself to go along with this concreteness, and definite structure, this set pattern and systematic method. On the opposite side of the spectrum it feels like a loose path, one that is not definite."	"I feel boxed in, closed in, stuck and trapped. It's almost as if I have been shut in this dark place with the lids shut on all four sides. This experience makes me feel completely crushed as if something is pressing on you."
The first patient's other song belonged to the mineral kingdom, because she speaks of concreteness and lacking a definitive structure.	The second patient's other song belongs to the animal kingdom, because she feels victimized by being trapped in and completely crushed.

Thus we concluded that just by looking at the doodle, it is very difficult to guess the sensation and experience or state of progress of the one who made it. What is reliable is the experience of the doodler as reflected in his description of it—his truth.

Our experiments with these pieces of "true artwork of inner reality" are still on. They help us invariably to get to the core sensation straight away as well as being a confirmation of the experience that we have gathered during the case taking.

Thus a doodle is one of the most spontaneous, natural and everyday expressions of the "Sensation". It can be a very powerful tool in our process of discovery of the Sensation, making it yet another way of helping people towards awareness.

You can use the following exercise to get in touch with your sensation.

Please draw something on a paper:

1. It should not be an object, person, scenery, etc.

2. It should be abstract.

3. It should be a shape.

4. If you are used to doodling something repeatedly in your everyday life, make that shape.

5. If you are not used to doodling then just draw any shape that comes spontaneously.

6. You can also draw more than one shape if it comes naturally.

Now go on... Do it...

If you have drawn more than one shape, please choose one that has the maximum impact on you.

1. Focus on the shape, just look at it.

2. Do not interpret it, or think about it or try to understand it or try to explain it.

3. On simply looking at it you are likely to experience something within you.

4. Observe the experience while focusing on the doodle.

5. This experience can be either a physical sensation or a mind experience.

6. Write about what's happening within you and not about the doodle.

7. Is ths something familiar to you.

Metaphors

When the cat pops its head out of the basket.

The human being is constantly revealing his other song in very many ways in his daily life and conversations. Some of the more common ways include metaphors, idioms, similes, gestures, verbalized images, and described sensations. The words and expressions from the other song keep popping up from time to time. They seem so casual, so natural, as to be imperceptible. But if one were to take

them out of their context, a unique pattern would be revealed that would show the energy and the sensation of the song within.

It is interesting, for example, how different people express a similar incident. When disappointed by another, one person may say he feels stabbed in the back, another feels a rug was pulled from beneath his feet, a third feels let down, a fourth feels betrayed, a fifth feels shattered, a sixth feels heartbroken, a seventh is shocked - and yet others are variously forsaken, neglected, shunned, isolated, attacked, hurt, and so forth.

"A man's character may be learned from the adjectives which he habitually uses in conversation."

Mark Twain

If we note how each one expresses his experience – the words and the metaphors used – we see that these utterances are not coincidental or casually chosen but come from his deep and constant experience.

Just observing others or ourselves with respect to the words we use to express, communicate or describe things or situations is a worthy exercise. It gives many clues to the deepest experience, the sensation. It may seem casual, or insignificant. But as you observe more, a repetitive pattern will be discerned. And much later we will begin to see how each of the expressions fit into place in the overall context of the source.

For example if we just ask three people to describe something as innocuous as the way to a particular place, it is quite amazing how there will be words and gestures unique to each one. When we pull out these unique words out of the context, they will reveal an inner pattern consistent to the individual's entire life.

This is also true for all those words and things which are unique and strange in a person, including so many things which are inexplicable like aversion or fascination for certain objects, colors, patterns, music, people, activities, etc, etc.

Have you wondered why someone likes a particular number, or a particular shape, or why someone is fascinated by ants or another cannot stand the fluttering of bird's wings. Why does someone like to wear black and another is attracted to high risk sport.

In a way, these forms of expression are involuntary and unconscious, and this makes them even more significant. The vehicle of expression rather than the ideas expressed is a very good starting point for further inquiry, because concentrating there leads directly into the experience and bypasses the context and the situation in which it happened. Then it will be seen to be an integral part of the person's core experience and one is amazed at the unfailing way in which these seemingly casual utterances are so rich with meaning. It is almost as if it were a coded language where the real message is hidden in words interspersed among "normal" sentences, which when strung together give a totally different message.

I recall a case of a woman who was brought to me unscheduled in an acute situation with severe weakness and vertigo. The first thing she said unscheduled to me was, "I hope I am not invading your space." Narrating her last dream she said she saw people "invading" her house, vandalizing and destroying it, and how she tried her best to ward them off.

One thing in nature that invades and destroys other things is the fungus. I selected a remedy (Agaricus) from the group of fungi – and this dramatically helped. The next day she came excitedly to me and said, "It came back to me suddenly that I spent many hours of my childhood drawing mushrooms (also a fungus) and said that it was my house."

Her unique use of the word "invade" gave the clue to her innermost experience. This was also the underlying experience in her dream. And then the obsession with mushrooms – that strange, inexplicable feature of herself as a child – now can be seen in context, and it makes total sense. This is true for all the inexplicable, unique phenomena and words of an individual – they all come from the sensation, they are the keynotes of the other song.

I am tempted here to use as an example some utterances of a man for whose courage and humanitarianism I have the highest respect: Nelson Mandela.

Here are some passages from his moving autobiography, "Long Walk to Freedom: The Autobiography of Nelson Mandela" (Boston: Little, Brown and Company, 1994):

"AT MIDNIGHT, I was awake and staring at the ceiling--images from the trial were still rattling around in my head--when I heard steps coming down the hallway. I was locked in my own cell, away from the others. There was a knock at my door and I could see Colonel Aucamp's face at the bars. "Mandela," he said in a husky whisper, "are you awake?"

I told him I was. "You are a lucky man," he said. "We are taking you to a place where you will have your freedom. You will be able to move around; you'll see the ocean and the sky, not just gray walls."

Here are some other passages:

"We were departing quietly, secretly, under a heavy police escort, in the middle of the night, and in less than half an hour we found ourselves at a small military airport outside the city. We were hustled onto a Dakota, a large military transport

plane that had seen better days. There was no heat, and we shivered in the belly of the plane. Some of the others had never flown before and they seemed more anxious about our voyage than our destination; bumping up and down in a plane at fifteen thousand feet seemed far more perilous than being locked in a cell behind high walls.

Warders walked among us to enforce the silence. During those first few weeks, warders from other sections and even other prisons came to stare at us as if we were a collection of rare caged animals. The work was tedious and difficult; it was not strenuous enough to keep us warm but it was demanding enough to make all our muscles ache."

If you read this with an eye to the words of the other song, if you ignore the actual context and see the metaphor, a pattern emerges.
Let us look at it again, with the non-human-specific words highlighted.

"AT MIDNIGHT, I was awake and staring at the ceiling--images from the trial were still ***rattling*** *around in my head--when I heard steps coming down the hallway. I was* ***locked*** *in my own* ***cell****, away from the others. There was a knock at my door and I could see Colonel Aucamp's face at the bars. "Mandela," he said in a husky whisper, "are you awake?"*

I told him I was. "You are a lucky man," he said. "We are taking you to a place where you will have your ***freedom****. You will be able* ***to move around****; you'll see* ***the ocean and the sky****, not just* ***gray walls****."*

Here are the other passages:

"We were departing quietly, secretly, under a heavy police escort, in the middle of the night, and in less than half an hour we found ourselves at a small military airport outside the city. We were hustled onto a Dakota, a large military transport plane that had seen better days. There was no heat, and we shivered in the belly of the plane. Some of the others had never flown before and they seemed more anxious about our voyage than our destination; bumping up and down in a plane at fifteen thousand feet seemed far more perilous than ***being locked in a cell behind high walls****.*

Warders walked among us to ***enforce*** *the silence. During those first few weeks, warders from other sections and even other prisons came to stare at us as if we were a collection of rare* ***caged animals****. The work was tedious and difficult; it was not strenuous enough to keep us warm but it was demanding enough to make all our muscles ache."*

When we read the highlighted words separately, we get an insight into the other song of Mandela. It is a song where freedom is very important (as the very title of his book suggests). It is a song of the oppressor versus the oppressed, where the freedom of the oppressed has been taken away by force and he feels locked like an animal in a cell. Ocean and sky too seem part of this song.

When we observe this pattern and ask ourselves where we can see this in nature, we come first to the animal kingdom: issues of one versus the other; and then we come to the class of birds, where the issues of freedom, being caged, ocean, sky, etc., are most significant.

(Please refer to the chapter 'A Map To The Inner World' and see the words of the 'bird song' on page 115.)

As an experiment, I randomly selected some prominent quotes of Mandela from the internet.

It is remarkable to see the consistency of the metaphorical images used in various speeches spread over time. **It is revealing to observe the energy of the animal and bird (particularly a soaring one like the eagle) in nearly all of these quotes.**

- *After **climbing** a great hill, one only finds that there are many more hills to climb*[1].

- *As we are **liberated** from our own fear, our presence automatically liberates others*[2].

1 Long Walk to Freedom: The Autobiography of Nelson Mandela. (544)

2 This quotation is often attributed to Mandela, though he never said this; the story that he did is an urban legend. The quotation is actually from A Return to Love: Reflections on the Principles of "A Course in Miracles" by Marianne Williamson. But so like Mandela's language is the Williamson quotation that it has been persistently attributed to Mandela despite the fact that it is someone else's work.

- *Communists have always played an active role in **the fight** by colonial countries for their **freedom**, because the short-term objects of Communism would always correspond with the long-term objects of **freedom** movements*[3].

- *Education is the most **powerful weapon** which you can use to change the world*[4].

- *For to be **free** is not **merely to cast off one's chains,** but to live in a way that respects and enhances the **freedom** of others*[5].

- *Never, never and never again shall it be that this beautiful land will again experience the **oppression of one by another***[6].

- *Only **free** men can negotiate; **prisoners** cannot enter into contracts. Your **freedom** and mine cannot be separated*[7].

- *The greatest glory of living lies not in never falling, but in **rising** every time we fall*[8].

---

3 Statement from the Dock at the Opening of the Defense Case. Rivonia Trial, Pretoria Supreme Court. 20 April 1964.

4 Speech. University of Witwatersrand. Johannesburg. 13 June 2004.

5 Mandela: An Illustrated Autobiography. (Boston: Little, Brown and Company, 1994). (202)

6 Statement at His Inauguration as President of the Democratic Republic of South Africa. Pretoria. 10 May 1994.

7 Response to 31 January 1985 Conditional Offer of Freedom by State President of South Africa, P.W. Botha. Soweto. 10 February 1985.

8 Remarks at a Whitehouse Reception in His Honor. Washington, D.C. 22 September 1998.

- *There is no easy walk to* ***freedom*** *anywhere, and many of us will have to pass through the valley of the shadow of death again and again before we reach the* ***mountaintop*** *of our desires*[9].

Some more, equally interesting, quotes:

- *'UNITE! MOBILISE!* ***FIGHT*** *ON! BETWEEN THE ANVIL OF UNITED MASS ACTION AND THE HAMMER OF THE ARMED STRUGGLE WE SHALL* ***CRUSH*** *APARTHEID*[10]*!'*

- *They think that we have brought about this transformation by defeating the White minority and that we are dealing with a community that is now lying prostrate on the ground, begging for mercy, to whom we can* ***dictate.*** *Both tendencies are wrong. We want men and women who are committed to our mandate, but who can* ***rise above*** *their ethnic groups and think in terms of South Africa as a whole*[11].

- *To have been asked to deliver the closing address at this conference, which in a very literal sense concerns itself with matters of life and death,* ***weighs heavily*** *upon me, for the* ***gravity*** *of the responsibility placed on one.............We have to* ***rise above*** *our differences and combine our efforts to save our people. History will judge us harshly if we fail*[12].

9 Presidential Address to the ANC Transvaal Conference. Read on his behalf. 21 September 1953.

10 Call after Soweto Uprising of 1976. Published 10 June 1980.

11 Address to the Constitutional Assembly on the Occasion of the Adoption of the New Constitution. Capetown. 8 May 1996.

12 Closing Address, International AIDS Conference. Durban. 14 July 2000.

- *But in this new century, millions of people in the world's poorest countries remain* ***imprisoned, enslaved, and in chains.*** *They are* ***trapped in the prison*** *of poverty. It is time to* ***set them free***[13].

Let us see if other passages from Mandela will lead to the same result. Here we examine sections of his Nobel prize acceptance speech:

- *It was during those long and lonely years that my hunger for the* ***freedom*** *of my own people became a hunger for the* ***freedom*** *of all people, white and black. I knew as well as I knew anything that the* ***oppressor*** *must be* ***liberated*** *just as surely as the* ***oppressed****. A man who takes away another man's* ***freedom*** *is a* ***prisoner*** *of hatred; he is* ***locked*** *behind the bars of prejudice and narrow-mindedness. I am not truly* ***free*** *if I am taking away someone else's* ***freedom,*** *just as surely as I am not* ***free*** *when my* ***freedom*** *is taken from me. The* ***oppressed*** *and the* ***oppressor*** *alike are robbed of their humanity*[14].

- *When I walked out of* ***prison,*** *that was my mission, to* ***liberate*** *the* ***oppressed*** *and the* ***oppressor*** *both. Some say that has now been achieved. But I know that that is not the case. The truth is that we are not yet* ***free;*** *we have merely achieved the* ***freedom*** *to be* ***free,*** *the right not to be* ***oppressed.*** *We have not taken the final step of our journey, but the first step on a longer and even more difficult road*[15].

---

13 Speech. Trafalgar Square, London. 3 February 2005.

14 Long Walk to Freedom: The Autobiography of Nelson Mandela. (544)

15 Long Walk to Freedom: The Autobiography of Nelson Mandela. (544)

One can see a persistent pattern – the remarkable, consistent energy pattern of a bird, particularly the eagle – in his speeches, no matter where and when they were given.

Mandela has been particularly eloquent and graphic. Not everyone is. However to a greater or lesser frequency the cat within each one of our baskets does keep popping its head out. And that is the moment to hold on to it and pull it out. These words, metaphors, idioms and images are doors to the inner world of our other song and often graphically evoke the source of that song, the kingdom from which it originates.

Awareness: The Way To Healing

"Why shouldn't truth be stranger than fiction? Fiction, after all, has to make sense."

Mark Twain

I remember a book that I was reading to my son, where there was a description of what was called a "gump"[1]. From what I understood, it is a raised portion on a hillock that has a secret door as an opening and when you open that door you enter into a world completely different from the one you see outside.

[1] Eva Ibbotson, The Secret of Platform 13 (New York: Dutton Children's Books, 1998) 3-4.

This is the story of every individual; the internal story is so different from the external one. Although external reality continues, it is as if the person is impervious to its changes and dwells more in his own inner world where co-exist his human song in its natural place and the other song which belongs elsewhere and creates discord within him.

In childhood, this language can be heard directly; its energy is clearly visible. There is neither any need nor any attempt to disguise it. As we grow older, however, it is not possible to survive in the human world if we are to live and talk the language of a non-human source. Hence we begin the process of concealing or suppressing this voice in order to sound more human.

This energy then gets hidden. And the more the energy of this source is suppressed, the more it will express itself at more superficial levels. It will first be expressed through dreams (delusion: Level 4), then through emotional disturbance (Level 3). Later it will find expression as physical symptoms (Level 2) and finally as pathology (Level 1). At each and every ascending level this "other energy" will speak the same language (that of the source), but at ever more socially acceptable levels.

The lower and more superficial the manifestation of a person's illness, the more social acceptance and understanding he will receive for it. Take the example of a person whose other song is characterized by "bursting" sensation. If that person has headache, asthma, or any other physical disease, his bursting sensation will be found throughout his physical illness and an expression will arise which is compatible with human society: e.g., you are allowed to have a bursting headache or feel like your lungs are going to burst. This is socially acceptable and makes sense to the world. Human society understands a head pain that feels as though something is bursting, yet there is no room in human society for the energy of "bursting" as a general attitude and way of life. If a person were to say that he feels he is bursting or wants to burst, this would be considered so illogical that his sanity would be questioned. The same sensation that is acceptable at the level of physical pathology is "not sense", or nonsense, at the level of the whole being. Therefore, the person unconsciously suppresses his general sensation, and then it is expressed at the level of his body parts as physical symptoms.

In contrast, as children we are allowed to be more ourselves. Generally we are allowed much freer expression of speech and action in childhood than in adulthood. There are reasons for this. First, the energy of a child is more vigorous and, therefore, harder to suppress. Second, society is generally more tolerant of imaginative, eccentric behavior in children.

For example, when you see a little boy rolling on the floor, growling like a lion, screaming, "I am strong, I am a lion," it is okay, and even amusing! There is therefore less need for a child to compensate and cover up his inner energy. As a result, compared to adults, children generally suffer from less severe pathologies. However, as the child grows into adulthood, he learns to suppress this inner energy in order to conform to the expectations of the society of which he is a member. So with age, the outer expression is altered. However the inner energy is unaltered and remains just as strong as ever. Without free channels through which to be expressed, it has to find other outlets at other levels. The suppressed inner dissonance starts to sound at mental, emotional, and – ultimately – at physical levels.

If you live on a deeper level of experience in your day-to-day life, you tend to have less pathology on the physical plane. The more you suppress your other song, the more the cat will pop its head out of the basket in some pathology -- physical or mental. Higher levels of experience in daily conduct lead to better health and quality of life. Higher levels of experience get portrayed in instances where we use more of our source words. That is, the more a person experiences the sensations of his other song in daily conduct at the higher levels (Level 4 through 7), the better his health and quality of life. When a patient is experiencing his sensation at these higher levels, he will use more words related to the source of his other song. Only persons who are able to live close to their sensation in everyday life can do this.

As a person's health improves, his levels veer more towards sensation and energy. Dreams begin to appear. Pathologies are reduced.

The Way to Health

What we need to do is retrace the path that we took when we learned to suppress the voice of the other song within us. This other song within us does not make sense to our rational mind or to the rational society we live in and has, therefore, been suppressed. Consequently, if we insist on that the inner journey be rational, we will not be able to travel far; our conscious mind will stop us. (Carl Jung said it beautifully when, according to his disciple Robert Johnson, he "compared the ego—the conscious mind—to a cork bobbing in the enormous ocean of the unconscious."[2]) We will never arrive at our goal which is awareness of ALL that is, if we are constantly judging and dismissing a part of that whole reality. When we ignore the parts of our other song that do not make rational sense, it is as if we have decided to set off on an unknown road having already made up our mind that any bends in the road are simply non-rational and are therefore to be dismissed and ignored. We can set off on this basis, but we will certainly not go far. Our prior conviction will utterly limit how far we can travel, how much we are able to experience and therefore be aware of.

Our rational mind is an excellent and useful tool for being selective when that is what the situation demands. However, in order to attain awareness, we need to develop the ability to drop this judging faculty of the mind; to still it. Only then

---

2 Robert A. Johnson, Inner Work: Using Dreams and Active Imagination for Personal Growth (San Francisco: Harper & Row, 1986) 8.

will we be able to experience all that is, and by experiencing the whole, journey towards awareness.

We begin this journey at the level the seeker is expressing or living, i.e. his state in the present moment. From here, we trace all his expressions to deeper levels, until finally we uncover the sensation and the energy pattern which forms the core of his unique disturbance.

Awareness can happen at any of the seven levels.
The deeper the level at which it is experienced, the better the effect.

Awareness has 3 basic steps:

1. Watching without judgment; simple, unconditional watching of all that is.

2. Dissociating from the phenomenon, distancing oneself from it.

3. Experiencing the phenomenon; allowing the experience to be fully felt while at the same time being the observer.

This detached, yet deeply involved, experiencing-and-observing is of all phenomena, both inner and outer: observing what is, in the moment, to the minutest possible degree, especially at stressful times. As stated before, stress highlights both our deepest sensation, and our way of coping with that sensation. Stressful times (when we experience, say, unpleasantness or excitement) are therefore key opportunities for deeply experiencing and observing our habitual inner patterns, our way of being in the world.

The technique necessary for detached observation can be practiced on oneself. One should sidestep the mind and simply and unconditionally watch what is going on at the level of fact, feeling, imagination and sensation (locally and generally), and lastly, in the energy pattern. One should carefully observe when there is a reaction on our part to anything; note when we respond emotionally, say with anger; and then note how we cope with that emotion or physical sensation e.g. do we accept it and try to avoid it in the future, or do we seek to control the situation? We should watch what is inside us, experience it to the greatest possible depth, without drawing conclusions, without wanting to change it. Just look at it as deeply, as long, and as often as you can, if possible all the time having one eye looking out and one eye looking in.

The process to be followed when you turn the attention inwards is first to become aware of your body and mind, of the sensations from various parts of the body, then the thoughts and the emotions. Then you reach an awareness of a deeper world of imagination, somewhat like a dream state.

From there, you go on to reach a deep experience of an overall sensation, a sensation which is felt in your whole being. This sensation when experienced even deeper, makes certain sounds and movements, and other energy patterns emerge and one's being is transformed as it were to a totally different state.

Deeper still than this experience is the experience of:

Silence, Blankness, Stillness.

This is the blank, still canvas for this whole experience. This empty canvas has no energy pattern, but as the receptacle of the person's energy pattern, it still has individuality. It is the screen that shows the movie. It is silent, yet it is the background or the container or, even deeper, the framework for the pattern within. Once awareness reaches to this depth, automatically a certain objectivity results and one is able to see one's true self as the witness in this whole phenomena and the other song as distinct from the true self. This kind of awareness, though not easy, can bring about significant changes. Awareness at this level produces deep effect, and problems at more superficial levels, like emotional conflicts, seem to get automatically resolved without even being directly addressed.

How Can One Become Aware?

There are two ways of reaching this awareness.

1. A process of enquiry aided by another.

2. Self-Observation.

Aided Enquiry

The process of enquiry with a guide is a good way of increasing awareness. The guide needs to be skilled in observation and in the art of keeping his own mind open, or blank.

Both the seeker and the guide should keep their logic and thought processes aside in order to embark on this unknown journey of discovery. The aim is to reach deeper levels, but without the accompanying expectation of reaching a definite conclusion; neither the seeker nor the guide has any idea of what may emerge. The questioning should lead the seeker step by step towards his core, often bypassing his story and emotional situations. The focus should always be on the seeker's energy pattern and sensations. The guide should be very vigilant of the seeker's hand gestures. When these are repeated, the guide should exactly imitate this gesture to the seeker and invite him to speak about it, not from his logic but from pure experience. In so doing, the guide is often helping the seeker to go on an inner, hitherto untravelled, journey.

(The illustrative cases later in this book make this point much clearer.)

Since this inner journey to the core pattern involves tracing the melody of the other song, at a certain point one reaches a level of absolute "non-sense". The seeker's words simply make no sense in terms of external reality. This is when the other song, the dissonant song, is sounding clearly. This is the point where one is very close to the core sensation and the seeker should not be allowed to backtrack to more superficial, apparently rational levels. Paradoxically, recognition of this other song is the one thing which ultimately makes complete sense of the dis-ease, of all that "does not fit" in the life of the seeker.

The focus must constantly be on the seeker's inner experience. Once some aspects of this experience (in terms of sensation or energy pattern) are revealed, one should hold on to this and enquire further until other aspects are revealed. Gradually, the full energy pattern of the other song is revealed in its entirety. At this point, every single expression of the seeker will be understood, as his whole inner song is heard clearly.

One can say this work is like that of an archaeologist who, when he sees part of a buried structure, recognizes it as a part of a whole. He excavates by gradually and carefully digging around it in order to unearth the structure which then stands revealed in its entirety.

Similarly the guide gently asks the seeker to unearth, to gradually uncover and reveal the other song within him. Parts of this other song can be seen at all levels of the seeker's life, but the whole can only be clearly seen and heard by traveling to deep levels. Journeying together, seeker and guide reach a point where this other song is heard so clearly and strongly that both seeker and guide can recognize it. The inner truth is then wholly revealed. When the other song is heard with complete clarity, the entire "non-sense" in the seeker's life suddenly makes complete sense. What is non-sense in the human context is perfect sense for something in nature. The other song is clearly heard and identified as a melody beautiful in itself, but out of place in the human being. It is recognized as an alien song. The recognition of this alien song is the path to awareness. The process of reaching such an awareness is both a difficult and deeply healing experience.

Self-observation

Objective observation of the self is not easy. What we need to see in ourselves is that which is bothering us most at the present moment. It could be a physical ailment, a pain, a paralysis, a tumor. It could be an emotional situation. It could be a spiritual dilemma. Whatever it is can become the starting point of observation into the self.

The first thing to ask is: "What exactly am I experiencing?" (locally in a part of the body or in a situation in life.) That experience should be perceived at deeper levels. How exactly does it feel? What is the sensation and what are the images that come? What movements arise? What colors and sounds are perceived? One needs to go beyond the mind to mindless, thoughtless perception. This experience can bring up unpleasant, frightful, disturbing sensations and images. But the experiencing must progress to deeper levels still. It is like being a witness without judgment, without action—just watching. The sensation can be experienced in the whole body. It may provoke memories of such experiences in various situations in life. One must stay with those sensations longer and longer until one observes them distinct from the self, as something that is a pattern which affects the self but is not a part of it.

Such observation is especially effective, though more difficult, during times of crisis. A crisis is the very moment when the inner state is excited and more vivid. At such times, if one can step back and observe the sensations and the underlying energy patterns that come up, awareness is enhanced. One begins to discern the exact melody of the inner song.

This process of awareness is not always instantaneous, nor is it a one-time phenomena. It is a process that can take place over a prolonged period of time. The ongoing task is to continuously and non- judgmentally observe oneself in various situations and difficult moments. Slowly, over a period of time, the self becomes more and more aware of, and therefore free from, the other song. People who have gone through this process find that they are better able to live in the Now. They feel freer to experience compassion for all beings and are inclined towards spiritual development.

As a seeker, one must persist until he or she reaches the core. As awareness dawns, health returns and so does your inner space. This gives you the flexibility and ability to be in the Now! It is beyond imagination and beyond sensation. It is an experience beyond the levels of experience. We may reach the innermost depths of our turmoil, become aware and get some space from it.

In the space thus created there arises the possibility of an even deeper awareness, namely the awareness of the transitory nature of all phenomena and of one's self. It is my observation that people who, through awareness or homoeopathic treatment, develop the inner space, often then are drawn to spiritual pursuits and more altruistic goals in life.

An example of self-observation on a day to day basis

I encountered a problem with a taxi driver on a day that I had to go downtown. Since I chose to take a cab my receptionist called a cab company asking it to send a cab at a specific time. As it did not arrive at the stipulated time we called them again and to our dismay were told (falsely) that someone from our office had called up to cancel the booking! She called for another taxi and was told that the fare would be eight hundred rupees (twice the official fare). It looked like he were taking advantage of our urgency and wanted to 'take us for a ride'. So I decided to take matters into my own hands and went to look for one on the road.

I found a cabbie who agreed to take me but insisted that it would cost five hundred and fifty rupees. Since I had no time to look for another one I agreed and got in. When I did, the cabbie, perhaps by way of confirming, repeated, "I hope you know that I will be charging you a fixed rate and not by the meter." So I told him, "I know that, and I have agreed to pay you five hundred and fifty rupees," then asked, "But aren't you supposed to charge me by the meter?" To which he replied that his taxi was associated with the hotel where they had a fixed rate. In a firm voice I conveyed my point to him, "As long as you drive a taxi of this city the same law applies to you, but obviously you people make your own laws and since we have no choice we have to listen to you." My tone was aggressive and somehow threatening. I was flustered. This startled the driver somewhat and alerted him.

On reflecting over this incident I realized that I was reacting from a victim mode. I perceived the whole situation as "Him versus me". He was taking advantage of me and I was powerless to do anything. Therefore my reaction was aggressive and threatening. I was reacting from the animal kingdom.

The healthy thing to do would have been to tell him, "I have agreed to pay the amount," then mention that while I can understand that he does not charge by the meter, this way of not going by the book is nevertheless self-propagating. I could have gotten my point across by using analogy and appealing to his better nature: "You may face a similar situation in another context. For example, if you apply for a license, you might be asked to shell out four times the legal fee by a corrupt official. And if we all as a society, individually decide to do what is right, it is possible that the country will prosper much better."

This is what I feel in my healthy perspective and in this stage there is no aggression, only observation of the situation as it is and the possible solutions. There is no stress in such a thought process; it is not connected with the issues in my life, with the past or future. It simply is watching and reacting to the now.

Such a healthy perspective is clouded by the other song within each one of us. Stressful situations excite us and the other song is more clearly to be heard. It gives us an opportunity to become aware of it, so that we might work towards lessening its intensity within us.

What is the Level in Health?

Health is synonymous with flexibility or freedom to act according to the reality of the moment. If this were true, then in health a person cannot be fixed at a particular level of experience. His experience has to vary depending on what is needed in the moment. A healthy person is therefore going to be in the **FACT level** when he is auditing his books of accounts. He is going to be in the **EMOTION level** when showing affection to his children. He is going to be in the **DELUSION level** while watching a movie or writing a verse. He will experience the **SENSATION level** when he is near a mountain or in nature. He will experience **the ENERGY level** when he sings or dances. He will experience **the SEVENTH level** in meditation. He will thus live in the moment and experience the level appropriate to that moment. Health is the freedom to be in the Now.

The Other Song And Homoeopathy

Though the concept is simple, it does require great skill in going with the other person into his experience and being able to identify the other song. Like all skills, it needs a firm foundation, guidance and a lot of practice. It requires a lot of honing before one can become adept at it.

So, how does it help one to just know that there is any other song and that one must try to identify it? The idea of writing this book is to introduce the general public to these concepts. And once they are understood, there will be many applications of it.

One area where it is being used is in homoeopathic practice. The identification of the other song in the patient has helped Homoeopathic practice immensely. As I have mentioned in the chapter "Origins", homoeopathic remedies are derived from the 3 kingdoms: animal, plant and mineral. So far, homoeopaths would find the remedy for the patient by matching his symptoms to the symptoms of various remedies. Now, with the discovery of the concept of the other song, a far more direct match is possible. By going deeper than the symptoms and the mind state, one can hear directly the song of the other entity within.

This has led to far greater accuracy and predictability in selecting the remedy than before. The ideas and techniques are now being taught and used by an increasing number of homoeopaths around the world.

The advantage of giving a homoeopathic remedy (which is made from the source in nature where the other song originates) has many distinct advantages. One is that it acts subtly. Secondly, it can be repeated when needed and in the right strength or potency (according to the level of experience of the patient). Thirdly, it is not mandatory for the patient to reach a level of awareness in the interview; the remedy produces this awareness unconsciously. Also homoeopathy has already a huge data base of symptoms recorded for each remedy which can confirm or help the choice of the remedy. This makes it possible to use homoeopathy in small children, in mental illnesses, and any situation where the patient is not capable of going through the awareness process with the practitioner.

Thus homoeopathy is a very potent tool, and can help people with physical symptoms and pathological conditions along with helping them generally and in their state of mind. It treats the person as a whole and sees all these as expressions of the underlying other song.

The case histories that follow are from homoeopathic practice and were all benefited by the suitable homoeopathic remedy (along with the awareness they got in the case taking process).

I must warn the reader that it would be very risky to try and prescribe homoeopathic remedies to oneself or to anybody by merely reading this or other books of this genre without a full and complete education in the fundamentals of homoeopathy and a proper guided training in practice. Such an education takes several years of dedicated and systematic learning which is offered in accredited colleges of homoeopathy, followed by clinical training by experienced practitioners. Knowledge of the concept of the other song enhances and complements such a formal study, but is not a replacement for it.

Case Studies

An Introduction To The Enquiry Process

"We are going on a journey to find out what is it that lies at the root of who you are and where your stress stems from. This journey is not to be an intellectual exercise but aims to uncover your deep experience within. In order to do that I will be asking certain questions.

I could ask the same question again and again, especially when it pertains to what you feel and what you experience. I will probably ask several times. It does not mean that you are not clear or that I do not understand you. It simply means that by asking the same question over and over again we have found that we were able to reach deeper levels. So each time I ask you the same question again, you simply need to answer me in different words, in a little more detail, and keep continuing like that. This is not a test and there is no right or wrong answer. It is your experience we are seeking to know."

With such an introduction the flow of the process of enquiry is far smoother.

Case Study I

A thirty-six-year-old woman suffering from urticaria (hives)

(**R** : Dr. Rajan Sankaran

P : Patient

Italics are author's comments.)

R : What is the problem?

P : This is the problem (pointing to the rash on her skin). I am basically fed up. I have done everything but nothing works. It comes at three in the morning, four in the morning. Till evening I am okay. When it comes I get desperate, very frustrated, very angry. I blast my husband. I become abusive. I use bad language against his parents. This urticaria has been a very hard lesson for me.

The story so far: -

Level 1: (name)

Urticaria.

Level 2: (fact)

Worse three and four a.m.

Level 3: (emotion)

Very, very frustrated and angry and abusive.

Level 4: (delusion)

It is a hard lesson.

Level 5: (sensation)

Blast, Against.

She sees the urticaria as a very hard lesson; this is peculiar. Also, ***'blast' and 'against'*** *are non-human-specific words, and they represent the Sensation.*

R : You said that the urticaria is a hard lesson for you. What is a hard lesson?

P : It comes at whatever time it pleases. It does not cater to my convenience.

She personifies the urticaria. She perceives the urticaria as a very definite 'it' which comes from outside and bothers her. The urticaria is against her.

P : But it comes like such a punch! (Punches one palm strongly with the fist of the other hand.) It burns. I am forced to take notice. It is telling me, "Get out! Take notice! Move! Do something!"

Although she experiences burning as well, the main sensation in the urticaria is ***the punch****, being accompanied by a hand gesture with energy. The kingdom gets clear early in this case. It is as if the urticaria has a life of its own and it is punching and telling her to get up and take notice. And she is against her* *in-laws and blasts her husband. We are talking here of 'a song' from the animal kingdom, one versus the other, fighting, blasting, punching.*

P : At least cancer is quiet and hidden. This comes right on the face.

Every word and every gesture of the patient reflects 'the song' of the source. One quality of the source in this case is that it is not hidden, and it comes right on the face. At this point we don't know what she is talking about, but we note 'not hidden, right on the face.'

P : In the last three years there has been one crisis after another. (Makes the same punching gesture.)

At this point in the case, it is very interesting that the hand gesture is completely unrelated to what she is saying. Through her words, she is saying something, but what her hands show has absolutely no logical connection with her words. It is the hand gesture, however, that speaks the truth. We have to take the case to that depth where the gestures and the sensation are saying the same thing.

P : My father-in-law is a major nut. He makes my life miserable. (Gestures as if going back and forth.) He accuses me of things which have not happened.

Nothing is hidden with her. She says what she feels quite openly and frankly.

P : People perceive me as very strong.

The issue is: Who is strong/who is weak.

P : Since they see me as strong, instead of blasting me, he blasts my eight-year old.

The weak one gets blasted.

P : I told my husband that I cannot stay with his parents. I want to get free. My husband has to choose them or me.

Them versus Me. Who will survive? Only one of us can survive.

P : I say, "Damn it! If your father can earn, so can you. So why do we have to live with him and bear this?"

In what way is he better than us? That is the question. Him versus Me.
She said many things along the way, and we make note of everything and make observations about her. But we will go back to the urticaria, which is her chief complaint, and is the most vivid and physical expression of her energy disturbance. As long as we follow and stay with the chief complaint, we stay with where the energy lies, where the other song sings most clearly. The energy is in the "punch" and from there we will get the sensation. So we hold onto that.

R : You said, "It comes like a punch". What do you mean?

We ask her to define "punch" because we want to know what the word means to her. In itself it does not hold. The punch is not like a hit, an injury. But it leads to many other things, and it always has something to do with 'me versus them'. That is the quality of the animal song. The sensation in itself does not hold. That punch is part of several different things that make up the animal. The other features that come up in the sensation are: suddenness and violence, comes at any time, it is violent, it punches, 'blasting', all expressions of violence.

P : 'Like a punch' means I am quietly sleeping at three in the morning and it suddenly comes and starts itching violently. I don't wake anyone up. I have to cool myself down. I used wrong lipstick and my whole face exploded. It is so strong. I am under so many dietary restrictions.

Restriction *is important. It is the opposite of the word 'get out', which she used with a lot of energy. This, we will find out later, represents the depth and degree of her desperation. This is the type of situation she perceives. One in which she is restricted and she must get out.*

Victim/aggressor is the deepest sensation, underlying and giving rise to all the other expressions of violence : punching, blasting, exploding, etc. She perceives and reacts to her father-in-law as an aggressor. That is her experience of reality. To what degree, with what intensity does she experience the sensation of victim/aggressor? To the degree of feeling very restricted and wanting to get out urgently. She is the claustrophobic type in her coping mechanism.

N.B. The sensation will almost always be accompanied by hand gestures, whereas the coping mechanism is almost never accompanied by hand gestures.

R : When you say 'punch', what do you mean?

She keeps wandering back into the external story, the situation where she experienced the sensation. Our task is to keep bringing her back to where the energy lies, until she takes us to the next level.

P : It comes very suddenly. I have to get up and take notice. It leaves me mentally very weak. I am shaken up.

The 'punch' has the effect of shaking her up. 'Shaken up' is non-human specific. It is out of context and has energy. So it is coming directly from the sensation, from the source. A punch that shakes you up.

R : 'Shaken up', meaning?

P : I start questioning many things. What did I do? It just shakes me up. It makes me feel.

We don't want feelings, so we go back to hand gestures and ask her about them.

R : You showed something with your hands?

P : (She shows a punch with her hands.) It is like this! Itching and burning. It is saying, "Get out and move! Don't just exist here. Live." Nobody has lived with in-laws and coped with them for so long. My allergy is very angry with me.

Again she personifies a symptom, this time 'my allergy'; as if it existed as an antagonist, distinct from her.

P : I have a lot of anger inside. Not just throwing something, but punching. I feel like holding my in-laws and shaking them up, but cannot do it.

What she feels is happening to her, she feels like doing to her in-laws, to others. She feels like breaking, punching, shaking up. This is what she experiences herself, and so wishes to do that to others, in accordance with postulate 1.

P : I do not feel like punching a soft pillow, but smashing something, like the television. I hate noises and my father-in-law watches the television very loud. I feel trapped in my room.

She specifically wants to smash the television. We have to understand what the television represents. Everything that she says is important. The television is a trap for her; that is what it means for her. 'Trap' suggests the level of desperation at which she experiences her sensation of victim/aggressor.

R : When you say 'trapped in my room,' what do you mean?

P : I feel shut in my room. The drawing room is my father-in-law's territory.

She is trapped by his hold on his territory. This is animal kingdom. What is the issue in her life? Domination by the father-in-law. How bad is this issue? 'He is trapping me, restricting me, and I have to get out.'

P : The drawing room is his private den. My children do not have the freedom to run around. The television is his property.

That is his territory. The main issue for her is her father-in-law. This situation between 'Him and Me' represents and expresses the core sensation and energy in her life. It is her delusion, her nightmare, her worst possible situation. Now we have the freedom to enter into that situation itself. We know the energy, we know the kingdom, and we know the situation. Now we want to understand this situation directly, in itself.

R : What is the issue with him?

P : He is a very dominating person.

There is nobody other than you. Anything, anybody, any situation you talk about, you are only describing your own sensitivity, about your own inner state - in accordance with postulate 3.

P : If you explain yourself they see it as answering them back. My confidence was very threatening to him. Everybody else was sucking up to him.

Here the question of confidence is coming. In the case of the mineral, the sensation would be 'I lack confidence, I cannot cope.' The mineral feeling is of an inner lack in capacity, in function. In contrast the issue for her is 'my confidence threatened him'. Here the issue of confidence is a comparison, a rivalry, a competition. It has to do with survival and external threat, that here is somebody who is a threat to my survival.

She spoke about how her father-in-law does not like it if his own son gets ahead of him. He falsely accused her, saying, "You know what this girl did with me?" She says she feels "Victim No.1 is me." He now picks on her daughter.

The main issue in her life is domination*. Her father-in-law dominates, doesn't allow her into his territory. She is trapped in her room as a result. He does not allow her to answer back. She is not allowed to challenge his authority. He is the boss. She has to abide by his wishes. Otherwise he blasts her, victimizes her. But she is strong and retaliates, so he picks on her daughter who is weak. She gets very angry and wants to smash, break things, shake up her in- laws. This is what she must experience as happening to her in her situation, and this is the sensation in the urticaria: a sudden punch, sudden violence. She blasts her husband. Her face explodes into hives. She is very open in the way she talks. She does not hide anything, makes no attempt to restrict herself. Like the urticaria* *which is not hidden, it comes on the face. These are her qualities, the qualities of the other song within her, the qualities of the source.*

It becomes evident quite early in the case that the main issue is one of survival: the father-in-law versus me. His authority versus mine. His territory versus mine. This is the animal kingdom. And the main sensations are punch, blast, smash, sudden violence, burning, angry. There is also the feeling of being trapped, of being restricted and of wanting to get out. These seem to indicate 'The Claustrophobic Type' of reaction (or coping mechanism) to the sensation experienced.

Apart from the sensation, what is also very apparent is the openness with which she talks.

The Source has to have the suddenness, the violence, the openness, and all the features that we have seen so far.

Having obtained the sensations in the chief complaint and in her situation we now go to the dreams. She describes one dream:

P : My whole body is shaken up. I am thinking of plants and flowers. Of very beautiful surroundings: a house on the beach, no noise, peaceful. Suddenly my whole body is vibrating. There was so much love pouring out of me. Snake dreams; they are in the temple. Just before the culmination of the dream somebody gets hit.

Hit is similar to punch.

P : I am scared of men. Had a dream where men are following me and I hide.

In the dreams, we see pursued and escaping, fear, snakes, beautiful surroundings that cause a reaction in her. We have reached the level of delusion. The next level is the sensation and the source itself.

R : How do you react to animals?

P : I am frightened of them. I am scared of stray dogs. Mosquito bites I can't stand. I am scared of insects. The house is full of cockroaches.

R : What about insects?

P : I am scared of insects, especially the bee.

This is where the whole case comes together. She tells us the name of her source. The bee sting is sudden with burning pains, excessive swelling of the skin with redness and heat. It has sudden effects; the symptoms develop suddenly and rapidly. Amongst the bees in a hive, there is violent anger and a lot of jealousy. Now we can appreciate how everything she says has to do with the source. It is not hidden, it comes on the face. It is like a punch: "It is telling me get up and move."

R : What about the bee?

P : I am scared of bee stings. If it stings me, I will get a massive reaction. The honey bee, the queen bee, that one. They are dangerous.

R : When you blast your husband, what do you do?

P : I blast him loudly, otherwise what is the use? I am vehement. Have been put here in a restricted atmosphere; it is slavish: I hate myself. When the maid or doctor is not around, I am there filling each and every role. I am not giving myself the choice. I am serving.

Subservient to the boss; like the workers toiling for the Queen bee.

As a child she was considered very, very active, running around, very dominating. Loves colorful flowers with aroma. "I don't like flowers without smell. I love the smell of roses, jasmine."

She is writing the script of a movie. She overheard her husband once, after watching a movie, discussing with his friends how men should go to Goa to ogle at women on the beach. She felt that these men should have done this in their twenties when single, not now when they have wives and children. So her script would have wives giving tit for tat to men. In her movie the wives would go to Goa and have one night stands with anyone, anywhere, to take revenge on their husbands.

The themes that come up here: sexuality, infidelity and lack of morals, jealousy and revenge. "What you do to me, I will do double to you." Even here there is a kind of competition. "Anything you can do, I can do better."

She says: "I can talk of revenge but not do it," but adds that if her husband ever had an affair, she would shoot the girl first and then him.

CASE ANALYSIS

The levels:

- ***Level 1: Name***
  - Urticaria.

- ***Level 2: Fact***
  - Worse three and four a.m.
  - Want someone to "bang my head, the harder the better".

- ***Level 3: Feeling***
  - Very very frustrated.
  - Angry and abusive.
  - Jealousy.
  - Revenge.
  - Sexuality.
  - Infidelity.
  - "Am I not good enough that you have to have an affair?"

- ***Level 4: Delusion***
  - It is a hard lesson.
  - Trapping, restricting, no freedom.

- ***Level 5: Sensation***
    - Blast against.
    - Comes like a punch. (Hand Gesture)
    - Exploding and blasting.
    - Shaken up.
    - Openness.
    - Right on the face.
    - Honey bee.

- ***Level 6: Energy***
    - Suddenness.
    - Violence.

CASE EXPLANATION

In every patient there is a human song and a non-human song, both sounding simultaneously. We should train our ears to hear the non-human song. As this case evolved, she revealed that song namely the song of the queen bee.

Interestingly, the life of a queen bee is as follows:

Swarming usually takes place in the late spring and early summer when a new queen is bred within the hive. Queens are no different genetically from other bees in the hive. They only attain royal status by dietary means, by being fed "royal-jelly", a secretion produced by the nurse worker bees during the larval stage. The larvae of the hive that are not fed this royal-jelly develop into smaller-sized bees, the workers.

Immediately preceding the emergence of the new queen, unrest pervades the hive. This causes some of the older drones and workers to rally around the old queen and leave the hive with her, before the new queen emerges from her royal cell. As soon as the new queen has emerged, she stings to death all the other occupants of the "queen cells", her potential young rivals in the hive (larvae who had also been fed the royal jelly). If the old queen has not left the hive (because she has aged to the point where she is no longer able to lay the number of eggs necessary to maintain the population of a hive), then she, too, is stung to death by the newly emergent young queen. When this is done the young queen has fully established her regal status.

With the patient who's 'Other Song' is so clearly from the animal kingdom, the insect sub-kingdom of the bee, we can clearly see the similarity as to how her entry into his house threatened her father- in-law's territory. She was young and confident. In her, this non- human song is that of Me versus the Other. It is her against her father-in-law. She perceives him as the aggressor and herself as victim. She cannot enter his territory; he is the emperor and she is the slave, the server. He has put her in a restricted area, and she feels the Claustrophobic response of needing to get out.

In the case of the husband having an affair, she feels : "If the men can do it, I can do it better." She gets a lot of pleasure in just saying that. She is very moral and faithful to her husband and consciously she would not dream of doing any such thing.

The survival of an insect depends upon it being active, being sexual, and being able to attack suddenly with great violence. Because the life of an insect is very short, it has to reproduce very quickly, and so there is a great deal of sexual activity. This is the kind of sexuality that the patient has in mind when talking about men going to Goa and ogle at women on the beach. One-night stands. Anybody is good enough, whoever you can get will do. If not here, then there. It doesn't make a difference

The activity of an insect is very fast, hasty. Death is sudden. It does sudden violence, but also experiences in its own life sudden death. The patient also said she would kill by a quick method, shoot. It means there is no cruelty, no hiding, and no deceit. You just take a gun and shoot. That's it. Not like a snake, where there will be deceit and planning. Here there is no plan. Nothing complicated, but very open, simple.

(Refer the qualities of the 'insect song' on page 115.)

In this way we can hear her non-human song ,tune for tune, note for note, as that of the queen bee, this is the Source, this is the other song that is playing within her, whose song she lives and whose melody colors every aspect of her life. And expresses finally in her body as urticaria.

Post script

She was given a homoeopathic ultra dilution (potency) of the bee (Apis mellifica). With this she had a significant reduction of her urticaria. Her attitude towards her life changed. She felt more at peace and grateful for everything. Her attitude towards her father-in-law became much more accepting and even caring.

Case Study II

A twenty-five-year-old woman with severe depression

(**R** : Dr. Rajan Sankaran

P : Patient

Italics are author's comments.)

R : What is the problem?

P : (It is some time before she starts to answer.) I have changed as a person. During the time of marriage, I had emotional problems (weeps). This shattered me totally. Parents, elders, religion, and culture: I alone am the target of everything.

Note her feelings: totally shattered, she is the target of everything. These are indicative of her inner turmoil and we definitely need to take notice of them. But we must keep in mind that her chief complaint is emotional and not physical, and so she will describe feelings rather than sensations. Feelings are individual-specific and can be misleading; therefore, , at the beginning of the case we need to be open and refrain from forming quick conclusions. For example, "feeling targeted" may seem to point in the direction of an animal song , but we must wait to see which kingdom her deeper constant sensation points to. This sort of confusion ceases with cognizance of the fact that these are feelings and not sensations. The level at this point in the case is as yet the emotional level, or Level 3, and the words or feelings that we can rely on to lead us further will be those that are used repeatedly, out of context with what she is saying. If they convey an image (for example, if she said that she felt totally shattered, like a glass pane that had shattered into a thousand tiny little bits), this would be conveying a very vivid image of "shattered" and would add weight to the conclusion that the deep sensation is of "shattered". Without such a vivid image, "shattered" may be regarded as no more than a mere expression. The words that have energy or form an evident pattern throughout her speech are non-human-specific. Such expressions are universal, are solid. For example, if you were to ask her about "shattered" and she were to say that it is like being torn to pieces, then one could say that "shattered" holds. We ask about a word that appears to be a sensation and she uses another similar word, also conveying the same sensation more clearly. Like the rock-climber who tests the foothold before he decides to use it to climb any further. Similarly, if we identify a potential sensation, and the person, on further questioning, is not able to lead us further in that direction, we might say that the word does not hold. For example, if we asked her about "shattered" and she said that she felt completely alone, we could appreciate that here "shattered" is a feeling (which will lead to another feeling) and so cannot be relied upon as being solid enough to lead us to the next step, away from the feelings. If we persist with it, there are chances of our getting lost in a maze of emotions. We must note synonyms or antonyms of words used earlier and whether they were accompanied by hand gestures, especially those not corresponding with the words of the person (A hand gesture that is incongruous with the words the person is speaking while making it should always be noted and the patient should be asked at some point what that gesture spontaneously brings up in that person). So although we note down "shattered" and "being targeted," we should not form any conclusions at this stage. We can be sure only at the level of sensation, Level 5. Here we are still at Level 3 (emotional, individual). At this level, we hear only possible directions, indications, early hints of a possible melody. We will completely mistake the melody and miss the other song if we draw conclusions at this level. We simply note, and wait for her to show us more.

Then she spoke of her lack of confidence in her bank job and how she would have continued the job, if permitted to, after her marriage.

She narrates a whole sequence of events which should be simply regarded as her "external" story. What we are interested in is the "story within the story," her "internal story" or inner song or turmoil. The "external" story is relevant, and provides the outer context within which she lives and experiences her life. The events of this "external story" are only facts, the backdrop or scene for her "internal story". What we are interested in is how she experiences that external story, what her own unique way of perceiving and experiencing life is. We listen, note the facts; and when there are feelings or anything peculiar, we note these. If there are words that meet any of the above-mentioned criteria, we give them more weight.

P : After marriage, dowry was demanded. (Weeps) It was a very big shock for me.

"Shocked and shattered" may make one think of the sensitivity of a plant, but she remains at the emotional level and has not yet moved onto sensations. We cannot infer the kingdom until she speaks at the level of sensation, Level 5.

P : I did not understand anything that was happening. Was this a marriage? What was happening?

It is as if she went through the marriage without being aware of what was happening.

After her marriage, she had pain in the abdomen and was diagnosed with a gall bladder stone. Although she had not been aware of the problem prior to marriage, her in-laws accused her of not declaring the condition before marriage. Her in-laws informed all the relatives about her condition, and her husband asked her to leave him if she couldn't bear living with his parents. Nobody was there to take care of her during pregnancy.

P : My mother-in-law kicked all the servants out. Not one sweet did she let me distribute after the birth of my child (as is the custom). The baby was small. I was brave enough at the birth of my child. Separation from husband was not possible.

Here we can note somewhat contrasting aspects of her nature: she is afraid to be alone and wants someone to take care of her, yet she is brave enough to handle the baby.

P : I can't handle even little, little problems. I can't even hear these things. I feel tension.

It is not the big things that she is concerned with, but the little, little things that bother her. These things reflect her nature; they are unrelated to the situation and are simply aspects of herself. So they become important for us.

P : I am not allowed to go to my own bedroom if my mother-in-law and husband are sitting there. She has ordered me not to call my son by the name I want. I should have a little bit of freedom at least. My husband also can't support me. I feel, "How unfair!" My father-in-law treats me like a bloody pig. If I go in front of him, he does this: (as if sweeping away something with her hand) "Go away from here!"

This is a comparison which corresponds to Level 4, the level of delusion. "I am treated like a bloody pig." This is her perception of how they react to her, how they perceive her.

Since her brother (the only wage earner in her own family) did not have a good income, she felt that if she left her in-laws' house there would be no security for her and the baby. She couldn't even kill herself because then what would happen to her baby?

There is desperation here. She seems to want support, a back-up, someone to take care of her. Without it, she is desperate enough to want to kill herself and the child. (In a part of her case not shown here, she talked of feeling that her only way out was to kill herself and her child.) This degree of intense desperation indicates one of the deeper coping reactions akin to "The Impossible type".

She speaks of lack of intimacy with her husband.

P : He knows I am capable of intelligent conversation, but he doesn't share things with me. (She keeps moving a napkin in her hand, fidgeting with it, turning and twisting it.) It as if I am dust or an object.

This, too, is at the level of delusion, Level 4: "as if I am dust or an object."
All the time, as she speaks, she is wringing the napkin in her hands vigorously.

P : I also want to feel independent. Even if I am capable, I don't have the confidence to start life afresh. What will I do without my husband's support? (She twists the napkin and then pulls to straighten it out.)

She has now finished telling her story, and we have to begin questioning. So what do we need to ask her? Where do we begin questioning? Her story is overwhelming, but if one has to understand what is at the very core of her turmoil, it would be best to steer clear of the story and the emotions and cut directly, if possible, to the level of sensation. So far, one is able to recognize her main complaint—depression, the name of her state—corresponds to Level l; Level 2 includes the facts of her story. At Level 3 the emotions are apparent through her weeping, and we can also see the fear of being alone and a lot of tension; at Level 4 are the delusions, viz., "I am treated like a bloody pig," "I am dust," etc.

And then what we note is that she is constantly twisting and stretching the napkin in her hands; she is doing this vigorously and continuously. This is very interesting. It was not evident from the beginning of the case, but it started only as the case proceeded. This means that from that point on, she has reached the level of sensation (Level 5) or gone deeper to the level of energy (Level 6). This constant and vigorous twisting and stretching of the napkin contains the energy of the case.

If we observe keenly enough, we may be able to appreciate that she has told us not only everything that she wanted to say, but also everything that we need to know. We need to train our minds and senses to recognize the sensation and energy when a person gives us these. We need to pick up the energy, which is contained in the hand gesture, and from there let her direct us to the sensation, as energy is closest to sensation. If one focuses on the energy, the sensation is revealed to us very clearly, and then we will be able to appreciate that she has expressed it earlier on. With this in mind, the first question I put to her was that she should describe what she was doing with her hands.

R : What are you doing with your hands?

P : I do this when. . . I don't know what to do. No self-confidence. Moving through borders, folding it properly makes it straight. I don't like crumpled things. I can't stay confused.

When asked to talk about confusion, she spoke of how life had been "clear" for her in the past–for instance, she did well in school, did not want to marry, and wished to become an air hostess and do something of her own.

We asked her about the hand gesture and she led us to "confusion" and "clarity". So "confusion" and "clarity," are at the level of sensation. There is no speed, no direction, no movement in these, indicating that she has come away from the level of energy. And the level closest to that of energy is that of sensation. Therefore, "confusion" and "clarity" have to be at the level of sensation; this much is clear to us. What is not yet clear is the kingdom that her "Other Song" belongs to. This is what we are now attempting to clarify. We will stick with the sensation of "confusion" until the kingdom-plant, animal, mineral-becomes clear to us.

R : When you say "clear and confused," what do you mean?

P : I know what I want to do, what I can do. I will do only what I know I am able to do. I will not depend on anybody. I don't want to depend on my parents, to say "I need you."

Being clear is related to the issue of her ability and inability, and of depending and not depending. Here is where we see the kingdom of the inner—the other song—expressing itself: the issue here is of ability or capability or function. This way of experiencing clarity and confusion is in the realm of mineral kingdom; the key to understanding to which kingdom her other song belongs is to see that she situates her core issues in terms of ability to cope and function.

If she had said "confused is like bewildered," she would be giving us yet another sensation to explain her experience. This would indicate that she experiences "confused" purely as a sensation and would locate her other song within the sensitive, always-bothered plant kingdom. If her other song were from the animal kingdom, with its constant awareness of competition and survival, she would have responded with something like, "Someone out there can get the better of me and attack me when I'm confused." But since her core issue is "Can I function?" with no deeper issues underlying that sensation, we can locate her constant inner experience within the mineral kingdom and its concern with ability, function, and loss. Probing into what her core words mean to her brings up the issue of independence versus dependence. The issue does not in itself indicate the kingdom: it is her reaction to the issue that will show the kingdom. For example, if in explaining her confusion she had said that she felt dominated by another person, unable to decide whether she should do as she pleases or what the other person wills her to do—constantly at odds with herself—then her other song would have been from the animal kingdom.

But she says, "I know how much capacity I have; I know what I am able to do. And I do only what I am able to do and I don't depend on others." This is definitely the mineral kingdom. In terms of sensation, this can be read as: my structure has a certain capacity to function, and if there is anything that is beyond its capacity, then it needs support from outside. In these instances where the task is beyond her ability, she needs to depend. You will remember that she had repeatedly referred to her ability and talked about wanting support and a backup; this is what becomes clear when we pick up the energy in the case.

Having determined the kingdom, we now need to establish what kind of dependence we are looking at, or in what area is she dependent or requiring support. That will give us the sub-kingdom (for the minerals, the subkingdom is found by placing the patient's sensation on the periodic table in relation to the characteristics of the table's rows and columns). Further, by understanding how the person deals with the sensation, we will be able to perceive the depth at which the sensation is experienced, and this will give us the coping reaction that the person tends to adopt.

We asked about the energy and we arrived at the sensation. We asked about the sensation and reached the kingdom. This is where we should train our mind and senses to be on high alert: what is going to be revealed to us now at the point of energy , the place where the patient's intensity of expression and hand gestures are expressing the same thing.

She wants to be financially independent, to take control of her life, to make decisions without anyone forcing her.

Money does not seem to be the main issue with her. The crucial issue for her is being able to make her own decisions. We have heard her entire story initially, and nowhere did money or financial security figure strongly. Her mother-in-law does not allow her to call her son the name she chose for him, does not allow her to talk on the phone, decides that she should have an abortion (issues she brought up in a part of her case not presented here), and interferes in everything. We can see now that the issue in this situation is that she does not have control and she cannot make her own decisions. In her case, the experience of not being allowed to make her own decisions equates with the sensation of someone forcing the course she takes, like the situation in which her mother-in-law tells her to wear a particular dress when she wants to wear something else and she feels: "My decision is not wrong."

The dependence is in the area of making decisions. She would like to decide independently, but someone forces her, and she is not allowed to decide for herself. She is not allowed to exert her independent, individual choice. The issue is of being an individual , something she is not allowed to be.

She is not allowed to have her own identity as an individual, as someone else takes the decision for her. This is where she experiences the confusion. The issue is that of identity, and in the periodic table this corresponds to the third row.

P : If I have made a decision, that person in front of me, instead of ordering me, if he moulds the way he puts it then I might do as he says. (She makes a hand gesture to express "mould".)

Force is what she does not like, and "mould" is what she wants. "Mould" is not an emotion; it cannot be a delusion. It is a word that is completely out of context as far as human experience goes. It is complete nonsense, in that one cannot conceive of human experience, perceptions, or emotions described in terms of "mould." One would have expected in this context that a person should say, "He should say it differently," etc. But "mould" is very peculiar. It has no human context; it is borrowed from something else in nature. We shall see later that this is related directly to the source - ***which is pure clay, a soft, mouldable substance.***

R : What is mould?

P : Say with love instead of in a rude manner. Then I am very willing to do it. Mould is a round object like a ball with a smooth surface and no disturbance.

Like to touch a round ball, smooth surface. It is very smooth, and rolls over, goes comfortably without bounce or disturbance.

This is the realm of nonsense. It is complete nonsense, has nothing to do with logic, nor is it related to her situation. And at the height of this complete nonsense, we find the source. Everything that she is saying now must be related to the other song singing within her, the source – clay.

R : Tell me about this, "I don't know what I want."

P : Don't know what to do. Decisions are made. I am just told. No discussions whatsoever. "What do you think? What is your opinion?" Instead it is, "Do this and do that." I was also something.

She has moved away and out of the level of sensation into that of the situation. She reached Level 5, or the level of the source. Now that the sensation is clear, we will attempt to understand the delusion (Level 4) in terms of the sensation, (Level 5).

R : What is the opposite of being something?

P : You are nothing. Treated like a doll, with a remote control in somebody else's hand.

This is her delusion.

P : If you press A, the doll will say A. If you press B, the doll will say B. If you press "Go there," the doll will go there. But the doll doesn't have a brain, I do. The doll is dead and cold, it will not affect her. It can't think or do anything. The doll is an object, but I am a human being. I get affected. I have my own emotions.

We are back to the level of emotions. This is her disease, that she is affected and depressed. But when we examine this depression in depth, we come to the issue of her identity not being her own but under the control of someone else.

R : How does it feel to be a doll with the remote in somebody's hands?

P : Very angry (angry expression on her face). I feel like just leaving everything and going away. Breaking something. Tearing something. Destroying something.

This indicates the depth of her anger, and points to the reaction and coping mechanism of **destruction** *which would indicate the* **Impossible Type**. *We have seen the degree of desperation earlier on, when she feels like killing herself and her child. Further, the action is always opposite to the perceived feeling or sensation. If she feels like breaking, destroying, killing, then she must feel that something in her is being broken, destroyed, or killed.*

With a childish look on her face, she describes that "lonely" for her is like having nothing in this world. "What will I do without him? How will I feed myself? How will I feed my son? Financially, how will I support myself? I will be without support. Who will help me? Who will stand with me? I want someone to lean on."

She is speaking the language of a very small child who cannot even feed itself. This is a very small child who cannot be by herself, is afraid to be alone, who still needs someone to care for and look after her, who needs love. It is the stage where the child still depends on the parents for love and food. At this stage, the parents decide what to feed the child, what to give her, where to send her. She cannot decide for herself, but her own individual identity is developing and she wants to exert it.

R : You said in the beginning, "I have changed as a person." What did you mean?

P : Earlier I was working and confident; I was doing something. I was independent. Now it has changed. I have to ask for everything. To go to my aunt's place, I have to ask. In childhood, I had plenty of conflicts with my parents. My father used to abuse and beat my mother. She used to be right, but he wouldn't listen to her. My mother, she never did anything for herself. Everything was for us. She was nothing.

We see the same words and feelings being applied to her mother as were true for her. The mother is no one but her. Once you reach the core of the case in every situation, every example will tell the same story.

Gesture alternates: folds napkin, then opens it up; keeps alternating.

P : I couldn't study in my college. My mother was so frustrated. She told me not to study. She used to beat me. She said, "Go to Hell! Your studies are not important."

She felt helpless not knowing what to do. "I knew I was doing the right thing. but I didn't know what to do."

R : You are again folding and re-folding the napkin. What's the significance?

P : To tidy things. I can't stand untidiness. It makes me feel confused, don't know what to do.

CASE ANALYSIS

The levels:

- ***Level 1: Name***
    - Depression
- ***Level 2: Fact***
    - Problem with parents, elders, religion, and culture.
    - "I have changed as a person"

- ***Level 3: Feeling***
  - Totally shattered
  - "I am the target of everything"
  - Afraid of being alone
  - Anger

- ***Level 4: Delusion***
  - Treated "As if I am a pig"
  - "I am dust"
  - Nothing
  - Treated like a doll with a remote control in somebody else's hand

- ***Level 5: Sensation***
  - Confusion and clarity
  - Ability and inability, depending and not depending
  - Being an individual (identity) or being a robot
  - Mouldable

- ***Level 6: Energy***
  - Hand gesture of constantly and vigorously twisting and stretching of the napkin

CASE EXPLANATION

The third row of the periodic table deals with the issue of identity.

Na	Mg		Al	Si	P	S	Cl	Ar

The elements of the third row are **Sodium, Magnesium, Aluminum, Silicon, Phosphorus, Sulphur, Chlorine, and Argon.**

The third row has to do with the issues of identity and individuality, nourishment and development, ego and insult. Struggles with or the attempted emergence of choice making, the definition of oneself and the relationship to others, care and dependence, and the development of ego are found in the third row. Within the framework of dependence, we see these persons expressing or attempting to express their individuality.

Let us examine each of these elements.

With **Sodium** the sensation is that of having no identity. Where a relationship is the main issue, we see the individual taking on the identity of the other person. One can envisage that this would be expressed in cases as "I am not me; I am he." It is as if her identity is not her own: "My own identity does not exist. Therefore, I need a relationship where the other person can be my identity. When I find that somebody, I will take his name, his identity. Then his choices will be my choices. His life will be the life I choose. There is nothing left that is me; everything is he." This is the Sensation with Sodium.

In the case of **Magnesium**, the beginnings of a sense of identity are there, but while coming into this sense of separate identity the person experiences loneliness, which is very frightening. The sensation is: "I am me but I don't want to be me, because it is very frightening." The feeling is that of a very small child abandoned by his parents and who does not get the care, protection, and nourishment that he needs. He has to make his own decisions but he feels too young and highly incapable of it. When he is expected to make his own decision he wonders, "Are you sure you want me to take the decision?" because he would like the other person to decide for him. When he has to decide what to wear, he feels, "Are you sure you are not going to choose what I should wear?" because what he wants is that the other person should choose for him. He has an identity but would prefer not to exert it (because exerting his separate identity does not yet feel safe for him) and he would much rather have the other person decide and choose for him He is afraid, always, of "What if I make my own decision and you reject me?" He needs the other person, because for him it is fearful to be alone. He feels that to keep the relationship he so needs, he must forego his own choice.

In **Alumina** (pure clay), which contains the element aluminum, is a confusion of identity: am I me or am I he? It is like a child who has his identity and choice, but is doubtful and unsure of it yet would feel forced if his parent were to make the decision for him. When the parents do not let him decide for himself, his sense of identity and his belief in his capacity are threatened. He begins to doubt these fundamentals of his being: Do I have my own identity or am I what these other people want me to be? Am I capable enough to be an individual in my own right or do I lack that capacity?

In this current case, she describes: When someone says A; I have to say A, and when he says B, I have to say B. Alumina is clay, which is soft and moldable. In moulding anything, you have to handle it softly and gently—and then you can turn it into any shape you want. If you are aggressive and try to force clay that is setting into a different shape, you will break it. Clay is soft and moldable, but it can be set: it alternates between not having a definite form and having a form. What it is can be either clear or unclear.

This is what she was showing us with the napkin.

In this case, her feeling is: I lack the ability to take care of myself and to decide for myself, though I want to. This creates a conflict: am I capable enough to look after myself and be independent, or am I incapable and dependent? We see this conflict expressed as confusion in her. Being independent means having to care for yourself and making your own decisions, and here she feels incapable. So she doesn't exert her choice or identity because of her inner experience of incapacity (a key mineral sensation). However, being dependent means that someone else is making your decisions for you, and here she experiences a desire to exert her own identity.

In **Silica** we see obstinacy and very fixed ideas, with a complete lack of flexibility. There is a strong, fixed, definite sense of identity: this is me. Silica is one of the components of glass. It is not moldable like Alumina, but has a fixed, rigid, and unchangeable shape. If someone tries to alter its shape, it breaks.

Phosphorus is friendly, affectionate, and sympathetic. He is the child who is not content with the identity that he has been given by his parents and family. He feels the need for his own identity apart from what they have given him. He goes and makes his own friends. He gains his sense of identity from being different. The feeling is: I am not you. I have an identity apart from you and apart from what you have given me. So you find that he is indifferent to his loved ones and friendly with strangers. He develops his own set of friends apart from his family and apart from what his parents may have chosen for him.

Sulphur is egoistic. If we trace this trait right down to the sensation level there he feels: I am proud to be me, and I know better than you. He believes he is individual enough to know what is right and pays little heed to what others may have to say. He feels he knows best; this is not a comparison that he makes, rather it is an assertion of his identity. He is the child who will say to his parents, "You know nothing." His sense of identity is now fully developed and he feels he knows it all.

Lastly, with **Chlorine** or the muriate (muriaticum) element in salts, we see the main sensation to be: "I am the opposite of you. Whatever you are, I will be the opposite." He is dissatisfied with doing what others may want him to do. If the parents want the child to obey, he will be obstinate and rebel. He has his own identity —very different from others'— and he keeps to himself.

Is there sense in the nonsense?

The words that she used at the deepest level were: smooth, ball, mould. These words are completely non-human-specific. They have no human context and are borrowed from something else in nature, and so they must represent the source itself.

I put in the words "Alumina" and "moulding" on the internet and obtained the following data:

> **"Alumina is one of the most mouldable substances on earth. It can be moulded into any shape."**

Next, I typed in the words "Alumina" and "balls" into the search. The result was a series of photographs of what are called Alumina balls. These balls are the way that Alumina is actually formed. One can actually order these Alumina balls on the internet! In its natural form Alumina is found in small, round balls. It is found in particles that are highly spherical.

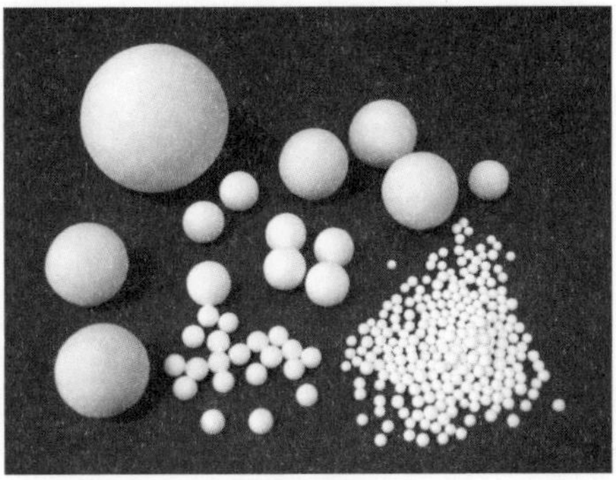

Alumina balls

Scanning with the electron microscope shows that they are spherical in nature, so they come in nature in that very form.

By its very nature, Alumina is a smooth, round ball! Also there are alumina grinding balls, which have a very good, smooth surface and very good roundness and can be used for a very long time.

I understand now that the source is very, very important. The entire expression of the patient's state is the human expression of the source itself.

Postscript

She was given Alumina in homoeopathic potencies, and the next few months showed a remarkable transformation in her. Her self-confidence went up; she could face her situation with a new perception, without the previous feelings of inadequacy, dependence, and self-doubt. Her manner of speaking changed from the childish whine to adult expression. Within months of the treatment, she grew by years to her natural stage of development.

Case Study III

A forty-year-old woman, dancer by profession

(**R** : Dr. Rajan Sankaran

P : Patient

Italics are author's comments.)

R : What is the problem?

P : Asthma.

Level 1: Diagnosis/Name.

R : Tell me about it.

P : It started as bronchitis in childhood. During pregnancy, it turned into full-fledged asthma. I just couldn't breathe well. Was fine for seven months, and then it was triggered again, and when my daughter was one and a half years old, it got aggravated and I was hospitalized. I have been trying to find out whether dust or change in season affects it. At times it suddenly flares up. At times it is under control. Sometimes at nights I need to take the pump when I have an attack; otherwise, for months there is nothing.

Level 2: Fact.

It is important to note the following facts about the symptoms at this level i.e. asthma aggravated near the seashore, better when away from it. What is also important to note is that for months there is nothing and then one night there is a severe attack; this is the pattern of the asthma. She says it suddenly flares up.

R : Tell a little more about this asthma.

P : Throughout the day I am busy and so I am not so conscious about this. But it comes in the night when I am lying down. So I try to sit up, but after a while again - when I get exhausted - I slide down. Though I try not to use the pump (inhaler containing bronchodilator), invariably I rush towards it.

It becomes an urgent need.

P : I have been trying different things. Cold things and fried I never eat, as I know it harms me. The other factors could be change of season, dust.

There are many factors that seem to affect her, but she does not know what triggers it. There is no single concrete aggravating factor. And she has to avoid many things as a result. This is not very uncommon with persons with asthmatic or allergic bronchitis. The peculiarity about the asthma is that its onset is sudden. This has the potential to lead us further, to understand the general disturbance. We should use this as a foothold in order to take our next step forward.

R : You said, it gets suddenly triggered.

P : It started with a cold that just would not go, in spite of steam inhalation. But very slowly and gradually it increased—and again I started taking a bronchodilator, but it did not help.

"Suddenly triggers" does not really lead much further and so we can try another route. We can ask about the effect of the asthma on her and in this way attempt to go further than Level 2. But we should keep in mind that the effect of the asthma has to be in tune with **suddenly triggers**.

R : What effect does this have on you?

P : On all these days I could not function. I stopped teaching and practicing dance for three weeks so as not to exert myself too much. In the past I could dance even when suffering from asthma, but this time it has really affected me.

It is a fact that she is a dancer; let us set that aside for the moment. It is important for us to know what dance means to her. We do not ask about dance. Dance is at a deeper level. At some point we will see that her dance and her asthma are two expressions of the same sensation. Then we shall be at the very centre of her being (Sensation level, Level 5). At this point in the case, we are still at the level of fact.

R : How does this asthma affect you?

P : This time it scared me. I remember the first time when I was hospitalized, I was shaken up so badly that I told myself that I would never get myself in this position again. That is how I started doing Yoga. For a long time that gave me relief.

Level 3: Emotion.

The asthma scared her and she was very badly shaken up and she does not want the situation to recur. This is in tune with 'suddenly triggered'. She is sensitive to things which are suddenly triggered and they have an effect on her: she feels scared and very badly shaken up. To take the next step, we use this as a foothold.

R : When you say, "It scared me," what do you mean?

P : In the night when I am very breathless, I feel it will do something to my lungs (hand gesture: she brings her hands close to her throat as if she is grasping it with both her hands), that it is going to bring an attack, heart attack, that this is going to be fatal, that is it! I feel that this is going to cause some extreme trouble. That is my fear: that I will not be able to function, that I will be bedridden. And that is something which I hate, just lying down, doing nothing for days; I become very restless. I hate anybody doing things for me. That scared me. I keep thinking, that's it! It is going to ruin my lungs and it is probably going to make me absolutely invalid.

Note how she describes the asthma: "It is going to bring an attack, it is going to do something to my lungs." She personifies the asthma, and it seems as if there are two entities here: the person and the asthma. It can make one think of the animal kingdom, where survival is the main issue, often expressed as me versus the other. The other thing she says is, "I will not be able to function," which can bring to mind the mineral kingdom. It is too early to decide the kingdom; the level is too superficial.

What is clear so far is this: The asthma is something that is suddenly triggered, that scares and shakes her up very badly so that she does not want to be in that position again. And when it comes, her reaction could be put into words something like this: "This is it! It is fatal." She experiences it as something sudden and highly disturbing to the extent of incapacitating her for life.

What is more important is that she starts using her hands at this point. Her hand gesture is indicating a sensation experienced in the lungs. From the fear, she has gone back to the local sensation through the use of hand gestures. If we keep our focus on her hand gestures and observe and follow those, then all confusion with regard to the sensation will vanish at some point.

R : Describe that sensation. What is your experience of what will happen to your lungs?

P : I feel that it is going to cause congestion, and there is no passage left to breathe (hand gesture, as if putting her hands around something to grasp it, with no space between the two hands, not even a little bit.) And that will probably lead to death, or even an attack, a heart attack. (Brings her palm with all fingers spread out very suddenly close to her chest.) It is the end; I cannot go beyond that. There is nothing left.

R : Just stick to that experience and describe it in more detail.

P : Choking. That the next breath I take will be the last one. (Gesture as if grasping her throat with both her hands. As if putting both her hands around something so as to encircle it.)

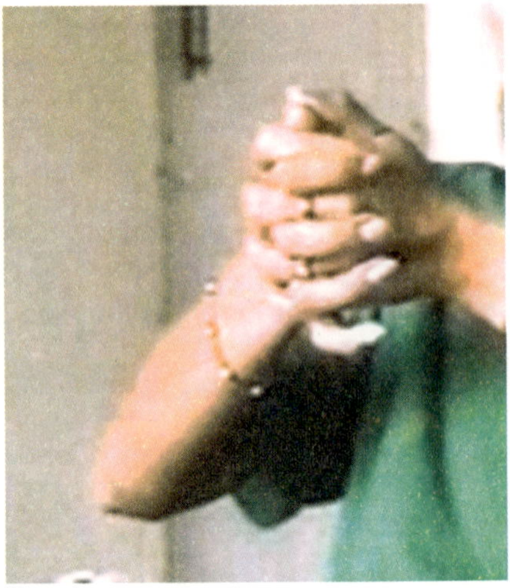

R : Tell me. What are you showing with your hands?

P : (Now every word is accompanied by a gesture.) As if there is nothing left, not even a little bit of space or passage for me to breathe. Congestion is accumulated. (With her hands again she shows something being encircled, as if very tightly, and when she talks of there being no passage, she gestures as if she is drawing something very fine or narrow from between her hands.)

What is significant in her hand gesture? All asthmatics feel choked, blocked, and so on. So what is the difference, what is special in her feeling of choked, blocked? The vivid description of sensation with so much use of hand gestures cannot be local only. With this much repetition and vividness, she is indicating a sensation which must be general as well. So when you keep asking about the local sensation again and again, at one point you will get the general sensation.

If a sensation is described with a hand gesture and this same gesture is repeated again and again, then it is a local expression of her whole general sensation. This general sensation expresses itself through every level of her being, in every aspect of her life.

This is why it is so important to respect and stay with the chief complaint : those symptoms troubling the person the most. This is where the person's energy is most vividly expressing its disharmony. This is where the deepest sensation will be most readily accessed. This is where the other song is singing the most clearly.

We keep asking about the chief complaint (in this case her asthma), and pick up that moment when the local sensation (choked and blocked with the asthma) is being expressed so vividly, so repetitively, that it has to be an expression something much deeper, something general to her entire being. As you continue exploring her case, it gradually emerges how this sensation pervades her whole life, her whole being. And then you see that the same sensation and coping method are present in every aspect, enveloping the whole case.

Therefore, I have learned to trust this sensation more than anything else. In the beginning, you would think that feeling choked/suffocating/congested is just a common experience for asthma patients, but actually every asthmatic will describe this breathlessness in a completely different way. For her, it is this choked/suffocated/no-room-to-breathe feeling that troubles her the most. We therefore stay with this, her chief complaint , and explore the exact nature of the sensations she experiences. She describes more, goes to deeper levels, and all along the hand gestures guide us and confirm that we are journeying towards her core sensation.

I ask the person again and again, "What comes up spontaneously when you make the gesture?" Every single aspect of a person is a part of their unique whole. In illness, every part, every aspect is singing the same particular discord that is unique to the patient. I have come to recognize that it is often the gesture which most truthfully portrays this deepest level of sensation and energy. Just hold on to what their hands are portraying; be aware that you don't know what the gesture signifies, but the person does. Only the person can describe to you what the gesture evokes. No interpretation can be more than a guess.

Hold on to the gesture and ask the person about it repeatedly, about what it brings up for her spontaneously.

At this point, she has told us what her hand gesture shows: no space to breathe, no space at all.

R : Can you just describe what you are showing with your hands? What is that?

P : (She continues to keep her hands locked into each other.) I just feel that there is so much of congestion that it is all blocking my lungs, that nothing is left, no space left inside for the next breath to go in. Nothing to take in, nothing to take out; that kind of a feeling and I won't be able to breathe. A choking. (She clasps her hands tightly together, stiffening her entire body with the gesture.)

She is using many words and many gestures. Keep asking her to describe the sensation further and further until it is crystal clear.

R : Forget the lungs for a while and only describe what you are showing with your hands. Describe this blockage a little bit more, whatever comes to your mind when you say, 'blockage' .

This is important, because here we are asking her to dissociate from the chief complaint, to dissociate the sensation from the local part and to generalize it. In this the person goes from Level 2 directly to Level 5. In bypassing Level 3, the emotional level, we avoid getting stuck and lost in these vivid but human specific emotions. Instead, we go straight to the deeper level of sensation, the level we need to understand, the level which, in fact, gives rise to such emotions. We go to Level 5 (Sensation) where we can reach clarity and a much deeper understanding of her whole state. Then we can go back to Level 3 and explore the emotions with a degree of understanding. We are much less likely to get lost at Level 3 if we already have some idea, some hint, of her deepest underlying sensation.

P : (Clasps hands very tightly that it is as if she is squeezing something between them.) I just think of death. That is it, this is the last. There is a block, there is no space, and I am going to die. Or it is going to lead to something like a heart attack? Total . . . absolutely blocked . . .darkness.

R : What comes to your mind? What is the picture like? When you say, "no space, darkness and suffocation", what picture comes to your mind? This way you can describe to us how and what it feels like. I cannot experience what you are saying. So I need an example from you as to how it feels.

We are now asking her to give an image or a delusion.

P : It is as if you were in a room (with the tips of both forefingers she draws a circle in the air) and there is no place to breathe and there is not even a little bit of air coming in. Suffocation because of that. As if you are locked in a room and there is no air coming from anywhere.

R : Describe this room and describe the block.

P : It is always associated with darkness. It is a small dark room (as if compressing something between her hands) with no sunlight, not even little bit of space to breathe; as if completely sealed. It is a slow death; you are not going to be able to breathe. (Crouches with her hands clasped in front of her.)

R : What is it that you are showing?

P : I do not know whether it is fear, or in some way I am protecting my lungs. I imagine myself like this, (hunches her shoulders and crouches again with hands clasped in front of her), helpless. As if everything is congested, not only the lungs. Your nerves are taut, your fingers, back. (stiffens her fingers) Absolutely numb feeling. Scared, shaken up and helpless. And in this image a sensation is emerging: numb and taut. We will explore the sensation.

R : Describe that sensation, the numb and taut feeling.

P : I feel at times that suddenly my whole body is very taut. (She stiffens her entire body and clenches her fists tightly in front of her.) That is when I have to relax my muscles.

This is the point where the local sensation can be seen as one and the same as the general one. She has been using the hand gestures right from the time that she was describing the asthma, she has been using them through out the description of the image, and now she is talking about her whole body rather than the lungs or nerves or any specific part. And the sensation here is taut, and it is accompanied by hand gestures. We will continue to explore this until she can go no further.

Note also that she started by saying, "It is going to ruin my lungs," evoking the possibility of an animal sensation. But when we asked her to describe the pure sensation in itself and the image, what we got was only a sensation. There was no victim-aggressor issue or survival issue there, there was no convincing "other" out there who is seeking to harm her, dominate her, and so we can rule out the animal kingdom. Nor was there anything to do with lost or missing structure or ability, so we can rule out also the mineral kingdom. And now one has come to Level 5 (Sensation) and so far there is nothing but a pure sensation. The issue here is only sensitivity, and this is the plant kingdom.

R : What is taut? What are you showing?

P : (She remains in the same posture.) I realize that I am very stiff all over my body, and I am not relaxed. I know that this is the problem, but why is it that my toes and my knees do not appear to be relaxed? My body and my nerves are taut, too tight.

'Taut' gives way to 'tight' . So we use 'tight' as our next foothold.

R : Describe this 'tight' a little bit more.

P : I feel that is an extension of the feeling I have in my lungs; I feel that it gets extended to all over my body.

Now you see that the local is nothing but the expression of the general. The same sensation and coping method applies to the lungs; it applies to the body and to every area in her life. The same thing has to be expressed in her dancing, dreams, delusions, and every single aspect of her life.

P : Just held up. As if my feet and hands are being tied up (gestures with hands as if winding a rope or chord around something) and I need to unwind it (makes the same winding gesture in the opposite direction), just relax them a bit. At times I can do that by taking my mind away from my chest and taking it to my knees, but I can do it only for a split second and again I come back to my chest. My whole body is restless, taut.

She started with "taut", then went to "tight", then to "held", and then to "tied" – all of these being accompanied by gestures. To understand the sensation clearly, or for one clear and fundamental sensation to emerge, repeat all these words to the person and ask her to describe them further.

R : Like what?

P : (Again the gesture of winding a rope, and then as if bundling something.) The way you feel when you tie something with a cloth. Something being tied with a cloth, wrapped with a string; that kind of feeling. Like you hold something in your fist, like this, (clenches her fist tightly), and when you open it, loosen the grip, you see the effect of it. As if it is a piece of something soft, like dough, and you see impressions on it. That is the kind of feeling, like some harm is being done to my body because of this taut feeling.

R : Tell me a little more about cloth being tied.

P : A tight feeling, absolutely tight, and the impressions you get when you open out the rope. (As if pressing something between the flat surfaces of both palms.) As if tied with something. (Winding something with her hands.)

The sensation is that of being tied up tightly, tied up so as to tauten, and the opposite is loosen, to unwind.

P : There is suffocation and scars. When you hold the wrist and it is very tight (encircles one wrist tightly with the other hand), and then you loosen the grip; that is what I feel all over my body. I realize that every part of my body is very, very, very taut.

R : This taut, tight feeling: in which situation do you experience it otherwise?

I do not ask this question anymore. It is a leading question, and when you lead the person it becomes possible to find and seemingly confirm even an incorrect sensation in his or her life and so be misled. For example, right in the beginning she used the word 'blocked'. If instead of maintaining a wide, open focus at that early stage, we had focused on 'blocked' and asked her: "Tell me. In which situation do you feel blocked?" it is very likely that she would have been able to give us an example of such a situation. And then we might have followed that whole story without ever reaching the true sensation (tied up). I prefer now to simply stay with the sensation until the person spontaneously leads me to another area in his life, to another situation. Or then to ask about the dreams or a stress situation and see if the same sensation is repeated there.

P : When tensed or late for something or trying to rush through something, but not to this extent; when you are edgy (stiffens fingers) and you are running late.

R : What do you feel when you are late?

P : At traffic signals I feel, Oh! I am going to be late! And I know I must relax, but my body becomes tense—the same taut feeling.

R : Was there any situation in your life that was very scary?

I used the word "scary" because in the past she had said of her breathlessness "it scared me."

P : Dogs used to scare me a lot. (Crouches a little, and throws her head back as if something is coming at her.) A dog in the colony had gone mad. I was wearing nice red sandals; I must have been around eight or nine years old. I was running and calling out for help, and in that process the sandals came off. And I saw the dog had ripped them apart. (Gesture as if stretching something tightly with both hands.) I was so scared that he could have done that to me. (Grasps her throat and widens her eyes as if frightened.) That image stayed in my mind, and I was so scared of dogs after that.

R : What was the feeling?

P : That it could have happened to me. (Again gestures as if stretching something tightly between both hands.) If the sandals had not fallen off, he could have done that to me. He could have ripped my leg. (As if stretching or pulling something tightly between both hands.)

R : What's the fear like?

P : Claws tearing open my skin. Dog will tear, rip. (Makes claws with both her hands facing outwards and then draws them apart, as if something is being ripped apart.)

The feeling of being caught or tied is always associated with something acute and panicky. How does the taut, caught feeling come to her (in relation to the dog in this instance)? It comes suddenly, it catches and it kills; and this is where the coping method and sensation intertwine all the time. We see that the 'tied' sensation always comes on suddenly, always comes together with panic.

The coping mechanism only occurs in response to the sensation, and always qualifies that sensation. In this case the coping mechanism (panic) only occurs in response to the sensation ("taut", "caught") If there is no underlying sensation, there is no need for any reaction; no coping mechanism occurs as none is required.

R : What dreams do you get?

P : If I have had a very hectic day, the same thing plays in my mind; it goes on and on and on. (Makes repeated circles with her forefingers.) I have a performance and so many things have happened that night, and the dream is like a replay of what has happened. (Again makes circles.) And if there is smoke in the room in my dreams, I feel the smoke is there everywhere. (As if something is encircling her.) Sometimes I am running, but my feet fail and I just can't run after a while. Sometimes it is related to aircraft; as if I am witnessing a disaster, or an air crash, or a mid-air crash. As a kid, I was scared on seeing aircraft; I would feel, "My God! This huge thing! What if it crashes? People will die, and I shouldn't be one." The first time I sat in a plane, I was scared and tense for a while, but after some time I relaxed a little. Then, later, sometimes scared of flying and sometimes not. This would be the worst death.

Note that in the dreams, too, she uses the same gestures. Also, from the dream of running she takes us to her childhood fear of air crashes. She describes the fear as an imagination of the airplane crashing. In this image we see the same sensation of being tied up in a sudden way. Of being in midair and dying; that's it! You have no warning, and you just die.

R : What is the feeling about no warning and dying?

P : You just fall down and die and there are pieces of you falling everywhere. (Brings her hands close together and then takes her arms far apart forcefully, as if showing something breaking and scattering.) Helplessness that you can't save yourself; you can't run away. (Crouches behind closed fists.) In a split second's time you are going to be nowhere. (Again takes her arms far apart forcefully.)

R : Explain 'you can't run away'.

P : In a train I wouldn't feel like that. I know that I would protect myself (as if covering her head with something like a hood); somehow you'll try to run out. But here the feeling is that you can't do anything. If in midair there is an explosion, you can't save yourself.

R : Because?

P : There is no time even to know that I am dying, (brings hands together with fingers closed, and then takes them apart, opening her fingers at the same time), for me to think. It will just happen. It won't happen slowly, just that explosion. (Takes hands forcefully apart, opening out all her fingers at the same time.)

R : What are you indicating with your hands?

P : Pieces everywhere; as if being ripped open (again takes hands forcefully apart), and there are pieces of me everywhere.

R : Talk a little bit more about this fear.

P : I feel the same way when I get these nightmares. I am standing on the beach and the plane has just taken off and right before my eyes there are so many people dying. (Again takes her hands forcefully apart, opening all her fingers out.) It is exploding--that's it: helplessness, fear (as if clasping her throat) that I might have to witness something like that one day.

She described helplessness and fear with regard to her asthma.

R : A little more about this helplessness...

P : Not being able to do anything, to rush out and help those people. *(She needs to rush for the inhaler. She is using the same words that she used to describe her experience of her asthma.)* Fear, people dying in front of your eyes, and the fear of watching something like that.

R : What is the fear like, where do you experience it?

P : In the chest. 'Dhuk' here. (Brings closed fists suddenly very close to the chest and forcefully opens them out.) You get a sudden push, a jolt.

R : What do you feel in the chest?

P : Fear. Restlessness. Choking. (As if clasping her throat.)

Again she experiences choking as she does with the asthma. The gestures are also exactly the same. The sensation is the same in the asthma as well as in the dream.

R : Describe this choking.

P : In the same way as I described before, but not so bad. It is for a split second. Choking. (As if cowering with fists clenched in front of her.) Taut, the same kind of feeling.

R : What's the feeling like?

P : Helplessness. (Takes hands apart.)

R : What are you showing with your hands?

P : Pieces that my body is going to be ripped into and thrown in different directions. (Takes hands very far apart.) Helplessness that I can't do anything about it; I can't run away, can't save myself.

R : Why can't you run away?

P : There is no time. In other circumstances, I can save myself, but not here. Because it's an explosion and I am dying in midair. (Takes hands far apart forcefully.) No time.

R : What is the feeling of no time?

P : It is just happening. There is going to be absolutely no time for me to get up, to save myself. Split second.

With the air crash, too, it is something that is sudden, something that happens in a split second, where she is scared and helpless and feels choked and taut. The sensation of being tied, trapped, and the coping method of feeling panic-stricken again come together, as they did in the chief complaint and the incident with the dog.

We have come to the point where our questioning of her—about the sensation she experiences with her asthma and other stressful events and dreams in her life – has led always to the same answer, the same sensation of "taut", "tied", "caught". Therefore, we move on to her dancing, to explore the relationship of the dancing to her chief complaint and core sensation.

R : Talk about dancing.

Dancing is both her hobby and her profession Dancing—the way she dances, what dancing means to her—will be an expression of her whole general sensation. It is important that we explore this area.

P : I have danced all my life, since I was a child. It gives me great pleasure. That's me.

R : What is that pleasure?

P : I feel there are so many outlets to expressions. (Takes hands far apart again.) Just the joy of moving the hand and facial muscles. I enjoy every aspect of it.

R : How?

P : As if I am living in a dancer's world. Everything is in the form of either a movement or an expression, artistic expression. Everything I see, flowers or trees, I see some aspect of dance in it. Maybe there is a movement in my body when I see something like that. It gives great pleasure.

R : When you say that it is an outlet, what do you mean?

We pick up the word, which is accompanied by the hand gesture.

P : As if there are things which you can't express yourself, but when I have danced I have succeeded in doing that; as if I have expressed everything that I have wanted to (takes hands far apart with fingers apart), all unsaid things. When I have finished dancing, I feel very nice, as if I have given vent to something that has been trying to come out.

R : How is it experienced, this outlet?

P : Relaxed. Facial muscles are relaxed and I have a broad smile.

R : What is the opposite?

P : The taut feeling that I described.

Again, the feelings of tense and taut on the one hand, and relaxed and outlet on the other.

R : What things make you tensed, upset?

P : Irritation with small things. Telling my daughter to get ready in time for school. Rush, rush, rush.

She has used the word 'rush' before, with regard to the asthma and the dream.

R : What is the feeling?

P : Irritation. Time-bound.

Here you see the sensation of bound or tied coming up once again.

R : What do you mean by time-bound?

P : As if I am bound by time (again the gesture as if winding something with a rope), and I am taxing myself by looking at the watch. I still keep doing it.

CASE ANALYSIS AND EXPLANATION

Levels:

Level 1: NAME

- Asthma: that is the diagnosis

Level 2: FACT

- Suddenly triggered
- Severe attack
- Aggravation night, lying down
- Danced even with asthma

Level 3: FEELING

- Scared
- Shaken up
- Fear that it will be fatal
- Helpless
- Fear of death

Level 4: DELUSION

- Closed room
- Dark place
- No outlet
- Airplane
- Dog

Fear of airplanes crashing is a very strong fear in the case; but it is not yet the deep point in the case; we need to get to her experience of it to that extent since what we need to know is her inner sensation when she imagines a plane crashing. I use delusions now only as a means to go to the next level.

Level 4 (Delusion) is just above Level 5 (Sensation). Therefore, I ask what the person feels and experiences within his delusion, what is their unique inner sensation. It is as if they give you the external story, set the scene, and tell you which play they are acting a part in. This is only partial information. What you need to know from the person is how he feels inside when playing that part in the play, what is actually his inner experience of that outer story.

You have the story of the dog ripping her sandals apart; the outer event, what happened; but what you need to then find out is the inner event: what she actually experienced within herself when she saw the dog ripping her sandals apart. Only then do you come to the deep level of Sensation (Level 5).

Level 5: SENSATION

- No passage to breathe
- Completely blocked
- No space left
- Choking

These are the initial views; they are not the deepest.

Description of hand gesture:

- Blocked, no passage

Body gestures will give the general sensation :

- Crouched, stiffened, tight, held, tied, by rope, string, need to unwind, loosen.

These are very specific.

Level 6: ENERGY

- Speed
- Sudden
- Coming towards
- Clasp

What is level 6?

This shows the energy level, what she is experiencing, her energy pattern, her gesture. The speed and the direction are shown at level 6. This energy is expressed in her sensation, in her delusions, and in the way her asthma comes on. The energy expresses, informs, and gives rise to all the other levels, throughout her whole case. The Sensation is based on this Energy, just as the Delusion is in turn based on the Sensation.

What she described as "tight" and "taut" is the energy expressed at the level of sensation (Level 5).

Arising from this sensation (Level 5) is the delusion (Level 4): I am in a closed room and cannot breathe. Delusion is experienced mentally and emotionally. In contrast, this movement that informs the whole of every person's case is at a much deeper, more basic level than either mind or body alone. This movement (in this patient's case, of coming together suddenly, rapidly) is pure energy (Level 6).

At the level of emotion (Level 3), it finds expression in, "I am scared."

Locally this energy is expressed in the physical symptoms (Level 2) as "My chest is tight and taut."

Finally, the expression of this energy is given a name, a diagnosis at the level of pathology i.e. Asthma (Level 1).

Postscript

The interview process itself gave this lady several insights, and she could see the commonality of her "sensation" in various spheres of her being. This had a healing effect. In addition, she was given a homeopathic remedy from the plant family Euphorbiaceae. This family has the sensation of tight, taut, tied, bound and the opposite of loose and untied. The remedy chosen for her was Croton tiglium, which within this family has the panic type of coping mechanism. Over the next six to eight months she not only recovered from the asthma but also experienced a significant reduction in her stress levels in various situations and a freedom in her being. Her dancing lost its compulsive nature and became a medium of creative expression for her.

Conclusion

This book is intended to share with you, dear reader, some observations based on just watching and listening to people and asking them to say a bit more about what they experience in the deeper levels of their being. What emerged was that our emotions, thoughts, likes and dislikes, dreams, fantasies nightmares—as well as our bodily illnesses—all have within them at a deeper level a particular language, a particular individual melody, if you may call it that.

This melody is a pattern, an energy field, which closely matches the energy field of a certain plant, animal, or mineral. This pattern colors the way we live, work, relate, and suffer. It almost rules our very existence. If we are able to perceive that our troubles come from that deep level where this non-human part of us resides, then the non-human melody is diluted and dispersed. But this is very difficult to do. Tackling emotions or dreams at a not-so-deep level could have only short-lasting effect, if any.

To see the shape and nature of that non-human thing that resides in us, we need the ability to distance ourselves from our problem which is easier said than done. But it is as if you have become your problem, and you cannot seem to stand back and observe. The other song is so loud that there is hardly any space for awareness.

An adjunct to becoming aware of the other song or another method of getting aware is to take homoeopathic treatment where the medication is the essence of the spirit of the other song that sings in us. The voice of the other song is heard all through the testing of the various substances from the animal, mineral and plant kingdoms. During the process of case taking as the individual (patient) unravels this inner story, enfolds his inner melody note by note, we match it with already available data of the various substances. And we try to locate a remedy that has the same melody, an ultra dilution (potency) of the substance from nature that has the same melody as the one playing within the patient.

We pinpoint the song in nature that matches the patient's other song as closely as possible by using descriptions from the subfamily level of plants, from the class level of animals, and from the row and column intersection point on the periodic table for minerals . The remedy produces significant change in the mind and the body, and consequently, the disease pathology gets better. Given sufficient time, one sees changes in the patient's perception of and reaction to life, resulting from a dilution of his other song. The changes are manifested in the way he perceives his relationships, his life, himself—in short, everything.

Homoeopathy acts at such a vital level yet without much effort on the part of the patient except during the process of initial case taking where he is led into the depth of his experience. Healing that happens in this way is at a very deep level. A treatment that touches lives in this fashion brings about that quantum jump that is required in the life of the patient; it effects change at the deepest level of his illness—beyond his physical symptoms and pathology.

The ideas in this book are broad and are not restricted to the realm of homoeopathy alone. People can use these to become more aware in their interaction with the world around them. We see these ideas being utilized in movies, art, architecture, politics, crime, news, art—truly, in each aspect of human life.

When we see a political leader saying, "We are being threatened by our neighboring country and we have to finish them so that we can survive in peace," we can hear the melody of the animal song playing in him. Advertisers use the sensitivity of our inner melodies to optimize the appeal of their products by striking the right chord within us. Advertisements cater to different types of people by using the main themes of the three kingdoms, animal, plant, and mineral. For example, an advertisement showing that one battery lasts 35% longer than another appeals to the buyer whose other song is from the mineral kingdom—with its themes of function and loss—since that person tends to base his purchases on quantifiable variables like usage and savings. Then there are those advertisements that highlight the fact that by the purchase of the detergent your clothes will be better, look whiter and last longer than those of your neighbors who will envy you. Here, their target buyers are the people with the animal song where their chords of competition and jealousy are struck. And consider those advertisements that mean to touch you deeply through a display of love, affection, and compassion, such as the one showing a mother whose annoyance turns to tender joy when the son whom she was about to scold for dirtying his clothes brings out flowers for her that he had been holding behind his back. This clearly softens the buyers with the sensitivity of the plant song.

The bulls and bears of the stock markets, the hawks and doves of international politics, speak of the animal songs in human society. The symbols that people use, the words they speak, and the choices they make all reflect a deeper melody from the non-human realm.

Nonetheless, what we are discussing here is the very essence of our life. It is that which is ingrained in our very existence and so should not be taken superficially or casually, like a coffee-table conversation. The ideas in this book are not a classification, for that would be a very left brain, analytical thinking. This book is about a journey that takes us on a path inwards. It is a process of discovery, not mathematical, logical analysis. It would be inappropriate to see it as deducing or drawing conclusions. If you follow the processes described here, then the inner world opens up. A totally new dimension gets revealed which runs parallel to but lies far deeper than the person's outer expression that the world sees.

I recall a time when I made a trip from Mumbai (India) to a holiday resort some seven hours away. I took a bus in which I assumed animals were not allowed, but I had to take my cat, since there was no one that I could leave her with. So I put her in a cane basket with holes. I chose to sit at the back of the bus. From time to time she would get restless in the basket and curiously stick her head out of it and meow. People would turn behind to look, wondering where the sound came from. As for me, I would push her head back in and pretend I had nothing to do with it.

The 'Other Song' is the cat in the basket that we carry around. It sticks its head out from time to time through words, gestures, expressions, and experiences that are not 'Human Specific'.

As the light of our awareness falls on the darkness of this other song, the other song's influence becomes lesser and lesser—making us healthier and, thus, more human—so that we can come closer to (as homoeopathy's founder, Samuel Hahnemann, put it) a healthy state wherein *"the reasoning spirit who inhabits the organism can thus freely use this healthy living instrument to reach the lofty goal of human existence."*[1]

This understanding for me personally has changed the way I see and listen on a daily basis to both myself and to those around me. I start seeing myself from where I am coming rather than just by the words I use or by what I do.

You listen to people's inner language and address it. You see the state each one of us is stuck in, and so you stop blaming. You start taking responsibility for yourself and your life and the situation you are in. There is less anger, fighting, and acrimony, there is more watching and being. It is calming in a major way.

---

1 Hahnemann, Samuel. Organon of Medicine: The First Integral English Translation of the Definitive Sixth Edition of the Original Work on Homoeopathic Medicine. Trans. Jost Kunzli, M.D.; Alain Naude and Peter Pendleton. Los Angeles: J. P. Tarcher, Inc., 1982.

Knowledge of the other song makes one quieter on many levels .The realization is that when we interact with someone else, we are often only interacting with ourselves. That there is really no dialogue of two people talking to each other but it is more a conversation with oneself. We come from such completely different worlds that we cannot even begin to comprehend what another is experiencing unless we see that person's other song emerge as his or her case is taken.

I believe that permanent and peaceful connections between people are possible only at the Seventh level. This is true friendship or oneness. At this level we are beyond our disease states, our sensations and delusions; hence we do not interact as one state with another, but as one observer with another, and we come to the common point of all humans—the silent witness state— where there is acceptance of self and the other as they are. Being in the now becomes natural.

Some Questions

1. **Is it possible for a person to have in him an animal song, a mineral song and a plant song at the same time? In the examples that follow, the subject seems to have an element from each of the three kingdoms. Is this possible, or is the case just not being assessed correctly?**

   Example 1: an architect feels ashamed (sensitive-plant) after he loses a competition (animal) to design the most efficiently structured house (mineral).

   Example 2: a person feels vulnerable (plant) in the cells of his body (mineral) to hostile microorganisms (animal).

   Example 3: "I am easily offended (plant) by rude classmates (animal) because of my internal weakness (mineral)."

The idea of kingdoms is this, when we go to the depth of a person's state, we find that it has a pattern that matches a substance from either one of these three kingdoms. A person has only one other song at a time, so this singular song presupposes only one kingdom; therefore, it is not possible for a person to have an animal, a mineral, and a plant song at the same time.

Here we have been given an example of an architect who has lost a competition for the most efficiently structured house. When we ask him what is his experience in that particular situation, he may say, for example, that he feels ashamed or embarrassed. We have to take him one step deeper. "Describe the experience of being ashamed or embarrassed." That question will take him into a deeper level, where he will present, not the emotion, but the actual experience of it, which will be a sensation.

Imagine the architect opening the letter that tells the winners of the competition and reading the names—his not among them. The mineral-kingdom response would be something like, "I must be losing my ability to work in the energy-efficiency field!" (a feeling of lacking something, being incapable of something, or having lost something). The animal-kingdom architect would think something like, "How could *he* have won? He's an *idiot!* I'm much better than he is!" (a feeling of competition). The plant-kingdom architect would say, "I reacted with a sense of shock and disappointment, with a feeling as if everything were sinking or that I were going downwards" (pure sensation and reaction).

So when you probe the case, delve into the same situation at a deeper level, you will find, at the core, the experience of the person; not his emotion, not his delusion, but his sensory experience. This will either be a sense of lacking something or losing something, which is mineral; a sense of competing, which is animal; or a sensation and a reaction to something, which is plant. At a superficial level, all of us have qualities of all the kingdoms. But we are not talking superficially here: we are talking about the Sensation level, and here it will be one and only one core sensation, one constant discomfort.

Drawing from the examples above, assume that a person feels vulnerable in the cells of his body, especially to hostile microorganisms, and also feels, "I am easily offended by rude classmates because of my internal weakness." The first feeling suggests the mineral kingdom; the second, the animal. This is a hypothetical scenario, but even if it were true, when you take this just a little further and ask, "How do you *experience* the situation of being offended by rude classmates?" What he will tell you will not come from all three kingdoms. He will come to one core sensation—from one kingdom only. This has been my experience in several hundred cases, and this is something for which you need to go deeper into your case and observe. Then you will see the truth of it.

2. **In your case-taking methodology, the doctor gently shepherds the patient to express deeper levels of his experience of his chief complaint, moving from its name and local sensations to the emotions, delusion, vital sensation, and energy. You use the words *deep, deeper, deepest,* and *depth,* so clearly the concept is important, but why is a feeling of being crushed (for example) deeper or more useful than a well-described pain? Why have you added this concept of *deeper*, and how it has made a difference?**

Particularly, how does one tell when one has gotten deep enough to have reached the vital sensation?

I think, again, the answer to this question will only come from practically seeing the method in action, either through a practitioner who follows this method or by trying it out in your own practice. Let me give you an example.

I had a case of a man with a tumor in his eyeball, and he described it by saying that this tumor caused a certain "imbalance" in his eyes. Then he described this imbalance as a sense of lack of coordination, and further, how coordination was the most important thing in his life, how everything needed to be coordinated. Pursuing this line of thought, he offered several examples of coordination: the kind a pilot needs when piloting his plane, a rocket scientist when making a rocket, an actor when performing live on stage and so on.

At some point, he described a situation where his mother-in-law had done something behind his back, and when I asked him what he had felt about it, he replied that he had felt very disappointed and betrayed. Now, these emotions of disappointment and betrayal are present in his case, and one might be tempted to come to conclusions from these. But if you state further, "Describe the disappointment," then you bring out the true individuality of the person's reaction to the circumstance.

When somebody does something behind your back, which is not expected, the feeling of disappointment is common, not individual. Hahnemann always emphasized the individualizing phenomena, the characteristic symptoms. Here, when we look at disappointment, it's not individual enough, not characteristic enough. Go further. When I asked him, "Describe the disappointment," he said, "It's as if somebody had punched me in my stomach." This now gets more characteristic. Take it one step further. I said, "Describe the experience of being punched" and he answered, "I feel completely suffocated." "Describe suffocation." And it opens out and you find that there is the suffocating sensation in many areas in his life, as when swimming, or in claustrophobic situations, etc. That suffocation sensation, along with a need for the type of precision coordination and control used by a stage artist or an airplane pilot, was the core sensation. (The homoeopathic remedy used in his case was Argentum nitricum.)

So 'ailments from disappointment' or 'delusion that somebody had punched his stomach', is a more superficial expression. The deeper expression is the tremendous sense of suffocation that he felt, not only in the situation with his mother-in-law, but in every area of his life. A sensation that is so individual, so completely unconnected with the external reality, that it becomes the most individualizing symptom (both physical and mental) of the person. It is at the Sensation level.

When you see that it is both physical and mental—that it encompasses his whole life, his whole story—and you see the *same thing* at the depth of *all* his expressions, be it his interests and hobbies, his occupation, his relationships, his physical symptoms, etc., you know that you have come to the depth, to the vital sensation. Everything comes together at this level.

3. **Some teach that the patient's way of responding to stress is very important. In your system, the doctor tries to go from the obvious levels of experience of the chief complaint to the deeper levels. During this process, is it accurate to say that he goes from a description of the complaint to understanding the patient's individual response to the complaint? Is this similar to the way that others teach us to explore the patient's individual response to stress?**

Yes, we explore the description of the complaint as well as the individual response to the complaint. At some point of exploring the description of the complaint and bringing out its nuances, you find that it is the same as the response to the complaint. Body and mind come together at the level of Sensation.

When we explore to its deepest level the person's physical experience of his symptom, then we come to how he reacts to that particular problem, and when that in turn is examined to its deepest level, it will come to the very same point, which is the Sensation.

4. Are the non-human-specific characteristics within each person always a problem?

The non-human-specific characteristics within a person, when they are persistent, when they form a pattern, and when that pattern fixes a person's life and he's stuck in it, then it becomes a problem, and that is the disease. If a person's sensations change along with the circumstance, if he is able to be in the moment, enjoying the wind and experiencing lightness and floating when on a mountain, when at work, experiencing his capability to work, when in a competition feeling competitive, then this is absolutely perfect. Anything becomes a problem only when it gets fixed and long-standing, and colors and limits the person's whole life.

5. Is differentiation or individuality possible among humans without non-human-specific characteristics?

Individuality will always be there. People are tall or short or intelligent or strong, etc. But these differences will not limit the individual; they will not be pathological. Hence, they will not be stuck. Each one will experience his individuality as well as his freedom. That would be health.

6. For a student who can only grasp very simple concepts, would it be helpful to say that 'mineral' patients believe their problem is within themselves, 'plant' patients believe their problem is from

some process or substance comes at them from outside themselves and 'animal' patients believe that their problem is caused by some external entity?

More or less, yes. You are right about the mineral and animal persons. The mineral person feels the problem as lacking something, losing something, or being incapable of something. The plant person does not see the problem as coming from anything outside. His problem lies in his own sensitivity and reactivity to something outside of himself.

Further Reading

General interest

- Ullman, Dana. *The Consumer's Guide to Homeopathy*, New York: Jeremy P. Tarcher, Putnam, 1995.
- Sankaran, Rajan. *Homoeopathy, The Science of Healing*, New Delhi: B. Jain Publishers Pvt. Ltd., 2005.
- Ullman, Robert and Ullman, Judyth R, *The Patient's Guide to Homeopathic Medicine*, Washington: Picnic Point Press, 1995.
- Vithoulkas, George. *The Science of Homeopathy*, New York: Grove Press, 1980.

RESOURCES

Homoeopathic Book Distributors

Homoeopathic Medical Publishers
201, Dinar
20, Station Road
Santacruz (West)
Mumbai - 400 054
India
Tel: +91 22 2660 5680
Fax: +91 22 2660 5776
www.rajansankaran.com
E-mail: office@rajansankaran.com
info@rajansankaran.com

Homeopathic Educational Services
2124B Kittredge St.,
Berkeley, CA 94704
USA
Tel: 800 359 9051; 510 649 0294

The Minimum Price Homeopathic Books
250 H St., PO Box 2187
Blaine, WA 98231
USA
Tel: 800 663 8272

Homoeopathic Organizations

Homoeopathic Research and Charities
F/2, Saraswat Colony
Niwas Path, Anusaya Road
Santacruz (West)
Mumbai 400 054
India
Tel: + 91 22 2660 5680
Fax: + 91 22 2660 5776
www.homeopathyindia.org
Journal: *Homoeopathic Links*

American Institute of Homeopathy
801 N. Fairfax Street, Suite 306
Alexandria, VA 22314-1757
USA
Tel: 888 445 9988
www.homeopathyusa.org
Journal: *American Journal of Homeopathic Medicine*

Homeopathic Academy of Naturopathic Physicians
12132 S.E. Foster Place
Portland, OR 97266
USA
Tel: 253 630 3338
Fax: 815 301 6595
E-mail: info@hanp.net
Journal: *Simillimum*
Directory of Practitioners

The National Center for Homeopathy
801 N. Fairfax Street, #306
Alexandria, VA 22314
USA
Tel: 703 548 7790
Fax: 703 548 7792
www.homeopathic.org
Journal: *Homeopathy Today*

North American Society of Homeopaths
PO BOX 450039
Sunrise, FL 33345-0039 USA
Tel: 206 720 7000
Fax: 208 248 1942
www.homeopathy.org
E-mail: NashInfo@homeopathy.org
Journal: *The American Homeopath*

British Homeopathic Association
Hahnemann House
29 Park Street West
Luton LU1 3BE
UK
Tel: 0870 444 3950
Fax: 0870 444 3960
Journal: *Health and Homoeopathy*

The Europeans and International Councils for Classical Homeopathy
ECCH and ICCH Secretariat
School House, Market Place
Kenninghall, Norfolk
NR16 2AH,
England
Tel/Fax: 44 1953888163

The Faculty of Homeopathy
Hahnemann House
29 Park Street West
Luton LU1 3BE
UK
Tel: 0870 444 3950
Fax: 0870 444 3960
Journal: *Homeopathy*

Liga Medicorum Homeopathica Internationalis
http://www.lmhint.net
Journal: *The Liga Letter*

Society of Homeopaths
11 Brookfield
Duncan Close
Moulton Park
Northampton
NN3 6WL
UK
Tel: 0845 450 6611
Fax: 0845 450 6622
http://www.homeopathy-soh.org
E-mail: info@homeopathy-soh.org
Journal: *The Homeopath*

Homeopaths Without Borders
33 Fairfax St.,
Berkeley Springs
WV 25411
USA
Tel: 800 336 1695
E-mail: joelillard@homeopathyworks.com

Other books written by

DR. RAJAN SANKARAN

Published By

HOMOEOPATHIC MEDICAL PUBLISHERS

THE SPIRIT OF HOMOEOPATHY

THE SUBSTANCE OF HOMOEOPATHY

THE SOUL OF REMEDIES

PROVINGS

THE SYSTEM OF HOMOEOPATHY

AN INSIGHT INTO PLANTS (2 VOLS)

SANKARAN'S SCHEMA 2005

THE SENSATION IN HOMOEOPATHY

AN INSIGHT INTO PLANTS (VOL 3)

SENSATION REFINED

STRUCTURE
Experiences with the Mineral Kingdom (2 VOLS)

SURVIVAL (VOL 1) THE MOLLUSC

Books by

DR. RAJAN SANKARAN

Published in other languages:

DUTCH

• Homeopathie En Materie (+ 2 Cds)
(Translation – The Substance of Homoeopathy)

FRENCH

• L'espirit De L'homeopathie
(Translation – The Spirit of Homoeopathy)

• Comprendre la Sensation Vitale en Homéopathie
De la plainte principale à l'énergie

• Le Schéma de Sankaran Edition 2005
(Translation - Sankaran's Schema 2005)

GERMAN

- Das Geistige Prinzip der Homöopathie
(Translation – The Spirit of Homoeopathy)
- Die Substanz der Homöopathie (+2 CDs)
(Translation – The Substance of Homoeopathy)
- Das System der Homöopathie
(Translation – The System of Homoeopathy)
- Die Seele der Heilmittel
(Translation – The Soul of Remedies)
- Einblicke ins Pflanzenreich Band 1 und 2
(Translation – An Insight into Plants Vol 1 & 2)
- Sankaran's Tabellen
(Translation - Sankaran's Schema 2005)
- Die Empfindung in der Homöopathie
(Translation - Sensation in Homoeopathy)
- Einblicke ins Pflanzenreich Band 3
(Translation - Insight into Plants Vol 3)
- Die Empfindung - Verfeinerung der Methode
(Translation - Sensation Refined)
- Struktur - Erfahrungen mit dem Mineralreich
(Translation – Structure – Experiences with the Mineral Kingdom)

SPANISH

- El Espiritu De La Homeopatia
(Translation – The Spirit of Homoeopathy)

- La substancia de la homepatia
(Translation – The Substance of Homoeopathy)

- El Esquema De Sankaran 2007
(Translation – Sankaran's Schema 2005)

- Sensación Vital en Homeopatía

HOMOEOPATHIC SOFTWARE:

VITAL QUEST - SANKARAN SYSTEM

The Next Generation Homoeopathic Software

WEBGROUP:

INSIGHT

Alliance Homoeopathic

DVD PACKAGE:

- **SPIRIT, SONG AND SENSATION (Set of 4 DVDs)**

- **SANKARAN LIVE (Set of 4 DVDs)**

A comprehensive exposition of the sensation method

Dr. Rajan Sankaran's books published in other languages by other publishers:

THE SPIRIT OF HOMOEOPATHY
Bosnian, Bulgarian, Czech, Hungarian, Italian, Japanese, Polish, Romanian, Russian, Serbian & Tamil.

THE SUBSTANCE OF HOMOEOPATHY
Bosnian, Hungarian, Italian, Polish, Romanian, Russian & Spanish.

THE SOUL OF REMEDIES
Czech, German (Audio book), Hungarian, Italian, Korean, Romanian, Russian & Spanish.

PROVINGS
Romanian

THE SYSTEM OF HOMOEOPATHY
Italian, Romanian & Russian.

AN INSIGHT INTO PLANTS (2 VOLS)
Bosnian, Croatian, French, Italian, Romanian, Russian, & Serbian.

THE SENSATION IN HOMOEOPATHY
Italian, Romanian & Russian.

SANKARANS SCHEMA 2005
Bulgarian, Hungarian, Italian, Japanese & Russian.

SENSATION REFINED
Russian

AN INSIGHT INTO PLANTS (VOL 3)
Russian

STRUCTURE – Experiences with the Mineral Kingdom
Russian

Homoeopathic Medical Publishers

201, Dinar, 20, Station Road, Santacruz (West), Mumbai - 400 054, India.
Tel.: +91 22 2660 5680; Fax: +91 22 2660 5776
www.rajansankaran.com
Email: office@rajansankaran.com • info@rajansankaran.com

NOTES

NOTES